# *Swimming*

## STEPS TO SUCCESS

## David Thomas, MS

**Professor Emeritus**
**State University of New York–Binghamton**

**Human Kinetics**

**Library of Congress Cataloging-in-Publication Data**

Thomas, David G., 1924-
  Swimming : steps to success / David G. Thomas.-- 3rd ed.
    p. cm.
  ISBN 0-7360-5436-7 (soft cover)
  1. Swimming.  I. Title.
  GV837.T47 2005
  797.2'1--dc22

                    2004019105

ISBN-10: 0-7360-5436-7
ISBN-13: 978-0-7360-5436-2

Developmental Editor: Cynthia McEntire
Assistant Editor: Scott Hawkins
Copyeditor: Jan Feeney
Proofreader: Sue Fetters
Graphic Designer: Nancy Rasmus
Graphic Artist: Francine Hamerski
Cover Designer: Keith Blomberg
Photographer (cover): © Harry How/Getty Images
Art Manager: Kareema McClendon
Illustrator: Roberto Sabas
Printer: United Graphics

Human Kinetics books are available at special discounts for bulk purchase. Special editions or book excerpts can also be created to specification. For details, contact the Special Sales Manager at Human Kinetics.

Printed in the United States of America      10 9 8 7 6 5 4

**Human Kinetics**
Web site: www.HumanKinetics.com

*United States:* Human Kinetics
P.O. Box 5076
Champaign, IL 61825-5076
800-747-4457
e-mail: humank@hkusa.com

*Canada:* Human Kinetics
475 Devonshire Road Unit 100
Windsor, ON N8Y 2L5
800-465-7301 (in Canada only)
e-mail: orders@hkcanada.com

*Europe:* Human Kinetics
107 Bradford Road
Stanningley
Leeds LS28 6AT, United Kingdom
+44 (0) 113 255 5665
e-mail: hk@hkeurope.com

*Australia:* Human Kinetics
57A Price Avenue
Lower Mitcham, South Australia 5062
08 8277 1555
e-mail: liaw@hkaustralia.com

*New Zealand:* Human Kinetics
Division of Sports Distributors NZ Ltd.
P.O. Box 300 226 Albany
North Shore City
Auckland
0064 9 448 1207
e-mail: info@humankinetics.co.nz

# Swimming

## STEPS TO SUCCESS

# ◨ Contents

# ◪ Climbing the Steps to Swimming Success

Commodore Wilbert E. Longfellow, founder of the American Red Cross swimming program, once remarked, "Swimming—you can't find a better sport to save your life." The statement is true, but it covers only one aspect of a sport that has much more to offer. Swimming is a wholesome, rewarding, invigorating sport that anyone of any age can enjoy.

This book offers a unique approach to learning swimming, one often overlooked by instructors—swimming is easy! It is so easy that it can be accomplished with less effort than is required for any other sport. The emphasis in the approach taught here is on relaxation, not on "kick, kick, kick" or "pull, pull, pull," an approach that exhausts a novice so quickly.

But be careful. Swimming may be habit forming. It may change your life and may even make you a national champion!

In the third edition of *Swimming: Steps to Success,* the steps have been redesigned so that you can move more quickly from the beginner level to the intermediate level. Also, more advanced skills have been added to challenge you. Safety is always a governing factor in each step.

The first few steps in this book, steps 1 through 3, introduce the beginning level of swimming. The next five steps, steps 4 through 8, guide you through intermediate and expert level swimming strokes, including the four competitive strokes. Steps 9 through 13 concentrate on auxiliary and related skills to enhance your aquatic expertise.

Along the way, follow this sequence for each step:

1. Read the explanation of what is covered in the step, why the step is important, and how to perform the skill.

2. Follow the numbered illustrations to learn how to position your body to execute each basic skill successfully. For most skills, there are three phases: preparation (getting into starting position), execution (performing the skill that is the focus of the step), and follow-through (recovering to the starting position).

3. Read the instructions for each drill and perform the drill as described. Drills help you improve your skills through repetition and purposeful practice, so practice accordingly and record your score. Pace yourself by adjusting the drills to increase or decrease the difficulty.

4. Have a qualified observer such as a teacher, coach, or trained partner evaluate your basic skill technique once you have completed each set of drills. Your observer can use the success checks in the drills as guidance. This is a qualitative or subjective evaluation of your basic technique or form.

Now it's time to begin your step-by-step journey to enhancing your swimming skills.

# ◲ The Sport of Swimming

The history of swimming is fascinating. In ancient times, people took to the water to avoid a forest fire, to escape an enemy, to search for food, or simply to find relief from the blazing sun. Women and men are drawn to the water by an unexplainable force. Children seek puddles to play in. Sailors march irresistibly to the sea. Vacationers flock to the seaside for the soothing sights and sounds of the water.

In 1883, William Wilson wrote in *The Swimming Instructor,* "The experienced swimmer, when in the water, may be classed among the happiest of mortals in the happiest of moods, and in the most complete enjoyment of the happiest of exercises."

This book is your key to sharing the enthusiasm of Mr. Wilson and beginning your quest for proficiency in the aquatic arts. You can experience the mysterious forces of the aquatic environment by learning to swim. Swimming gives you amusement, relaxation, challenge, competition, and the ability to save your life or someone else's in an aquatic emergency.

Swimming does not require a set pattern of arm or leg movements. You may use any arm and leg movements that allow you to remain at the surface and move from one place to another. Certain combinations of motions, however, are more efficient than others. Swimmers package these efficient motions into recognized strokes. The best known swimming strokes are the sidestroke, crawl stroke, breaststroke, back crawl stroke, and butterfly stroke. In this book, you will learn all of these strokes as well as some that are not as well known.

In addition to the standardized packaged traditional strokes, this text will lead you on an adventure in watermanship, the mastery of the aquatic element. You will be introduced to skills that transcend the traditional and awaken you to a new joy in accomplishment. You will be introduced to new motions, positions, and strokes that will challenge your creative abilities.

On completion of this series of steps, you will be ready to participate in the other facets of the world of aquatics: lifesaving, speed swimming, synchronized swimming, scuba diving, water polo, underwater hockey, and waterskiing. The governing associations of these aquatic activities, along with their Web addresses, are listed in the next few paragraphs.

If your interest lies in swim instruction or lifesaving and lifeguarding, seek further information and training from organizations such as the American Red Cross (www.redcross.org) or the Young Men's Christian Association (YMCA) (www.ymca.net/index.jsp).

If competition is your forte, you may want to become involved in speed swimming through a national organization such as USA Swimming (www.usaswimming.org). Other opportunities in aquatic competition also are available: water polo (USA Water Polo; www.usawaterpolo.com), synchronized swimming (USA Synchronized Swimming; www.usasynchro.org), underwater hockey (National Underwater Hockey Association; www.underwater-society.org), springboard diving and platform diving (USA Diving; www.usadiving.org), and competitive lifesaving (United States Lifesaving Association; www.usla.org).

If you are interested in scuba diving, contact the National Association of Underwater Instructors (www.naui.org), the Professional Association of Diving Instructors (www.padi.com), or the YMCA. For waterskiing, contact USA Waterski, (www.usawaterski.org).

## SAFETY CONSIDERATIONS

Water demands the respect of all who enjoy its many charms. Good swimmers are safer than nonswimmers, but being a good swimmer does not guarantee immunity from injury or drowning. Even the best swimmers can find themselves injured or fatigued, which can lead to distress and drowning. Fear of the water is not a helpful emotion. Respecting the power of water and showing good common sense when dealing with unexpected situations may save your life. Consistently follow these rules to minimize your chances of injury while swimming:

- Never swim alone. Always have someone with you who can help or who can get help if necessary.
- Know the area where you plan to swim. Know where the deep and shallow areas are. Find out about any hidden hazards that are not apparent from above the water. Learn about eddies, currents, tides, and runouts that are common to the area.

- Do not chew gum while swimming. Breathing patterns in swimming require a clear mouth and throat.
- Do not overestimate your ability or endurance. Don't assume that your endurance is the same at the beginning of the swimming season as it was at the end of the last season. Start easy.
- Never swim immediately after eating a heavy meal. Wait at least 30 minutes after eating a light meal, and longer after a heavy meal.
- Use great care when diving. Do not dive into water less than 5 feet deep.
- Do not run, push others, or indulge in horseplay on a pool deck. The pool deck is usually slippery, and accidents can easily happen.

## EQUIPMENT

Technically all you really need for swimming is an area of water, but certain types of equipment may make it easier and safer for you to learn various techniques and strokes. The following pieces of equipment will help you climb the steps to successful swimming (figure 1):

- Kickboard
- Leg float (sometimes called a *pull buoy*)
- Face mask
- Swim fins and socks or boots
- Snorkel
- Deep-float leg float
- Float belt
- Swim goggles
- Nose clip
- Hula hoop
- Stopwatch or timer
- Hand paddles or webbed gloves

Many of these items will help you minimize the length of time necessary to master a given skill, but of course many people have learned to swim without using them. We urge you to make use of these items for your comfort and swift learning progress.

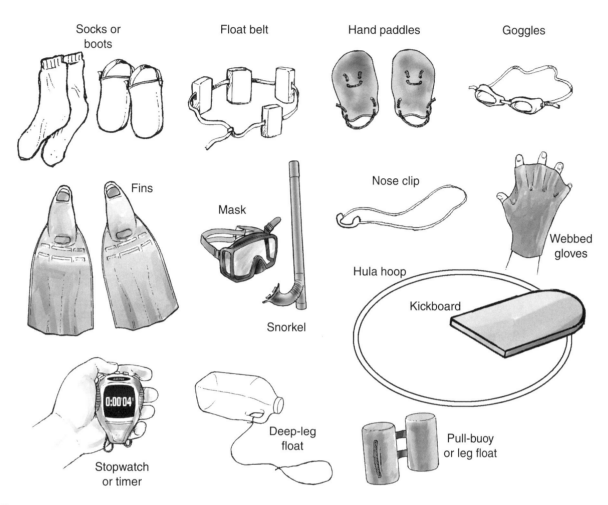

**Figure 1** Aquatic equipment will make learning easier and safer.

The first two items, kickboards and pull buoys, are standard equipment at most pools. You may be permitted to use them, or you can buy your own inexpensively. The next three items—face mask, swim fins, and snorkel—are all personally fit items. You'll want to buy your own for proper fit and personal hygiene. Masks and fins are the most expensive items. Swim goggles and nose clips are not essential items, but they add greatly to your comfort and confidence in many of the skills.

The deep-float leg float and float belt are very easy and inexpensive to make. Make a deep-float leg float by tying a piece of light cord to the handle of an empty half-gallon container that has a good top, such as a milk or juice container. Make the cord long enough so that a 4-inch (10.16 centimeters) loop at one end will hang 10 inches (25.4 centimeters)

under the water when the container is floating. Use the float by inserting one ankle into the loop. This will give you some leg support at a depth of about a foot for some of the swimming drills.

You will need a safety float belt for added confidence and safety when you try some of the deep-water drills. The float belt should be large enough to keep you afloat to chin level. Those few people who are not buoyant (only 3 percent of the general population) will need a smaller float belt for the first few skills.

You can make a float belt by cutting blocks of a closed-cell plastic foam, such as polyethylene, about 2 inches (5.08 centimeters) square and 6 to 8 inches (15.24 to 20.32 centimeters) long. Each of these blocks (you may need four or six of them) should be split so that a 2-inch-wide webbed nylon belt can pass through them. A belt like the ones that scuba divers use for a weight belt is ideal. You can also purchase a float belt, but do not buy one that is inflatable.

A stopwatch or timer will be used only in a few of the advanced skills. Many wristwatches have built-in timers. A hula hoop may aid you in obtaining better height when first learning to dive. See step 11 for more details. The hand paddles and webbed gloves are used when learning to scull, as explained in step 12.

# WARMING UP AND COOLING DOWN

Swimming is one of the very best exercises for body conditioning, flexibility, and endurance. It is best to prepare your body for the activity before attempting each step to success by performing a few warm-up exercises.

## Breathing

Stand erect with your arms at your sides. As you take a deep breath, slowly lift both arms out and up until they meet directly overhead. Bring your arms slowly back down as you exhale. Repeat 10 times, trying to breathe more deeply with each breath.

Stand erect with your hands clasped behind your head. Take a deep breath and hold it while you count 5 seconds. Exhale very quickly and completely, then fully inhale through your mouth as quickly as you can. Hold for 5 seconds. Repeat five times, emphasizing the quickness with which you get rid of one breath and take in the next.

## Stretching

Stand erect with your feet apart and arms at your sides. Slowly raise your arms overhead and stretch up as high as you can while rising on your toes. Lower your heels and slowly bring your arms down until they are extended to the sides at shoulder height. Twist slowly to the left from the waist. Face the front and twist to the left as far as possible. Face the front again and bend forward at the waist to touch your toes with your fingertips. Straighten to standing position and repeat the exercise, twisting to the right.

## Tapering

At the end of your activity in the water, take a minute to relax before you go. In chest-deep water, bob and breathe slowly and deeply for 30 breaths, then lie back, leave your heels on the bottom, and float motionless. Inhale deeply, hold for 5 seconds, then exhale and inhale quickly and hold again. Float for 3 minutes. Then go about your business relaxed, refreshed, and ready to enjoy the rest of the day.

# Buoyancy and Back Float

Even the most complicated swimming stroke involves only two basic skills: floating and adding propulsive movements to move from place to place. Floating is the basis of all swimming, and it is so easy you can't fail. In fact, for the majority of people, holding a full breath makes it impossible to sink even if they wanted to do so. When you discover that fact for yourself, you will be well on your way to swimming.

Some people who are fair swimmers still think that they will sink to the bottom if they stop pressing down on the water. They waste a lot of energy, tire quickly, and will never be really good swimmers until they discover that moving their arms and legs is not necessary to keep them up. How lucky you are that you will learn about buoyancy before you learn to swim.

Buoyancy is an inherent body characteristic and does not need to be learned. Only about 3 percent of the general population have such heavy musculature and limited lung capacity that they can sink when immersed. Even the few nonbuoyant people can float by adding small, slow hand movements.

Learning to control the natural buoyancy of your body makes it really easy to float in any position you desire. Three elements control buoyancy: breath control (the amount of air in your lungs), body position (balance to achieve any position you desire), and relaxation (you weigh the same whether you're tense or relaxed).

## PROVING BUOYANCY

Human bodies do not float *on* the water: they float *in* it! Only a specific percentage of your body will remain above the surface, and that percentage varies with every person. For your own safety and peace of mind, *always* have a skilled swimmer right beside you whenever you attempt a new skill.

To discover how much of your body remains above the surface, find a place at the edge of the pool where the water is chin deep. Hold on to the side with two fingers of each hand and keep your abdomen tight against the wall (figure 1.1a).

Take a big breath until your lungs are totally filled with air. Hold that breath, bend your knees so that your feet are off the bottom, look straight forward (do not tilt your head back), and lower yourself *slowly* (the key word here) until only the very top of your head is above water (figure 1.1b). Bring both hands slowly under the water. You are floating! Take hold of the edge and stand again (figure 1.1c).

Some portion of your head was above water. To swim, you need to learn how to make the portion of your head above water be the portion that contains your mouth so that you can breathe.

## Figure 1.1    You Can Float!

### GET READY

1. Hold head straight
2. Grasp edge with two fingers of each hand
3. Hold abdomen tight against wall
4. Bend knees

a

### DESCEND

1. Take a big breath
2. Slowly lower your body into the water
3. Hold your breath
4. Pull hands underwater

b

### RECOVER

1. Extend arms
2. Grasp edge
3. Stand

c

2

**Misstep**

Your head drops beneath the surface.

**Correction**

Lower your body *very slowly.* Hold all the air you can hold.

If you are one of those rare adult males who has neutral or negative buoyancy, try wearing a solid foam buoyancy belt that will give you enough positive buoyancy to float at eye level. The belt should attach under your armpits. The buoyancy may support you completely around your body or may support you on each side (figure 1.2). Wear the belt throughout step 1.

**Figure 1.2** A buoyancy belt.

## Buoyancy Drill 1.   *Vertical Buoyancy*

Repeat the vertical buoyancy discovery drill illustrated in figure 1.1 five times. Try it with your eyes shut and with your eyes open. Do not tilt your head back. Lower yourself to floating position *very slowly.*

**To Increase Difficulty**

• Push yourself under gently before releasing the wall, and float slowly to the surface.

**To Decrease Difficulty**

• Try to take in even more air.
• Wear goggles or a mask and look at the wall.
• Wear a small float belt.

• Have a friend stand beside you for confidence.

### Success Check

• Take in all the air you can hold.
• Look straight ahead.
• Pull your fingers underwater.

### Score Your Success

Earn 1 point each time you complete the drill and prove that you will not sink, for a maximum of 5 points. Add 1 additional point each time you push yourself under and float to the surface, for a maximum of 10 points.

Your score ___

# Buoyancy Drill 2.   *Deep-Water Adjustment*

Repeat the vertical buoyancy discovery drill illustrated in figure 1.1 (page 2) in deep water. Ask a skilled swimmer to stay in the water beside you to help you recover and to give you confidence (figure 1.3). Keep your knees straight. Hold the float for 10 seconds. Repeat one time.

**Figure 1.3**   Deep-water vertical buoyancy drill.

**To Increase Difficulty**

- Push yourself underwater and drift to the top.
- Hold the float for 15 seconds.

**To Decrease Difficulty**

- Wear a mask or goggles.
- Wear a small float belt.

## *Success Check*

- Keep knees straight.
- Look ahead.
- Hold still for 10 seconds.

## *Score Your Success*

Hold float for 10 seconds = 2 points

Push underwater, drift up, and hold float for
10 seconds = 4 points

Your score ___

# LEARNING THE BACK FLOAT

You must be able to control your buoyancy to produce a body position that will allow you to breathe while floating. Most beginners attempt to float horizontally. A balanced back-float position may be vertical, semivertical, or horizontal.

The back float is one of the most useful skills you will ever learn in swimming because it allows you to rest and breathe in deep water. A back float requires almost no effort and may save your life in the event of an aquatic emergency. The back float also teaches you how to balance your body in a close-to-horizontal position.

To learn to float on your back, stand in chin-deep water facing the pool wall. Hold onto the wall with two fingers of each hand, but extend your arms until your elbows are straight. Turn your face up to the ceiling (figure 1.4a).

Lower yourself carefully until your ears are completely submerged. Take a deep breath and hold it. Release the edge of the pool and bring your hands underwater. Hold still and keep your eyes open as you drift slowly away from the wall (figure 1.4b).

When you are steady in the water, very quickly exhale and inhale through your mouth. Hold that breath for 5 seconds, then quickly take another one. Remain perfectly still. Allow your knees to straighten. When you are confident, relax. Slowly bring your arms out underwater to shoulder height. Stop. Continue very slowly to extend your arms above your head, but keep them fully submerged (figure 1.4c). Your feet will rise slowly as your arms move up. Quickly breathe again.

To recover, bring your knees up to your chest, drop your chin forward, and sweep your arms down behind you and forward past your hips, palms forward (figure 1.4d). Stay tucked until your feet are under you, then stand.

## Figure 1.4    **Back Float**

### GET READY

1. Hold pool wall
2. Bring head back
3. Bend knees
4. Straighten elbows

*a*

### FLOAT

1. Take a deep breath
2. Arch back
3. Let go of wall
4. Quickly exhale and inhale

*b*

### RECOVER

1. Slowly move arms out
2. Reach back
3. Tuck knees
4. Scoop arms

*c*

### STAND

1. Return to vertical position
2. Bend knees, press feet against bottom of pool, and stand

*d*

**Misstep**

Your face submerges when you exhale.

**Correction**

Exhale and inhale more quickly.

## Back Float Drill 1.    *Land Drill for Breathing*

Correct breathing techniques ensure proper buoyancy and enable you to hold a back float for more than one breath. This drill will prepare you to breathe while you float.

Stand or sit at the edge of the pool. Take in all the air you can hold and hold your breath for just 5 seconds. Exhale and inhale as quickly as possible through your mouth, making sure you get all the air you can hold. Hold your breath for only 5 seconds, then quickly exhale and inhale again.

Total exhalation is not necessary; total inhalation is. Breathe off the top of your lungs. Continue for 20 breaths. See how quickly you can get a new breath. Open your mouth wide to breathe.

**To Increase Difficulty**

- Hold each breath for 8 seconds.

**To Decrease Difficulty**

- Sit or stand erect.
- Breathe from your diaphragm and use your abdominal muscles.
- Close your mouth while holding your breath.

### Success Check

- Open mouth wide.
- Exchange air quickly.
- Fill lungs completely each time.

### Score Your Success

Complete 20 breaths successfully = 1 point

Your score ___

## Back Float Drill 2.    *Beginning Back Float*

Have a friend stand directly behind you to give you confidence. Stand in chin-deep water facing the pool wall. Hold onto the wall with two fingers of each hand, but extend your arms until your elbows are straight and turn your face up to the ceiling. Lower yourself carefully until your ears are completely submerged. Take a deep breath and hold it. Release the edge and bring your hands underwater. Hold still, and keep your eyes open as you drift slowly away from the wall.

When you are steady in the water, very quickly exhale and inhale through your mouth. Hold that breath for 5 seconds, then quickly take another one. Remain perfectly still. Allow your knees to straighten. When you are confident, relax. Slowly bring your arms outward underwater to shoulder height. Stop. Then continue very slowly to extend your arms above your head, but keep them fully submerged. Your feet will rise slowly as your arms move up. Breathe quickly again. To recover, bring your knees up to your chest, drop your chin forward, and sweep your arms downward behind you and forward past your hips, palms forward. Stay tucked until your feet are under you, then stand. Repeat five times.

**To Increase Difficulty**

- Float for 3 minutes.
- Move forward by pulling arms strongly back to your sides.

**To Decrease Difficulty**

- Have a friend hold two fingers behind your neck as you recover.
- If you feel your face is bobbing, hold each breath a little longer.
- Use a float belt.
- Use a nose clip to keep water out of your nose.

## Success Check

- Fully inflate lungs.
- Arch back and extend arms overhead.
- Breathe very quickly.
- Move very slowly.
- Tuck and scoop to recover.

## Score Your Success

Earn 1 point for each full minute you hold the float, up to 5 minutes.

Your score ___

## Back Float Drill 3. *Deep-Water Back Float*

With a skilled swimmer holding a large float belt in the water at your side, try the back float in deep water (figure 1.5). Recover by taking hold of the float belt and kicking your way back to the edge. Do three deep-water back floats, holding the float position and breathing for 30 seconds.

### To Increase Difficulty

- Keep your arms at your sides and do a nearly vertical float with your chin fully extended.
- Maintain a deep-water float for 10 minutes.

### To Decrease Difficulty

- Wear a nose clip.
- Wear a float belt.

## Success Check

- Keep eyes open.
- Breathe quickly and fully.
- Move slowly.

## Score Your Success

Float for 30 seconds = 1 point
Float for 1 minute = 2 points
Float for 3 minutes = 3 points
Your score ___

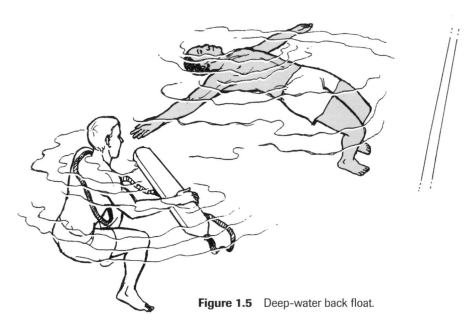

**Figure 1.5** Deep-water back float.

7

## Back Float Drill 4. *Back Float From a Standing Position*

In chin-deep water, stand on the bottom of the pool, arms out at shoulder height, palms up. Tilt your head back until your ears are underwater. Take a deep breath, arch your back, and drift back into floating position. Do not try to lift your heels from the bottom. When you are floating, move your arms slowly overhead underwater and allow your heels to drift up. Breathe and hold the float for as long as is comfortable. Relax your neck muscles, shoulder muscles, arm muscles, and legs in that order. Recover. Do three floats for 2 minutes each.

Ask an expert swimmer or an instructor to watch your back float and to make suggestions for improving it according to the success checks.

**To Increase Difficulty**

- "Step" up to the surface with your feet while you float.
- Use your arms to pull yourself toward shallow water.

**To Decrease Difficulty**

- Have a friend stand directly behind you with one finger behind your neck for confidence.
- If your heels stay on the bottom, bend your knees as you drift back.

### Success Check

- Submerge ears.
- Stretch arms overhead, underwater, until heels lift.
- Keep hips up.

### Score Your Success

Earn 1 point for each 2-minute float, for a maximum total of 3 points.

Your score ____

# SUCCESS SUMMARY OF BUOYANCY AND BACK FLOAT

If you have scored a total of 8 points in this step, you have mastered the hardest part of learning how to swim. You proved to yourself that your body is lighter than water when you hold your breath. You can breathe and control your buoyancy and body position in the water. This knowledge can be a lifesaver. If you fall into deep water, simply hold your breath until you surface, then go into a back float until you can attract attention and get help. Your clothing may actually hold enough air to help you float.

Rate your progress as excellent if you scored 20 to 26 points. Good progress is indicated by a score of 10 to 19 points. If you scored 9 points or fewer, go back through the drills and fine-tune your technique before moving to the next step.

*Buoyancy Drills*

  1.  Vertical Buoyancy     ___ out of 10

  2.  Deep-Water Adjustment     ___ out of 4

*Back Float Drills*

  1.  Land Drill for Breathing     ___ out of 1

  2.  Beginning Back Float     ___ out of 5

  3.  Deep-Water Back Float     ___ out of 3

  4.  Back Float From a Standing Position     ___ out of 3

*Total*     ___ *out of 26*

# Basic Backstroke

Now that you know you have the natural ability to remain at the surface of the water just by breathing deeply and quickly, you need to learn how to move from place to place while floating. This step will show you how.

Pulling or pushing on the water while your body is floating is the basis of all forward motion in the water. Floating is effortless, and your arms and legs can pull or push on the water as gently or as forcefully as you wish. Pulling and kicking for support and propulsion can move you through the water as you float on your back.

## BACKSTROKE SUPPORT KICK

Leg and foot motions in swimming serve three functions: support, propulsion, and balance. The relative importance of these three functions varies greatly from person to person. Learners who have buoyant legs will need very little, if any, support from the leg and foot motion. They may spend less time on this skill and move on to backstroke kicking for propulsion.

For all swimmers and for all strokes, kicking supplies at least one of the functions of support, propulsion, or balance. Therefore, you need to learn proper methods of leg and ankle motion and the variations within a kick that aid in determining which of the functions will be maximized. At this stage we are more interested in support than in propulsion.

While floating on your back, extend the toes of your right foot (figure 2.1a). Press down on the water with the sole of your right foot. Then draw your foot toward your body by bending at the knee and the hip. Just before your knee breaks the surface, hook your ankle and step up to the surface (figure 2.1b). Your left leg and foot perform the same motions in opposition to the right leg and foot. The result is very similar to pedaling a bicycle with emphasis on pressing the pedals downward with your toes extended (figure 2.1c). Keep your feet and knees under the surface of the water. Your ankle should be hooked when moving up, and your foot should be pointed when moving down as you press the water with the soles of your feet. Do not make a splash. Recover as from a back float.

| Figure 2.1 | Support Kick With Back Float |

## BACK FLOAT

1. Extend legs
2. Point toes of right foot

*a*

## KICK

1. Press down with sole of right foot
2. Bring foot toward body, hook ankle
3. Step up to surface
4. Press with left leg as right leg recovers

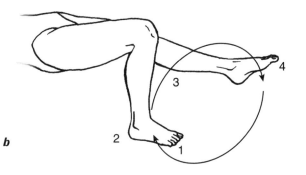

*b*

## CONTINUOUS MOTION

1. Move feet and legs as if pedaling a bicycle
2. Continue to circle
3. Keep knees and feet below the surface

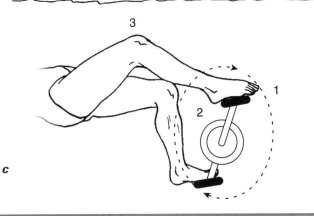

*c*

**Misstep**

Your hips sink to a sitting position.

**Correction**

Arch your back. Push your hips up by pressing your foot down.

# Support Kick Drill 1. *Support Kick at the Wall*

In shallow water with your back against the pool wall, stretch your arms out to the side and hook your elbows over the edge of the overflow trough. With your hips bent, extend your legs in front of you. Extend the toes of your right foot. Press down on the water with the sole of your foot. Then draw your foot toward your body by bending at the knee and the hip. Just before your knee breaks the surface, hook your ankle and step up to the surface. As the right foot steps up to the surface, press down with the left foot in the same manner. The result is a motion very similar to riding a bicycle, with emphasis on pressing the pedals down with your toes extended. Step your feet up to the surface. As your feet move up, straighten your hips until your whole body is nearly horizontal. Do not allow your feet to break the surface. Step to the surface five times and hold the position for 2 minutes each time.

**To Increase Difficulty**

- Do a back float from a standing position away from the side, kicking your legs and feet to the surface.

**To Decrease Difficulty**

- Have someone stand behind you and hold you under the armpits instead of hooking your arms over the side.

## Success Check

- Step your feet to the surface.
- Raise hips until body is nearly horizontal.
- Keep knees and feet underwater.

### Score Your Success

Complete five step-ups to the side = 1 point each

Step up from back-float position with no help = 1 additional point each time

Your score ___

# Support Kick Drill 2. *Support Kick With Kickboard*

In shallow water, hold a kickboard overhead. Lie back on the water, head resting on the edge of the kickboard (figure 2.2). Keep your back arched and hips up. Use the support kick to step up to the surface. Avoid dropping your hips. Keep your chin up. Kick continuously for 3 minutes. Note your forward progress.

**To Increase Difficulty**

- Do not use the kickboard and start in back-float position with your arms overhead.

**To Decrease Difficulty**

- Have someone hold the kickboard.
- Wear goggles, a nose clip, or both.

## Success Check

- Step your feet smoothly to the surface.
- Maintain a horizontal position.
- Do not splash.

### Score Your Success

Kick continuously for 3 minutes with kickboard = 1 point

Kick continuously for 3 minutes without kickboard = 3 points

Your score ___

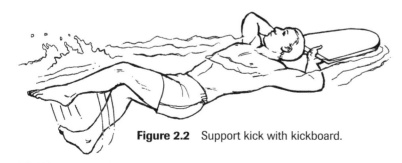

**Figure 2.2** Support kick with kickboard.

# BACK CRAWL KICK FOR PROPULSION

Another function of the kick in swimming is to propel the swimmer. Propulsion from your legs varies greatly with the type of kick and the flexibility of your ankles. In some strokes, the kick supplies a major portion of the propulsion. In other strokes, the gain in propulsion may not be worth the expenditure of energy. Because it resembles the forward-and-back motion of walking, the back crawl kick is the easiest to learn for propulsion in a back-float position.

The back crawl kick is the first propulsive movement of the legs you will learn. It is not a necessary motion for floating on your back, but rather an optional motion for moving forward. There is a natural tendency to move your legs while swimming. If you don't need your legs for supporting movements, you need to move them in an efficient, propulsive manner rather than allowing them to cause resistance by dragging. This kick will also be useful to you later when you learn the back crawl stroke.

To perform the back crawl kick, start from a back-float position with both arms extended overhead. Relax your ankles completely so that your feet can flop fully relaxed. Drop one leg down about 24 to 30 inches (60.96 to 76.2 centimeters), keeping the other knee straight (figure 2.3a). Water pressure will force your ankle to hook during the downward motion. Move your leg up again, allowing your knee to bend slightly as in a forward walking step (figure 2.3b). The upward movement will press your ankle into a pointed-toe position. Raise your leg until your knee is just under the surface. Stop your knee at this point and straighten your leg. Your foot will spoon the water up and back, raising a mound of water. Move your other leg in the same manner, but in the opposite direction, causing an alternate up-and-back thrust of your feet against the water. If your ankles are truly relaxed, your toes will naturally turn slightly inward. Recover by dropping your hips into a sitting position and scooping your hands forward from behind your hips.

## Figure 2.3    Back Crawl Kick

### DROP RIGHT FOOT

1. Drop right leg 24 to 30 inches
2. Keep left knee straight

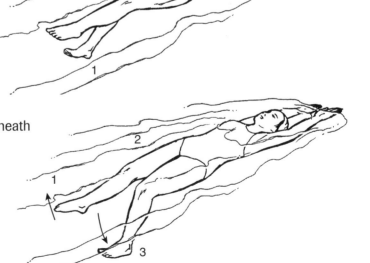

a

### DROP LEFT FOOT

1. Raise right leg until knee is just beneath the surface
2. Straighten right knee
3. Lower left foot

b

**Misstep**

You get little or no propulsion.

**Correction**

Relax your ankle and allow your foot to turn in on the upthrust. Bend knees to only 45 degrees.

# Back Crawl Kick Drill 1.

# *Back Crawl Kick With Kickboard*

For this drill, you may wear goggles if you wish. In shallow water, hold a kickboard against your chest. Assume a back-float position (figure 2.4). Lift your chin slightly. Kick up and back, but try not to produce a splash. Instead try to raise a mound of water above your feet as you kick. Emphasize the backward thrust and keep your hips at the surface. Note your forward progress. Kick for 15 yards (13.716 meters) without stopping.

 **Be alert when approaching the end of the pool. Do not bump your head. Look for a ladder on the side of the pool near the end, place a piece of equipment on the side of the pool, or use the backstroke turn flags hanging over the pool to indicate that you are near the edge.**

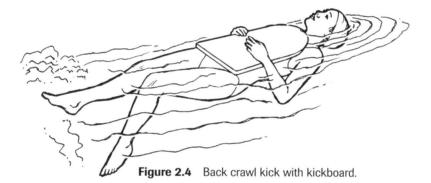

**Figure 2.4** Back crawl kick with kickboard.

**To Increase Difficulty**

• Repeat the drill without the kickboard and keep hands at your sides.
• Repeat the drill without the kickboard and extend hands overhead.

**To Decrease Difficulty**

• Think about the up-and-back pressure of the water on the tops of your feet.
• Wear goggles, a nose clip, or both.

## Success Check

• Keep hips straight.
• Dig in with toes and lift.
• Raise a mound of water over your feet.

## Score Your Success

Kick for 15 yards = 1 point
Kick for 15 yards without a kickboard = 3 points
Your score ___

## Back Crawl Kick Drill 2.

## *Backstroke Kick With Board Overhead*

Float on your back in shallow water with both arms stretched straight overhead. Hold the trailing edge of a kickboard in both hands. Keep your head back between your arms so that both ears are underwater, and keep your hips up as you kick across the pool. Keep your knees and feet underwater, but try to raise a mound of water above your feet. Goggles are optional. To avoid getting water in your nose, inhale through your mouth and exhale through your nose. Practice until you can kick three times across the pool (about 45 yards, 41.148 meters), stopping only to turn at the sides.

**To Increase Difficulty**

- Let go of the kickboard and continue kicking.
- Start the next lap without the kickboard.

**To Decrease Difficulty**

- Wear goggles, a nose clip, or both.
- Have someone hold the kickboard until you get your kick started.

### *Success Check*

- Keep your hips at the surface.
- Raise a mound of water over your feet.

### *Score Your Success*

Kick for 45 yards = 2 points

Kick for 45 yards without a kickboard = 4 points

Your score ___

# BASIC BACKSTROKE ARM PULL

To be safe in the water, you need a method of propulsion that will get you from one place to another. Your have seen how a back crawl kick can move you through the water, but you need skills that will enable you to swim for some distance without tiring. The basic backstroke arm pull will solve that problem.

Several types of arm motions are possible with a backstroke. The basic backstroke arm pull is not only powerful but also conserves energy. It follows the back crawl kick in the most efficient learning progression.

The basic backstroke arm pull propels you with considerable speed and incorporates a long glide phase that allows you to rest between strokes. Some swimmers have actually saved their own lives with the basic backstroke arm pull when they were too fatigued to continue swimming by any other means. This is a stroke to use for long distances.

Start the basic backstroke arm pull in the back-float position with your arms along your sides. Slide both thumbs up along your sides until your thumbs are touching the tops of your shoulders and your wrists are fully flexed (figure 2.5a). Rotate your forearms until your fingertips point out. Extend your arms, fingertips leading, slightly above shoulder level (figure 2.5b). Take hold of the water with your hands and arms. Think about fastening your hands to the water and pulling your body past your hands. Pull horizontally just beneath the surface, from shoulders to thighs. If your pull is level, your arms will finish the pull slightly in front of your thighs. For the recovery phase, perform a long glide in a streamlined back-float position (figure 2.5c).

## Figure 2.5 | Basic Backstroke Arm Motion

### BACK FLOAT

1. Float on back, arms at sides
2. Slide thumbs up sides to shoulders
3. Turn hands outward

*a*

### REACH AND PULL

1. Extend arms out and up
2. Stretch arms just above shoulder level
3. Pull arms toward feet
4. Keep arms level under the water

*b*

### GLIDE

1. Glide in the water
2. Keep arms at sides
3. Relax and recover

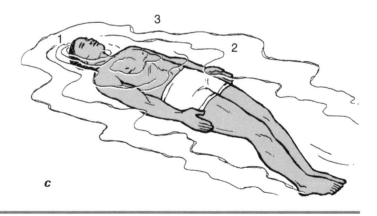

*c*

**Misstep**

Your body rises in the water and then sinks.

**Correction**

Keep arms level when pulling just under the surface of the water.

**17**

## Basic Backstroke Drill 1. *Basic Backstroke Arm Pull*

In shallow water at the edge of the pool, start the basic backstroke arm pull in a back-float position. Slide both of your thumbs up along your sides until your thumbs are touching the tops of your shoulders and wrists are fully flexed. Rotate your forearms until your fingertips point out. Extend your arms, fingertips leading, slightly above shoulder level. Take hold of the water with your hands and arms and pull evenly and forcefully down toward your feet. Your feet will be a little deeper in the water, so your pull will finish slightly in front of your body. Stop and glide in a streamlined back-float position with your arms at your sides. When your forward motion slows almost to a stop, reach and pull again. Continue across the pool. Count how many strokes it takes to get across the pool (about 15 yards, 13.716 meters).

**To Increase Difficulty**

- Try to travel 5 feet (1.524 meters) per stroke.
- Reach well above shoulder height.

**To Decrease Difficulty**

- Use a slow support kick.
- Wear a nose clip, goggles, or both.

### Success Check

- Slide thumbs to tops of shoulders.
- Keep hands and arms underwater.
- Pull long and strong.
- Stop and glide.

### Score Your Success

Swim 15 yards without stopping = 2 points
Swim 15 yards in 9 strokes or fewer = 4 points
Your score ___

## Basic Backstroke Drill 2. *Deep-Water Backstroke Pull*

With a skilled swimmer beside you, begin with a back float in deep water and pull into shallow water. Try to extend your distance to 25 yards (22.86 meters).

**To Increase Difficulty**

- Stay away from the edge of the pool.
- Have the skilled swimmer watch from the side of the pool.

**To Decrease Difficulty**

- Stay close to the edge of the pool for confidence.
- Use a slow support kick.
- Wear a nose clip, goggles, or both.

### Success Check

- Make long, full pulls.
- Keep your arms and hands underwater.
- Glide after each stroke.
- Keep your hips up.

### Score Your Success

Swim 25 yards from deep water without stopping = 2 points
Swim 25 yards from deep water without stopping, away from edge of pool = 4 points
Your score ___

## Basic Backstroke Drill 3.

# *Deep-Water Basic Backstroke*

Start in deep water in a back-float position with a skilled swimmer beside you. Begin kicking with the back crawl kick, then add long, full arm pulls toward shallow water. Continue to kick while you glide with your arms at your sides. Swim for 25 yards without stopping.

**To Increase Difficulty**

- Swim in the middle of the pool.

**To Decrease Difficulty**

- Stay close to the edge of the pool.
- Breathe deeply.
- Wear goggles, a nose clip, or both.

## *Success Check*

- Keep your hands underwater.
- Take long glides while kicking.
- Keep your hips up and back straight.

### *Score Your Success*

Swim 25 yards from deep water = 3 points

Swim 25 yards from deep water, away from edge of pool = 4 points

Your score ___

## Basic Backstroke Drill 4.

# *Basic Backstroke Turn*

In shallow water, begin the basic backstroke across the pool. Use the back crawl kick as you pull. After three full strokes, stop pulling and hold one arm at your side (figure 2.6). Continue to kick and pull with the other arm. Expect to turn in a direction away from the pulling arm. Continue to pull with one arm until you have completed a full circle, then pull with both arms again. During the turn, stroke continuously with no glide. Repeat the drill using the other arm to turn. Do three circles in each direction.

**To Increase Difficulty**

- Turn a half circle, then shift arms and turn back again.
- Do not wear goggles or a nose clip.

## *Success Check*

- Keep your body straight.
- Do not splash with your feet.
- Turn slowly 360 degrees.

### *Score Your Success*

Complete one circle = 1 point

Complete three circles = 2 points

Complete three circles without using goggles or a nose clip = 3 points

Your score ___

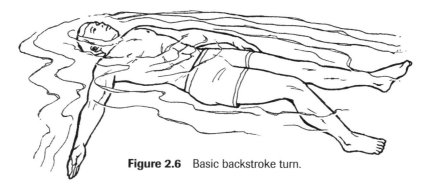

**Figure 2.6** Basic backstroke turn.

**19**

## Basic Backstroke Drill 5.   *Deep-Water Swim and Turn*

Start in shallow water. Use the basic backstroke to swim into deep water, then turn and swim back into shallow water. For safety, have a skilled swimmer watch you. Do five deep-water turns in each direction.

### To Increase Difficulty

- Swim from the deep end to the shallow end of the pool, turn, and return to the deep end.

### To Decrease Difficulty

- Swim completely around a skilled swimmer in deep water.
- Use goggles, a nose clip, or both.

### *Success Check*

- Keep your hips at the surface while turning.
- Glide after each stroke while swimming straight.

### *Score Your Success*

Complete three deep-water turns = 1 point

Complete five deep-water turns = 2 points

Complete a turn without using goggles or a nose clip = 1 additional point each time

Your score ____

# SUCCESS SUMMARY OF BASIC BACKSTROKE

The basic backstroke is the first stroke in your swimming repertoire. It is the greatest confidence builder and best safety maneuver in swimming.

Review your scores for the drills in this step. If you have earned 30 or more points, you have mastered the backstroke and can proceed to step 3. If you have fewer than 30 points, repeat the drills that gave you the most trouble and ask for additional help before starting step 3.

| | |
|---|---:|
| *Support Kick Drills* | |
| 1. Support Kick at the Wall | ____ out of 10 |
| 2. Support Kick With Kickboard | ____ out of 3 |
| *Back Crawl Kick Drills* | |
| 1. Back Crawl Kick With Kickboard | ____ out of 3 |
| 2. Backstroke Kick With Board Overhead | ____ out of 4 |
| *Basic Backstroke Drills* | |
| 1. Basic Backstroke Arm Pull | ____ out of 4 |
| 2. Deep-Water Backstroke Pull | ____ out of 4 |
| 3. Deep-Water Basic Backstroke | ____ out of 4 |
| 4. Basic Backstroke Turn | ____ out of 3 |
| 5. Deep-Water Swim and Turn | ____ out of 7 |
| *Total* | ____ *out of 42* |

# Prone Float and Crawl Kick

This step to success in swimming rests on the basic premise that if you float and push or pull, you are swimming! In this step, you'll float in a prone position (on your front so that you can see where you are going) while you push or pull. You'll also be introduced to some items of equipment that will allow you to learn swimming skills without experiencing the discomfort that beginners occasionally experience. A mask, fins, and snorkel will help you on your way to success in swimming.

## FACE MASK, SNORKEL, AND SWIM FINS

A face mask should have a soft, flexible skirt that fits your face snugly, and it should have a face plate of safety glass or tempered glass (figure 3.1). A face mask performs two functions: It keeps water from your eyes and nose, and it allows you to see clearly underwater. Check the fit of a mask by placing it against your face without using the strap. Then inhale gently to create suction. If the mask remains on your face until you exhale, then it fits. Keep the mask from fogging by applying four drops of dishwashing detergent to the inside of the glass. Rub the detergent around and rinse thoroughly at least twice.

Masks may be split into two separate eye pieces or consist of a single faceplate that can be round, oval, or rectangular. Let fit and comfort determine the shape you use.

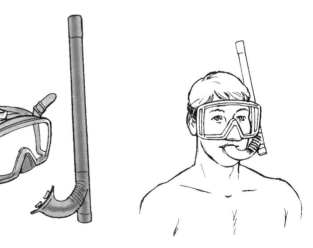

**Figure 3.1** Face mask and snorkel.

The mask strap should be split into two sections so that it will fit your head. It should have an easy adjustable mechanism at the side. Some masks come with built-in purge valves to clear water that leaks into the faceplate. You can purchase masks with prescription lenses if you need them.

Masks come in many colors and materials. Most have frames of colored plastic with skirts of black rubber or silicone compounds. Those with skirts made of silicone are translucent, allowing more light into the mask. They are also less susceptible to damage from exposure to the sun.

A snorkel should have a soft, flexible curved section and a comfortable mouthpiece. When attached to the mask strap, it will fit comfortably in your mouth, remain upright while you swim, and allow you to breathe normally while your face is submerged. You can expel any water that inadvertently finds its way into the open end of the snorkel by puffing sharply into the snorkel to clear it. A little practice will allow you to clear your snorkel easily.

Snorkels come in various lengths but should never be more than 16 inches (40.64 centimeters) long. Those with purge valves near the mouthpiece are considerably easier to clear of extraneous water than those without.

The diameter of the snorkel tube also varies. In general, snorkel tubes with wider diameters supply more air with less effort than those with smaller diameters. Several attempts have been made to attach devices to snorkels to keep water from entering the top. None of them have been successful. Beginners should use only a basic snorkel with a purge valve.

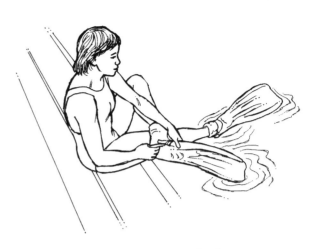

**Figure 3.2**  Proper way to put on swim fins.

Swim fins (figure 3.2) provide much more effective propulsion than legs and feet alone. Such power aids greatly in increasing the confidence of a beginning swimmer. Fins may encompass the full foot and heel in a shoelike cup, or they may have only an adjustable strap around the heel area. It is common practice to wear heavy socks or scuba boots inside swim fins, but you may wish to use them on bare feet. Fins that are too tight can cause foot cramps; fins that are too loose may cause blisters on bare skin. Some fins sink if dropped, and others float. Beginning swimmers might be better served with floating fins.

Never put fins on by pulling the strap or heel socket. Wet the fins and your feet, then slide your foot all the way into the pocket before slipping the strap or heel pocket onto your heel. It is dangerous to walk in swim fins, but if you must walk, walk backward to prevent tripping or breaking the fins.

# PRONE FLOAT

You learned in previous steps that your body is lighter than water (or that you need a small float belt). Your body retains its buoyancy regardless of the position you assume. It floats just as well facedown as faceup. That's common sense.

The prone float is the basis for the most popular swimming strokes, such as the crawl stroke and the breaststroke. Remember that all swimming strokes simply involve floating while you push or pull yourself through the water. Note: If

you needed a float belt for the back float, you will also need one for the prone float.

For the prone float, put on your mask and snorkel and be sure to adjust them properly for comfort. Stand in shoulder-deep water and cautiously place your face in the water (figure 3.3a). Breathe normally through your mouth. Notice that you can see the bottom clearly and that breathing is easy. Take a few moments to get used to the sensation.

Take a deep breath and hold it. Slowly slide your hands down the fronts of your legs to your ankles (figure 3.3b). You will notice that your feet want to leave the bottom. Hold your breath as you fully extend your arms forward and your legs backward (figure 3.3c). Take a new breath quickly and hold it.

When you're ready to recover, bend at the waist to bring your legs back down, and put your hands on your knees again. Slide your hands back up to your thighs as you stand. Breathe.

## Figure 3.3    **Prone Float**

### PREPARATION

1. Put on mask and snorkel
2. Stand in chest-deep water
3. Bend forward, putting face in the water
4. Place hands on thighs

### BEGIN TO FLOAT

1. Breathe deeply
2. Slide hands down legs toward ankles
3. Feet leave the pool floor

### FLOAT AND RECOVER

1. Hold breath
2. Extend arms and legs
3. Put hands on knees
4. Slide hands to thighs and stand

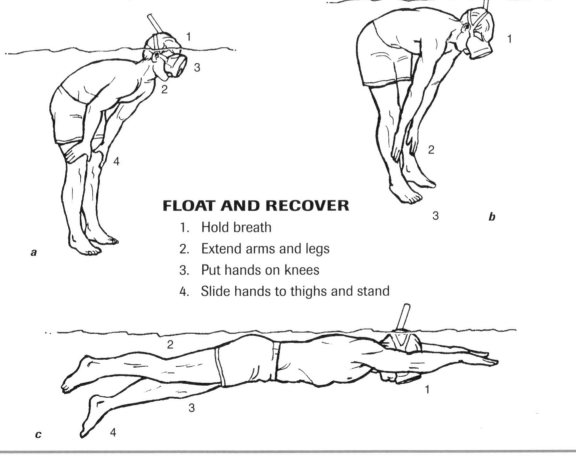

### Misstep

Your feet remain on the bottom of the pool.

### Correction

Take a bigger breath. If you needed a float belt for the back float, you may need one now for the prone float.

## Prone Float Drill 1. *Pick Up an Object*

Adjust your mask and snorkel so that the fit is snug and comfortable. Breathe through your mouth. Stand in shoulder-deep water with the toes of one foot on a coin or any object that sinks. Put your hands on your thighs. Place your face in the water and breathe through your snorkel. Take a deep breath and hold it, then slowly slide your hands down your legs and try to pick up the object. Your feet will come off the bottom, but you will not be able to reach the object. Slide your hands back up your legs and stand. Try three times to pick up the object, holding a deep breath each time. Prove to yourself that you cannot sink even if you tried.

**To Increase Difficulty**

- Hold the jellyfish position for 10 seconds before standing.
- Perform the same drill without the mask and snorkel.

**To Decrease Difficulty**

- Have a friend stand directly in front of you for confidence.
- Wear a float belt only if you need it.

### Success Check

- Move slowly.
- Hold all the air you can take in.
- Hang suspended like a jellyfish.
- Slide hands back up to thighs.

### Score Your Success

Score 2 points if you find you *cannot* pick up the object. Score 2 more points if you can do the drill without the mask and snorkel.

Your score ___

## Prone Float Drill 2. *Prone Float*

Put on a mask and snorkel as shown in figure 3.1, page 21. Stand in shoulder-deep water and place your face in the water. Breathe normally through your mouth. Take a deep breath and hold it, then slowly slide your hands down the front of your legs to your ankles. Your feet will float up from the bottom. (Use a float belt at your hips only if your feet stay on the bottom.)

Hold your breath as you fully extend your arms forward and your legs backward. Exhale and inhale deeply very quickly and hold it. Hold this position and take quick breaths as needed. When you are ready to recover, bend at the waist to bring your legs back down, and put your hands on your knees. Slide your hands back up to your thighs as you stand. Repeat the drill and hold the prone-float position for at least 20 seconds.

**To Increase Difficulty**

- Perform the drill without a mask and snorkel for 20 seconds.

**To Decrease Difficulty**

- Take deeper breaths.
- Spread arms and legs slightly when extended.
- Have a friend stand directly in front of you to assist you to your feet.

### Success Check

- Take and hold deep breaths.
- Slide hands down your legs slowly.
- Watch your feet lift.
- Stretch out flat.
- Put hands on knees again to recover.
- Stand.

### Score Your Success

Float for 20 seconds while wearing a mask and snorkel = 2 points

Float for 20 seconds without a mask and snorkel = 4 points

Your score ___

# Prone Float Drill 3. *Prone Float and Glide*

Put on your mask and snorkel and stand with your back against the wall. Extend your arms in front of you. Place one foot against the wall and place your face in the water (figure 3.4a). Push off the wall into prone-float position (figure 3.4b). Streamline your body, especially your feet and toes, and lift your hands to the very top of the water. Glide. When your glide is finished, press down forcefully with both hands while drawing your knees into a tight tuck (figure 3.4c). Keep pressing until you are upright before attempting to put your feet down. Repeat, trying for a glide of 20 feet (6.096 meters).

**To Increase Difficulty**

- Eliminate the mask and snorkel.

**To Decrease Difficulty**

- Decrease the distance of the glide and try to glide for 20 seconds.
- Have a friend stand by to help you recover.

## Success Check

- Streamline your body.
- Lift hands to top.
- Press hands and tuck knees simultaneously.

## Score Your Success

Glide for 20 feet or for 20 seconds = 2 points

Glide for 20 feet or for 20 seconds without a mask or snorkel = 4 points

Your score ___

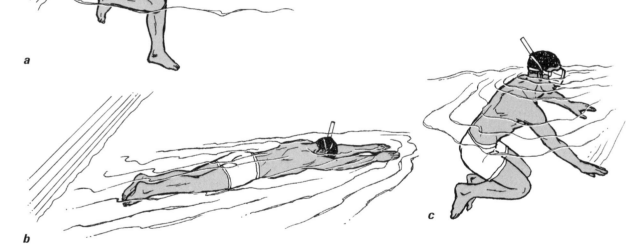

**Figure 3.4** Prone float and glide: *(a)* one foot on wall, face in the water; *(b)* glide in prone-float position; *(c)* recover.

# CRAWL STROKE KICK

The crawl stroke kick is nearly identical to the back crawl kick, but it is performed in the prone position. It varies in power from person to person, depending on ankle flexibility, timing of the knee bend, and speed of the kick in relation to the arm stroke. Some people find that the crawl stroke kick requires more energy than they are willing to expend for the results they obtain, but in this step you will use swim fins, which enhance the power of the kick to make it an exciting experience for any swimmer.

The crawl stroke is the stroke that defines swimming. If you mention swimming, the image that comes to mind immediately is of a person swimming the crawl stroke. No other stroke is as well known. The crawl stroke kick is an integral part of this stroke; it contributes to its speed, power, and usefulness.

To perform the crawl stroke kick (figure 3.5), wear your mask and snorkel and get in a prone-float position with arms extended in front of you. Relax your ankles completely so that your feet can flop fully relaxed. Remember the up-and-down motion you used in the back crawl kick.

Kick easily in an up-and-down motion. Make your kick very narrow. Keep your knees nearly straight; kick your whole leg from the hip with loose, floppy ankles. Only your heels should break the surface. Tilt your head up so that you look forward under the water. Breathe normally. Kick for propulsion. If your ankles are loose and your feet extend well, you will get good forward motion.

To recover, press down with both hands and pull your knees up into a tuck position simultaneously. Continue to press down until your feet are under you, then stand.

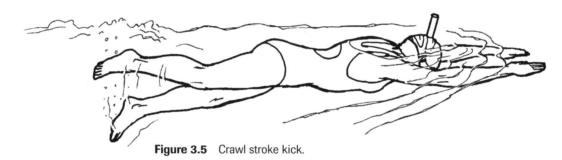

**Figure 3.5** Crawl stroke kick.

## Crawl Stroke Kick Drill 1.

## Crawl Stroke Kick With Mask, Snorkel, and Swim Fins

Put on swim fins as shown in figure 3.2, page 22. Wear a pair of athletic socks with the swim fins to prevent chafing by fins that may not fit perfectly. Put on your mask and snorkel. Hold a kickboard with both hands extended in front of you. Do not try to kick the fins. Kick your legs from the hips with straight knees, and let the fins do whatever they may do. Your ankles must be relaxed so that the fins can flop properly to provide propulsion. You will be aware of tremendous propulsion. Keep your chin up so that you look ahead and slightly down. Breathe normally. Kick one pool width or 15 yards (13.716 meters).

**To Increase Difficulty**

- Discard the kickboard and keep arms extended.
- Increase the distance to 30 yards (27.432 meters).

**To Decrease Difficulty**

- Kick slowly, resisting the urge to go fast.

### Success Check

- Kick your legs, not the fins.
- Keep ankles relaxed and floppy.
- Tilt head and look forward underwater.

## Score Your Success

Kick 15 yards = 2 points

Kick 30 yards = 3 points

Kick 30 yards without kickboard = 4 points

Your score ___

# Crawl Stroke Kick Drill 2.

## Crawl Kick Without Fins

Repeat crawl stroke kick drill 1 without swim fins. Notice the difference in propulsion. Keep your knees fairly straight and ankles relaxed. Do not kick your feet. Kick your legs from the hips and let the feet flop. Kick for 15 yards (13.716 meters).

### To Increase Difficulty

- Try to kick for 30 feet (9.144 meters) without mask or snorkel. Keep head down, but press on kickboard and raise your head forward to breathe when needed.

### To Decrease Difficulty

- Decrease the distance to 10 yards (9.144 meters).

## Success Check

- Use a narrow kick with floppy ankles.
- Lift the kickboard with your hands.

## Score Your Success

Kick 15 yards = 1 point

Kick 30 yards = 2 points

Kick 30 feet without mask or snorkel = 3 additional points

Your score ___

# Crawl Stroke Kick Drill 3.

## Deep-Water Kicking

Wear mask, snorkel, fins, and a float belt at your hips. Have a good swimmer beside you. Start at the deep end of the pool. Hold a kickboard at full arm extension in front of you. Kick to the shallow end or at least 30 feet into shallow water. Repeat the drill.

### To Increase Difficulty

- Remove the float belt on the second trip.
- Perform the drill close to the edge of the pool with a good swimmer beside you, but without the mask and snorkel. Press gently on the kickboard to raise your head to breathe.

### To Decrease Difficulty

- Stay close to the edge of the pool.
- Start only 20 feet from shallow water.

## Success Check

- Keep knees straight and ankles loose.
- Keep head down.
- Breathe normally.
- Use a narrow kick.

## Score Your Success

Kick for 30 feet with mask, snorkel, and fins = 2 points

Kick for 30 feet with fins only = 4 points

Your score ___

# SUCCESS SUMMARY OF PRONE FLOAT AND CRAWL KICK

To be sure you perform the prone float and kicking correctly, have a swimming expert or instructor check your skills against the success checks listed with each drill.

If you scored at least 15 points in the drills for this step, your progress is satisfactory. If you scored 16 to 20 points, you are making good progress, and 21 points or more indicates excellent progress. You have learned a lot in step 3—your body is equally buoyant in any position, and you can easily do a prone float. Kicking can provide support as well as propulsion, and masks, fins, and snorkels make swimming easier. You have even sampled the joys of skindiving. You are ready now to move on to step 4, where you'll learn some actual facedown swimming and breathing without a snorkel.

---

### Prone Float Drills

1. Pick Up an Object                                          ___ out of 4
2. Prone Float                                                ___ out of 4
3. Prone Float and Glide                                      ___ out of 4

### Crawl Stroke Kick Drills

1. Crawl Stroke Kick With Mask, Snorkel, and Swim Fins        ___ out of 4
2. Crawl Kick Without Fins                                    ___ out of 5
3. Deep-Water Kicking                                         ___ out of 4

### *Total*                                                   ___ *out of 25*

---

# Crawl Stroke and Breathing

Pushing and pulling on the water while you float get you to your goal. Any pushing motion of your feet and any pulling motion with your arms will fit the definition of swimming. Efficiency in swimming, however, is highly desirable, and to swim efficiently we must put together a package of pulling and pushing movements that apply the most pressure to the water with the least expenditure of energy.

The crawl stroke is the most efficient stroke known. It propels a swimmer faster than any other combination of arm and leg motions.

It's the choice of all competitive swimmers for freestyle races, which allow the swimmer to swim in any fashion he or she desires. The crawl stroke is not the easiest stroke to swim, and for survival you will turn to other strokes. Nevertheless, it will likely be your stroke of choice when you go swimming. The crawl is the stroke on which people will judge your swimming ability. They will not pay much attention to your ability to swim backstroke or breaststroke, but they will notice how well you swim the crawl.

## CRAWL ARM STROKE

The crawl arm stroke is the most visible part of the stroke. It is the part of the stroke that is seen by spectators, and it defines your proficiency in the crawl stroke.

The arm stroke is the most powerful part of the crawl stroke. The feet and legs contribute a driving force as well, but they use a great deal of energy and are somewhat less useful in this stroke. The arm stroke will determine your speed in swimming.

To learn the crawl arm stroke, attach a deep-float leg float to one ankle (figure 4.1). Keep your legs together and still while learning this skill.

Put on your mask and snorkel. Push off the wall in a prone glide with arms stretched in front. The arm stroke may begin with either arm. For the sake of clarity and brevity, however, we will describe the stroke as beginning with the right arm and moving through an S-shaped path (figure 4.2).

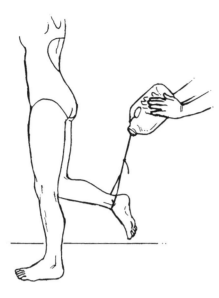

**Figure 4.1** Deep-float leg support attached to one ankle.

**Figure 4.2** S-shaped arm path.

Relax the hands, but keep the fingers straight. Do not squeeze the fingers tightly together. A small space between them will not greatly affect the pulling power but will allow greater relaxation.

Bend your right wrist and rotate the entire arm medially (inward), pointing your fingers down and out at about 45 degrees. As your arm rotates, allow a slight bend in your elbow, which will turn your hand slightly palm out. Lock your hand, wrist, and elbow rigidly in that position and move your arm out so that the hand moves laterally about 10 or 12 inches (25.4 to 30.48 centimeters). This outward motion, if done properly, produces pressure on the palm of the hand. This sculling motion also uses Bernoulli's principle (which is a factor in airplane wing lift)

to create a pulling force over the back of your hand. This first propulsive force of the arm stroke is shown from two viewpoints in figure 4.3.

As your hand reaches the end of its short outward movement, smoothly rotate the forearm, straighten the wrist, and bend the elbow to an angle of about 90 degrees so that your fingertips point down and slightly in (figure 4.4). Your hand should then slice down, across, and back to the centerline of your body at about the level of your chin. This movement is partially sculling motion and partially pulling motion. The sculling component of the movement adds Bernoulli lift forces to the back of the hand while the palm of the hand presses backward. This is an important part of the propulsive force of the arm stroke.

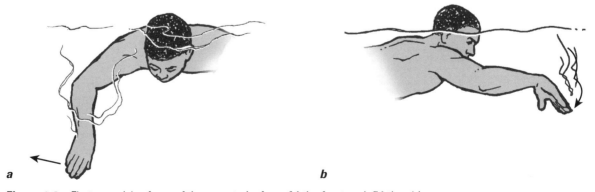

*a*  *b*

**Figure 4.3** First propulsive force of the arm stroke from *(a)* the front and *(b)* the side.

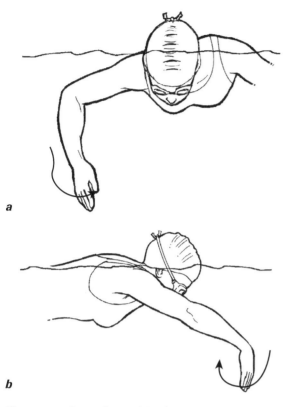

*a*

*b*

**Figure 4.4** Second propulsive force of the arm stroke from *(a)* the front and *(b)* the side.

Continue the 90-degree bend in your elbow as your entire arm begins to pull from the shoulder. At this point, the upper arm should be at the level of your shoulder but slightly slanted out so that, with the elbow bent 90 degrees, your hand is directly under your chin on the centerline of your body (figure 4.5). Your entire arm—forearm, wrist, hand, and upper arm—is perpendicular to the direction of the pull.

Pull your arm directly back with the hand about 6 inches (15.24 centimeters) under the centerline of your body. At this point, the pull transforms into a push. As the push progresses, begin to relax your wrist, and allow the water pressure to bend your wrist back so that the palm remains

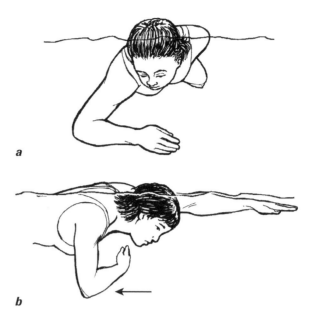

*a*

*b*

**Figure 4.5** *(a)* Front and *(b)* side views of the propulsive force generated by the entire arm.

perpendicular to the direction of the push (figure 4.6). You must straighten your elbow to continue pushing, and you move your hand out slightly to a position just beside your upper thigh.

During the pull–push, roll your body to the left so that your right shoulder clears the surface. At this end-of-pull position, your thumb should be within an inch of your thigh, your elbow should be straight, and your palm should be turned up (figure 4.7).

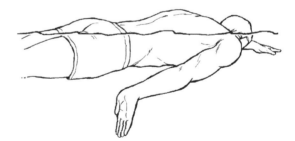

**Figure 4.6** Propulsive force of the hand.

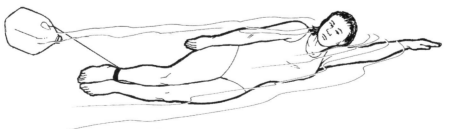

**Figure 4.7** End-of-pull position.

**31**

Begin the arm stroke recovery using only your shoulder muscles. Lift your elbow directly up and forward, keeping the elbow, wrist, and hand perfectly relaxed (figure 4.8).

Be sure to retain full medial (inward) rotation of your arm from the shoulder as your arm moves forward until your forearm is at shoulder level. As your hand passes shoulder level, begin to straighten your elbow. Keep your right shoulder elevated, and begin to reach over the barrel to touch the water with your fingertips as far forward of your head as possible (figure 4.9).

Do not drop your elbow until your fingertips touch the water and you begin to roll to the opposite side. As your right hand enters the water, stretch forward with your arm and shoulder to reach and hold a straight position about 6 inches (15.24 centimeters) deep.

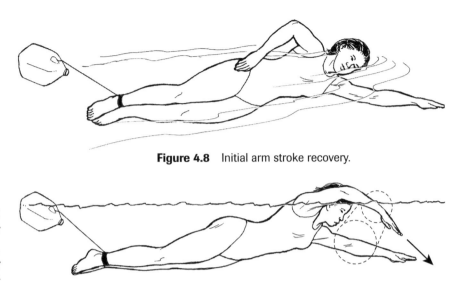

**Figure 4.8**   Initial arm stroke recovery.

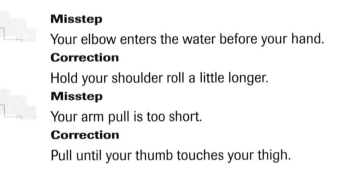

**Figure 4.9**   Over-the-barrel reach position.

Begin to pull with your left arm when the fingertips of your right hand are still about 8 inches (20.32 centimeters) above the water on the right-arm recovery. The left-arm stroke follows an S-shaped pull–push pattern identical to that of the right arm.

**Misstep**

Your elbow enters the water before your hand.

**Correction**

Hold your shoulder roll a little longer.

**Misstep**

Your arm pull is too short.

**Correction**

Pull until your thumb touches your thigh.

## Crawl Arm Stroke Drill 1.

## *Crawl Arm Stroke, Right Arm*

Use the deep-float leg support on your right ankle. Put on your mask and snorkel. Hold a kickboard by its trailing edge in your left hand with your fingers on top of the board and thumb underneath. Assume a prone-float position, keep your face down, and breathe naturally. Stretch your right hand forward beside the kickboard. Pull through with your right arm and roll onto your left side, but leave your face in the water. Finish the pull with your palm up at your thigh, then lift your elbow and return your hand to a forward stretch as you roll back onto your front. Stop and glide for 3 seconds. Repeat, using only your right arm at least 10 times.

**To Increase Difficulty**

- Eliminate leg support.
- Perform 15 consecutive right-arm strokes.

**To Decrease Difficulty**

- Pause momentarily in side glide position with hand on thigh, palm up.
- Use a pull-buoy type of leg support.

## Success Check

- Use an S-pull (review figure 4.2, page 30).
- Pull–push all the way to your thigh.

- Keep the palm up, lift the elbow, and reach over the barrel.
- Roll, stretch forward, and glide.

### Score Your Success

Execute 10 consecutive right-arm strokes = 2 points

Execute 15 consecutive right-arm strokes = 3 points

Execute 15 consecutive right-arm strokes with no leg support = 4 additional points

Your score ___

## Crawl Arm Stroke Drill 2.

## Crawl Arm Stroke, Left Arm

Repeat crawl arm stroke drill 1 using your left arm. Attach a deep-float leg float to your left leg. Hold the kickboard with your right hand. Roll onto your right side for arm recovery.

**To Increase Difficulty**

- Eliminate the leg float.
- Eliminate the kickboard.

**To Decrease Difficulty**

- Use a pull-buoy type of leg float.
- Pause in side glide position with hand on thigh, palm up.

## Success Check

- Use an S-pull (review figure 4.2, page 30).
- Pull–push all the way to your thigh.
- Keep the palm up, lift the elbow, and reach over the barrel.
- Roll, stretch forward, and glide.

### Score Your Success

Execute 10 consecutive left-arm strokes = 2 points

Execute 15 consecutive left-arm strokes = 3 points

Execute 15 consecutive left-arm strokes with no leg support = 4 additional points

Your score ___

## Crawl Arm Stroke Drill 3.

## Touch-and-Go Stroke With Leg Support

Put on a mask and snorkel. Attach leg-support float to one ankle. Do not use a kickboard, but extend both arms forward in prone-float position. Start stroking with your left arm (figure 4.10). Keep the right arm stretched forward until the left hand catches up and touches it. Thus "touch" the forward hand to tell it when to "go." Continue touch-and-go alternate arm strokes. Keep the forward hand and arm stretched at the surface until touched by the recovering hand. Make 10 consecutive touch-and-go strokes, 5 with each arm.

**To Increase Difficulty**

- Continue for 20 strokes, 10 for each arm.

**To Decrease Difficulty**

- Pause momentarily at the touch of each hand.

### Success Check

- Begin to roll as you begin to pull on each side.
- Keep the forward hand at the surface.

### Score Your Success

Complete 10 consecutive strokes = 2 points

Complete 20 consecutive strokes = 4 points

Your score ____

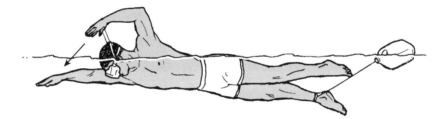

**Figure 4.10** Touch-and-go stroke with leg support.

## Crawl Arm Stroke Drill 4.

## Touch-and-Go Stroke Without Support

Repeat crawl arm stroke drill 3 without the leg support. Allow your legs to kick for support. Do 10 touch-and-go strokes, alternating arms.

**To Increase Difficulty**

- Do 20 touch-and-go strokes.

**To Decrease Difficulty**

- Pull back; don't press downward.
- Start kicking before you start to pull.

### Success Check

- Each hand touches the other before it begins to pull.
- Begin to roll as each arm starts to pull.
- Pull under the centerline of your body.

### Score Your Success

Complete 10 consecutive strokes = 2 points

Complete 20 consecutive strokes = 3 points

Your score ____

## Crawl Arm Stroke Drill 5.

## Deep-Water Stroke With Mask and Snorkel

Put on a mask and snorkel. With a skilled swimmer or lifeguard watching you, swim the crawl stroke the length of the pool from the deep end (or 25 yards, 22.86 meters). Remember to keep your face in the water and breathe naturally through your mouth. Roll your body nearly into a side-float position for the arm recovery on each side. Continue to touch and go. Crawl kick as you wish.

**To Increase Difficulty**

- Pause and glide momentarily as your hands touch each other.
- Make a 90-degree turn near the end of the swim.

**To Decrease Difficulty**

- Stay close to the edge of the pool.
- Have a skilled swimmer swim with you.
- Use swim fins.

### Success Check

- Keep your face down so that the snorkel remains clear.
- Maintain the touch-and-go stroke.

### Score Your Success

Swim 25 yards from deep water with fins
  = 3 points

Swim 25 yards from deep water without fins
  = 6 points

Your score ___

# BREATHING WHILE SWIMMING

Breath control is an essential ingredient in all swimming. Recreational swimmers, speed swimmers, and synchronized swimmers all need to learn correct breathing habits to be good at what they do. In this section, you will learn to integrate breath control into prone swimming technique.

While swimming, you cannot just breathe when you want to; you must breathe when you can. Often the rhythm of a stroke allows only a very short breathing time. Your nose is not large enough to allow you to take in the amount of air you require in the short interval. You can solve this problem by breathing through your mouth. Exhaling through your nose helps you to keep the water out, but the volume of air you must exhale in the time allowed requires that you exhale partly through your mouth as well.

Buoyancy depends on the amount of air in your lungs. You cannot hold a full breath all the time you are swimming, but you can keep your lungs inflated by inhaling fully and exhaling about half the air on each breath. Thus you can breathe off the top of your lungs. If this technique leaves you breathless, you must resort to full exhalations and inhalations. The drills in this section will help you establish proper breathing techniques gradually.

Learning to control your breathing to make it fit your stroke pattern is probably the most difficult and the most rewarding skill required in the sport. Practice breath control until it becomes a habit. When you become truly proficient, you will probably find yourself practicing swimming breathing patterns involuntarily every time you step into a shower. Correct breathing patterns differentiate the polished swimmer from the novice.

During the breathing exercises, you will probably discover it seems easier to breathe on one side than on the other. Most people have a favorite breathing side. In the drills for this section, we refer to your favorite side as your breathing side.

When learning to breathe, do not use a mask or snorkel. You may wear goggles if you wish, but no nose clip. Lie in prone position with your hands on the edge of the pool, and a float (pull buoy) between your knees (figure 4.11a).

Take a breath through your mouth and place your face in the water (figure 4.11b). Look slightly forward so that the water line is on your forehead. Exhale fully through your nose. The air will come out more easily if you hum it out using your voice. After exhaling completely, turn your head to the side until your mouth is just at water level. Do not lift your head, but leave your ear in the water. Open your mouth wide, inhale quickly, and turn your face into the water again to exhale. Repeat this sequence, turning your head to the opposite side. After several trials, choose the breathing side you prefer. It will become your breathing side.

## Figure 4.11   Learning to Breathe

### INHALE

1. Get in prone position
2. Hold float between knees
3. Turn head to side
4. Inhale through mouth

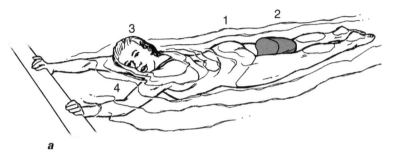

### EXHALE

1. Put your face in the water
2. Exhale through nose and mouth
3. Turn head to the other side and repeat the inhalation

**Misstep**
Water gets in your nose when your face is down.
**Correction**
Keep the waterline at your forehead. Exhale partly through your nose.

At this point, you know how to pull and how to breathe. Combining the two skills adds a new element to breath control: timing. Until this point you were free to breathe at any time you felt the need. Now you will learn to make your breathing fit the timing of your stroke rather than stroking to fit your breathing. If you follow this drill sequence, you will breeze through this traditional stumbling point with very little difficulty and be on your way to successful swimming.

# Breathing Drill 1. *Bracket and Leg Float, Side Breathing*

Wear goggles if you wish, but do not wear a mask or snorkel. Hold onto the side of the pool with both hands. Use a leg float (pull buoy) to support your legs. Turn your head to one side, lay your ear on the water, and keep your mouth at water level. Inhale through your mouth, turn your face down, and exhale through your nose. Continue breathing to the side. If you have difficulty, do not lift your head. Instead, leave your ear on the water and roll your shoulders to help get your head in position. Try turning to each side until you discover a favorite side. Get 10 consecutive breaths without choking.

**To Increase Difficulty**

- Discard the leg float.
- Try 20 consecutive breaths.
- Let go of the edge. Press with your breathing-side hand to roll your body to breathe.

**To Decrease Difficulty**

- Move your arms a little farther apart.
- Hum the air out.
- If you get water in your nose, time your exhalation so that you are still humming as your nose breaks the surface.

## Success Check

- Keep your ear in the water.
- Inhale quickly.
- Exhale slowly.

### Score Your Success

Complete 10 breaths without choking = 2 points

Complete 20 breaths without choking = 3 points

Complete the drill without holding the edge of the pool = 2 additional points

Your score ____

# Breathing Drill 2. *Floating and Breathing With Kickboard*

Repeat breathing drill 1 while floating with a kickboard held at arm's length in front. Do not try to move forward; just float motionless. Lift on the kickboard as you exhale to help keep your feet up. Get 10 consecutive breaths without choking.

**To Increase Difficulty**

- Take 20 consecutive breaths.
- Perform the drill without a board. Press with your breathing-side hand to roll for breath.

**To Decrease Difficulty**

- Take the breathing-side arm off the board and press on the water while inhaling.

## Success Check

- Keep your ear underwater.
- Inhale through your mouth.
- Exhale slowly.

### Score Your Success

Complete 10 consecutive breaths without choking = 2 points

Complete 10 consecutive breaths without choking, no kickboard = 5 additional points

Your score ____

## Breathing Drill 3.   *Kick and Breathe for Distance*

Use goggles if you wish. With a kickboard, kick while inhaling on the side and exhaling facedown. Kick and breathe for 15 yards (13.716 meters). Breathe with your ear on the water. Turn your head without lifting.

**To Increase Difficulty**

- Discard the board and roll your body to breathe.
- Breathe on alternate sides.

**To Decrease Difficulty**

- Remove your breathing-side arm from the board and press with it while inhaling.
- Wear swim fins.

### Success Check

- Keep your ear on the water.
- Inhale through your mouth.
- Hum the air out slowly.

### Score Your Success

Kick and breathe 15 yards with swim fins and kickboard = 1 point

Kick and breathe 15 yards without swim fins = 2 additional points

Kick and breathe 15 yards without kickboard or swim fins = 2 additional points

Your score ___

## Breathing Drill 4.   *Pulling and Breathing With Deep-Leg Support*

Wear goggles if you wish. Attach a deep float to the ankle on your better breathing side. Assume a prone-float position. Keep your feet together and start by exhaling as you pull with your nonbreathing-side arm. Turn your head to the breathing side and inhale with the pull of your breathing-side arm. Leave your ear underwater. Turn your head back down to exhale while you pull with the opposite arm. Continue to pull and breathe for 10 consecutive breaths without choking.

**To Increase Difficulty**

- Discard the float. Kick.
- Try for 20 breaths.

**To Decrease Difficulty**

- Roll your shoulders as well as your head.

### Success Check

- Finish each arm pull before beginning the next.
- Continue to exhale until your nose breaks the surface.
- Keep your ear on the water.

### Score Your Success

Complete 10 consecutive breaths without choking = 2 points

Complete 20 consecutive breaths without choking = 4 points

Complete 20 consecutive breaths without choking, no leg float = 4 additional points

Your score ___

## Breathing Drill 5.    *Fine-Tune Your Timing*

Repeat breathing drill 4, but this time emphasize the timing. Take your breath quickly while your breathing-side arm pulls, not while it recovers. The inhalation should be complete before the recovery begins. Exhale slowly during both the pull and recovery of the opposite arm so that you are still exhaling as your mouth breaks the water for the next inhalation. Allow your shoulders and body to roll to the side as you turn to breathe, and to roll to the opposite side as you exhale. Pull and breathe for 15 yards.

**To Increase Difficulty**

- Discard the float. Kick.
- Concentrate on timing.
- Try breathing on the opposite side.

**To Decrease Difficulty**

- Wear swim fins.

### Success Check

- With your mouth open, grab a quick breath.
- Keep your face down while your breathing-side arm recovers.
- Exhale slowly.
- Pull all the way through.

### Score Your Success

Score 2 points if you *think* your timing is correct. Score 4 more points if your coach says your timing is correct. Earn points whether or not you use swim fins and a leg float.

Your score ____

## Breathing Drill 6.    *Pull, Kick, and Breathe Without Support*

Start from a prone-float position. Begin to kick gently. After four or five kicks, begin to pull and breathe to the side. Start with an exhalation and a pull of your nonbreathing-side arm. Continue to kick while pulling and breathing. If you lose your coordination, stop and start over. Keep the kick small; do not concentrate on it. Breathe on *every* pull of the breathing-side arm. Swim for 15 yards.

**To Increase Difficulty**

- Breathe on the opposite side.
- Breathe on every third arm pull on alternate sides.
- Swim for 20 yards (18.288 meters).

**To Decrease Difficulty**

- Wear goggles.
- Roll onto your side while breathing.

### Success Check

- Roll your head, shoulders, and body.
- Breathe during the pull, not the recovery, of the breathing-side arm.

### Score Your Success

Swim for 15 yards = 2 points

Swim for 20 yards = 3 points

Your score ____

## Breathing Drill 7. *Swim, Breathe, and Turn Without Support*

In shallow water, repeat breathing drill 6. After a few strokes, reach and pull to one side to effect a turn. Swim across the pool, make a wide turn, and return. Continue to breathe on every breathing-side pull while turning. Make at least two round trips.

**To Increase Difficulty**

- On the second round trip, turn in the opposite direction, but in shallow water.
- Breathe on the opposite side.

**To Decrease Difficulty**

- Wear a float belt, swim fins, or goggles.

### Success Check

- Take long, easy pulls.
- Kick gently.
- Keep head low.
- Look and reach in direction of turn.

### Score Your Success

Earn 2 points for each round trip, up to 10 points.

Your score ___

## Breathing Drill 8. *Deep-Water Pull, Kick, Breathe, and Turn*

**CAUTION** Do not attempt this drill without a safety float belt unless you have an instructor or trained lifeguard with you.

Have an expert swimmer nearby or wear a safety float belt as you begin to swim from the shallow end of the pool. Swim to the deep end of the pool, make a wide turn, and return to the shallow end. Breathe on every breathing-side pull. Complete two pool lengths or 50 yards (45.72 meters).

**To Increase Difficulty**

- Breathe on alternate sides.
- Swim a full circle in deep water before returning.

**To Decrease Difficulty**

- Wear a safety float belt or goggles.
- Swim into deep water and back, but not the full pool length.

### Success Check

- Look and pull to the side for your turn.
- Kick gently.
- Keep your head low.

### Score Your Success

Turn successfully in deep water = 1 point each time, up to 3 points

Complete two pool lengths or 50 yards = 2 additional points

Your score ___

# CRAWL STROKE COORDINATION

The modern crawl stroke allows more leeway for swimmers when selecting an arm–leg coordination pattern than when the classic six-beat American crawl stroke or the older four-beat Australian crawl were taught. Coordination aids in the efficiency of the crawl stroke, but the pattern of coordination can be quite different for different swimmers.

The importance of the crawl stroke kick diminishes as you realize the crawl stroke kick requires more energy than its propulsive force is worth. There is great variance in the coordination patterns used by world-class swimmers. Some, especially sprinters, use the classic six-beat stroke. Others, especially distance swimmers, use a four- or two-beat stroke, and some appear to use the kick only for balance.

We will describe the classic six-beat American crawl stroke, but if the coordination process proves too cumbersome to master, it is perfectly

acceptable for you to adopt a different kick pattern that is more natural for you.

Start in a prone-float position. Wearing a mask, snorkel, and swim fins will allow you to concentrate on the arm–leg coordination without thinking about breathing, but you should discard the equipment as soon as you establish coordination so that you can incorporate breathing.

Until it becomes a habitual pattern, you will have to count each downward leg beat in a six-beat cycle. Begin the pull of your right arm as your left leg kicks downward on the count of 1. Allow your left arm to remain in a relaxed, straight glide position. Pull your right arm through as your right leg kicks downward on the count of 2, and recover it as your left leg kicks downward on the count of 3. Your right hand should reenter the water in front of your shoulder, fingertips first, on the right-leg count of 4 (figure 4.12).

## Figure 4.12   Crawl Stroke Arm–Leg Coordination

### COUNT 1

1. Kick downward with left leg
2. Pull right arm as left arm enters the water
3. Begin to roll right shoulder up
4. Exhale gently

*a*

### COUNT 2

1. Kick downward with right leg
2. Finish the pull with right arm
3. Roll right shoulder out of the water
4. Exhale gently

*b*

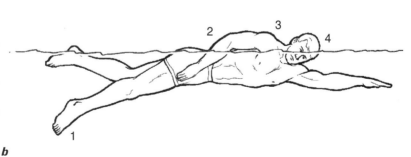

*(continued)*

**Figure 4.12** *(continued)*

## COUNT 3

1. Kick downward with left leg
2. Recover the right arm, elbow high, over the barrel
3. Roll head and shoulders to prone position
4. Exhale gently

## COUNT 4

1. Kick downward with right leg
2. Pull left arm as right arm enters the water
3. Roll head and shoulders to the left
4. Exhale forcibly

## COUNT 5

1. Kick downward with left leg
2. Finish the pull with left arm
3. Roll left shoulder out of the water
4. Inhale on left side

## COUNT 6

1. Kick downward with right leg
2. Recover the left arm, elbow high, over the barrel
3. Roll head and shoulders to prone position

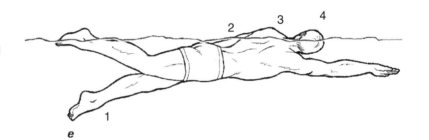

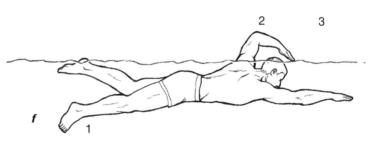

From a glide position, begin to pull with the left arm just before the count of 4, hand about 8 inches (20.32 centimeters) deep. The left arm pulls through on the left-leg count of 5, recovers on the right-leg count of 6, and reenters the water on the next count of 1. Emphasize counts 1 and 4 as the key counts in maintaining coordination between arm and leg movements. Note that each arm begins its pull as the other is about to enter the water. To recover, repeat counts 1 through 6 rhythmically.

When you have mastered the arm–leg coordination, remove the mask and snorkel and concentrate on coordinating your breathing with the arm stroke rhythm. Turn your head on the count of 1 or 4 and inhale on the count of 2 or 5, depending on whether you wish to breathe on the left or right side. Note that your head should *turn,* not *lift,* for a breath. Inhaling on the count of 2 (or 5) indicates that you take the breath during the last half of the pull, not during the recovery of the arm. At the count of 2 (or 5), your arm is finishing its power stroke, the hand is still in the water, and your shoulders are rolled to facilitate lifting your arm in recovery.

If you were to wait to breathe until your arm was in the air for recovery, the added weight of an arm not supported by buoyancy would necessitate a supporting downward push of the forward hand to keep your mouth above water. Your forward arm would then be too deep when the next pull was started. Consequently, coordination and some propulsive force would be lost.

Roll your head back into the water on the count of 4 (or 1). Begin to exhale immediately when your face submerges. Some swimmers prefer to exhale during the entire pull of the arm on the nonbreathing side. Others prefer to allow only a trickle of air to escape most of the time the arm is pulling, holding most of the air until just before the face breaks water for the next breath. They then get rid of the major portion of the held air in an explosive exhalation as the mouth rises above the surface. The latter method of breathing, called the *explosive method,* has the advantage of forcefully expelling water from around the mouth, making it less likely that the swimmer will inhale water.

## Crawl Stroke Coordination Drill 1. Crawl Stroke With Kickboard, Mask, Fins, and Snorkel

Put on a mask, snorkel, and swim fins; hold a kickboard in both hands at arm's length in front of you (figure 4.13). Kick slowly, beginning the six-beat count with the leg on your breathing side. After two full kick cycles, begin stroking with your nonbreathing-side arm. Pull the arm through and return the hand to the board at the count of 4. Begin pulling with the breathing-side arm on the count of 4 and return the hand to the board on the count of 1; the board will float free for just an instant as one hand returns and the other begins to pull. Stroke and kick *very* slowly in order to facilitate the transfer of the board from one hand to the other. Exhale through your snorkel on counts 1 through 4, then inhale on counts 5 and 6. Continue to kick and stroke for 25 yards (22.86 meters). Repeat the drill four times.

**Figure 4.13** Crawl stroke with kickboard, mask, fins, and snorkel.

### To Increase Difficulty

- Gradually pick up speed.
- Discard the fins.

### To Decrease Difficulty

- Start over if you lose coordination.
- Have someone swim beside you when in deep water.

### Success Check

- Swim *very* slowly.
- Kick two full cycles before starting to stroke.

### Score Your Success

Complete 25 yards successfully = 1 point

Complete the drill four more times
  = 2 additional points each time

Your score ___

## Crawl Stroke Coordination Drill 2. Crawl Stroke Without a Kickboard

Repeat crawl stroke coordination drill 1 without a kickboard. Imagine the kickboard is there and follow the same pattern. Stop and restart anytime you lose coordination. Keep your head down and breathe through your snorkel in proper coordination with your arms. Swim 100 yards (91.44 meters), stopping only to turn at the end of the pool.

**To Increase Difficulty**

- Discard the fins.
- Discard the mask and snorkel; turn head and roll to breathe.

**To Decrease Difficulty**

- Have someone swim beside you.

### Success Check

- Use slow, smooth strokes.
- Roll your shoulders, not your head.

### Score Your Success

Earn 1 point for every 25 yards completed successfully, up to 100 yards. Give yourself 3 additional points for each 25 yards if you do not use the mask, fins, or snorkel.

Your score ____

## Crawl Stroke Coordination Drill 3. Crawl Arm Stroke and Breathing, No Kick

Use only goggles and a pull-buoy leg float between your thighs. Begin in a prone glide position. Do not kick at all, but count as if you were kicking. Pull with your nonbreathing-side arm on counts 1 and 2; recover on count 3; and place the arm back in the water, fingertips first, on count 4. Start the breathing-side arm stroke on count 4; pull through on count 5; recover on count 6; and place it in the water, fingertips first, on count 1. Roll your face out of the water and inhale on count 5, roll it back into the water on count 6, and exhale the rest of the time. Keep your legs together and hold them still. Swim 100 yards, stopping only to turn at the end of the pool.

**To Increase Difficulty**

- Move your feet *slightly* in time with your count.
- Pull for 200 yards (182.88 meters).

**To Decrease Difficulty**

- Pull the distance in shallow water.

### Success Check

- Pull slowly.
- Breathe deeply.

### Score Your Success

Successfully complete 100 yards = 3 points
Successfully complete 200 yards = 5 points
Your score ____

## Crawl Stroke Coordination Drill 4.
## *Fully Coordinated Crawl Stroke With Goggles Only*

Wear goggles but no mask, fins, or snorkel. Begin with a prone glide, kicking in six-beat cycles. Start the count on a kick with your breathing-side leg. Count two full cycles before beginning the arm stroke.

Start the arm stroke with your nonbreathing-side arm. On counts 1 and 2, leave your face in the water and exhale, but roll your nonbreathing-side shoulder up out of the water as the arm pulls through. Keep your shoulder high, but leave your face down and continue exhaling as your arm recovers and stretches forward. Roll your shoulders back through the horizontal on count 4, and begin the roll to your breathing side as your nonbreathing-side hand enters the water, fingertips first, and the breathing-side arm begins its pull. Roll both face and shoulder out of the water, and inhale on count 5. Keep your breathing-side shoulder out of the water as your breathing-side arm recovers on count 6 and stretches forward. Roll your shoulders and face back through the horizontal on count 1, then begin to exhale as your breathing-side

hand enters the water and your nonbreathing-side arm begins its pull.

It's really very easy if you swim very slowly and think. Complete five swims of 100 yards each to be sure you have the coordination correct. Take a 30-second rest between swims.

**To Decrease Difficulty**

- Go slowly, emphasizing the hand hitting the water on counts 1 and 4.

## *Success Check*

- Breathe on the pull, not on the recovery.
- Start slowly; remember, a hand hits the water on counts 1 and 4.

### *Score Your Success*

Successfully complete 100 yards = 1 point for each 100 yards (5 points maximum)

Successfully complete all 500 yards (457.2 meters) = 5 additional points

Your score ___

## Crawl Stroke Coordination Drill 5.
## *Discover Your Natural Coordination Preference*

Use goggles but no other aids. Begin with the idea that you will swim lengths continuously for at least 10 minutes. Alert your coach or instructor to what you are doing, and ask him or her to watch your efforts sometime during the middle of the period when you are not thinking about your legs. After several observations of this sort over a period of several days, your coach or instructor should be able to tell you what arm–leg coordination is natural for you. (You probably won't believe it when you are told.)

Begin swimming the crawl stroke, concentrating on the correct timing of your arms (that is, one arm beginning to stroke just before the other arm enters the water). *Do not count.* Concentrate so hard on the arm stroke and breathing that you forget all about your legs. Let them do whatever

they want, but do not consciously hold them still. Concentrate on breathing on the last half of the pull, not on the recovery. Concentrate on the pull–push and the S-shaped arm motion, but do not think about your legs.

## *Success Check*

- Swim the drill each day for several days with your coach watching.
- Concentrate on your arms and breathing.

### *Score Your Success*

Score 4 points for determining your natural kicking pattern.

Your score ___

# CRAWL STROKE OPEN TURN

Swimming in a pool or other enclosed area necessitates frequent reversals as you reach the end of the area. It is desirable to change course with a minimum expenditure of energy and minimum disruption of rhythm and swimming form. An *open turn* is a course reversal in which your head comes above the water, allowing you to get a breath on the turn. A turn in which your head remains underwater is called a *closed turn*.

The open turn is the choice of most recreational swimmers for changing direction at the end of a swimming course. It is the smoothest, quickest turn that allows breathing. There are different open turns for each style of swimming.

The closed turn for the crawl stroke is called a *tumble turn* because it employs a somersault motion. It is universally recognized to be the quickest turn yet discovered, and it will cut more from your competitive swimming time than any other turn. It is used by all freestyle swimmers in the Olympic Games. There are many books on competitive swimming that explain the intricacies of the tumble turn.

It is essential to judge your distance from the end wall accurately to make an open turn safely. Two options are available for judging this distance: Either raise your head slightly to look forward above the water, or look for underwater turn targets. All pools designed for competitive swimming have lines on the bottom of the pool in each lane. A large cross or T on the bottom at the end of the lane line and a cross on the end wall are turn targets. The target on the bottom may be either 6 feet, 7 inches (2 meters) or 5 feet (1.524 meters) from the wall, depending on whether the pool is designed for competition in meters or yards. In pools not marked for competition, you must raise your head to see the end of the pool. Wearing goggles or a mask greatly facilitates your judgment of distances underwa-

ter. With a little practice, you will be able to judge your distance from the wall.

Swim a slow crawl stroke toward the end of the pool and judge your distance from the wall. When about 5 feet (1.524 meters) from the wall or when over a turn target, pull through to the end of the arm stroke, roll onto your side, and glide with your pulling hand resting on your thigh (figure 4.14a). Leave the bottom arm fully extended in glide position just under the surface. As your forward hand reaches the end wall, absorb the shock by placing your hand flat against the wall and allowing your elbow to bend, keeping your forearm between your head and the wall (figure 4.14b). As your elbow bends, remain on your side and tuck both knees up to your chin.

Leave your top arm pointing toward the other end as you push with your palm against the wall, raise your head sideways, inhale quickly, and use the momentum from your glide to pivot sideways so that your feet come directly under you to the wall (figure 4.14c). Keep your knees tucked, and lay your ear on the other arm. Bring your arm from the wall, over the water (figure 4.14d), and beside the other arm as you roll onto your face. Push off the wall with your feet into an underwater prone glide position (figure 4.14e). Glide until your speed slows to equal your swimming speed, then begin stroking for the next length.

If the pool design is such that you can take hold of the end wall, either by the edge of an overflow trough or by a low coping, grasp the end, pull yourself into the wall, and press down to accelerate your pivot. Pulling yourself into the wall is faster and will keep you closer for a better push-off.

The entire process should have rhythm. You should be able to count it off with the key words *pull, touch, pivot, arm over, push, glide*. The turn should be smooth and fluid without hesitation.

## Figure 4.14    Crawl Stroke Open Turn

### PULL
1. Pull arm to thigh
2. Roll to opposite side

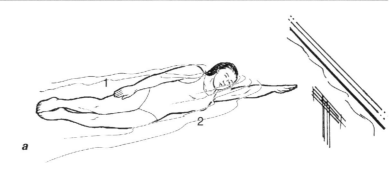

*a*

### TOUCH
1. Touch palms against wall
2. Bend elbow
3. Tuck legs

### PIVOT
1. Lift head
2. Pivot sideways
3. Inhale

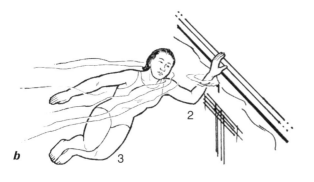

*b*

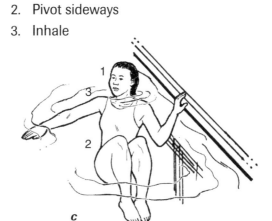

*c*

### ARM OVER
1. Bring arm from wall over the water
2. Stay tucked with feet on the wall

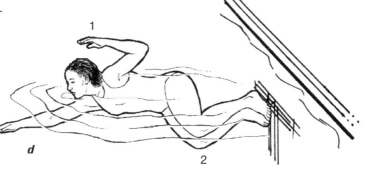

*d*

### PUSH AND GLIDE
1. Push off underwater
2. Glide until you slow to swimming speed

*e*

**Misstep**

Your turn finishes too far from the wall, resulting in a poor push.

**Correction**

Bend your elbow as you touch the wall.

**Misstep**

You push off from the wall with your arm in the air.

**Correction**

Release the wall before your feet touch it, and delay the push-off until both arms are together.

## Crawl Stroke Open Turn Drill 1.
## *Open Crawl Turn, Push, and Glide*

Put on swimming goggles. Stand at arm's length from a pool wall in water 3 to 4 feet (0.9144 to 1.2192 meters) deep. Turn your side to the wall and extend both arms out to your sides. Grasp the edge of the gutter or the coping with one hand, and lay your other arm, pointing straight out and slightly downward, on the water. Sink down until your chin is on the water. Lean your head away from the wall and lay your ear on your outstretched arm.

Continue to hold the edge as you tuck both knees and place both feet against the wall just under the surface. You should now be floating on your side, tucked, with one hand on the wall to steady you and your feet against the wall. Keeping your knees tucked, *do not push off* but bring your hand quickly from the wall *over* the water and place it beside the forward hand. This movement will turn you facedown as you float.

Lift your chin so that you look straight ahead underwater. Push off slightly downhill. (If you do not raise your chin before pushing off, the water may push your goggles off.) Streamline your whole body. Stretch your arms and legs and point your toes. Turn your hands up to guide you to the surface about three body lengths from the wall. Swim two strokes of the crawl stroke and stop. Repeat, starting with your other side to the wall. Make five push-offs in good form on each side.

**To Increase Difficulty**

- Before shoving off, hold your tucked, floating position with feet against the wall for 5 seconds without drifting away from the wall.

**To Decrease Difficulty**

- Hold your tucked position with hand on the wall until you are ready to push off, then bring your arm over *quickly* and get it in the water as you push off.

## Success Check

- Hold your tuck; do not drift away from the wall when you bring your arm over.
- Glide before you start to swim away.

### Score Your Success

Complete 1 good push-off on each side = 2 points

Complete 3 good drill turns on each side = 2 additional points

Your score ___

## Crawl Stroke Open Turn Drill 2.

## Approaching the Open Crawl Turn

Put on swimming goggles. Stand in water about 4 feet (1.2192 meters) deep, facing the end wall of the pool from about 6 feet (1.8288 meters) away. Stretch both arms toward the wall and lower your body until your chin is at water level.

Push off gently into a prone glide toward the wall. As soon as your feet leave the bottom of the pool, begin a crawl stroke pull with your left arm. As your left arm pulls, roll onto your right side. Stop the left-arm pull when your hand reaches your thigh, then do a side glide into the wall. Remain on your side as you grasp the rim of the overflow trough, tuck your knees quickly, and pull yourself toward the wall. Drop your feet directly under your body and complete the open turn as in the previous drill. Repeat the turn on the other side. Do five open turns on each side.

**To Increase Difficulty**

• Swim in from 20 feet (6.096 meters) away.

**To Decrease Difficulty**

• Walk through it a couple of times first.

### Success Check

• Glide, touch, pull, tuck, pivot, put arm over, push off.

### Score Your Success

Complete at least 3 good turns on each side = 3 points

Complete 1 good turn from 20 feet away = 2 additional points

Your score ___

## Crawl Stroke Open Turn Drill 3.

## Open Crawl Turn With Free Pivot

Put on swimming goggles. From about 30 feet (9.144 meters) away from the end of the pool, swim the crawl stroke toward the end. Judge your distance from the end either by lifting your head momentarily and looking forward over the water or by using the turn targets on the bottom of the pool.

Swim into an open turn, but do not maintain a hold on the edge of the pool during the pivot. Use your forward hand to press quickly on the wall to initiate the pivot. As soon as your feet are moving under you in tucked position, release the wall and bring your arm over the water as your body floats through the pivot. By the time your feet touch the wall, your arms should already be in position for the push-off. You can even initiate the push-off a split second before your feet touch. The result of this free-floating pivot should be a much smoother turn without any hesitation just before the push-off. The turn should have a more fluid rhythm. Do five free-floating pivot turns on each side.

**To Increase Difficulty**

• Thrust with your feet just before they touch the wall.

**To Decrease Difficulty**

• Practice the first three times *very* slowly.

### Success Check

• Glide in, touch and tuck, press and release, put arm over, push off.

### Score Your Success

Complete at least 3 good turns on each side = 3 points

Complete 5 good turns on each side = 5 additional points

Your score ___

**49**

## Crawl Stroke Open Turn Drill 4. *Open Turns on a Flat Wall*

Put on swimming goggles. Swim the crawl stroke toward the end of the pool. Judge your distance and glide into an open turn, but do not grasp the edge. Keep your hand just below the surface of the water and place the palm of your hand flat against the pool wall. Keep your arm directly in front of your head.

As your head touches your forearm, push gently down and away on the wall to initiate the pivot. Use just enough pressure on your forward hand to initiate the pivot without pushing yourself so far from the wall that you cannot get a good push-off. As soon as you begin the pivot, bring your forward hand over the water, float through the pivot, and push off. Repeat on the other side. Obtain solid push-offs from a flat wall on five consecutive turns on each side.

**To Increase Difficulty**

- Allow your head to touch your forearm before pushing away.

**To Decrease Difficulty**

- Be sure you have momentum going into the turn.

### Success Check

- On some pools, the edge is too high to grasp. Practice flat-hand turns.

### Score Your Success

Complete 3 successful flat-wall turns on each side = 3 points

Complete five successful flat-wall turns on each side = 5 additional points

Your score ____

# SUCCESS SUMMARY OF CRAWL STROKE AND BREATHING

Step 4 is arguably the most difficult step in the book because it covers principles that apply to all prone strokes and introduces the most complicated coordination.

You can count the number of yards you swim, but you cannot see yourself swimming except on a videotape. Expert human observers are much better at analyzing stroking ease and smoothness than the video camera. Have your coach or instructor study your stroke and turn for a few lengths and evaluate it according to the success checks in each drill.

In general, if you scored at least 75 points during step 4, your progress is adequate. If you scored 76 to 110 points, you made good progress, and a score of 111 points or more indicates excellent progress.

## Crawl Arm Stroke Drills

1. Crawl Arm Stroke, Right Arm ___ out of 7
2. Crawl Arm Stroke, Left Arm ___ out of 7
3. Touch-and-Go Stroke With Leg Support ___ out of 4
4. Touch-and-Go Stroke Without Support ___ out of 3
5. Deep-Water Stroke With Mask and Snorkel ___ out of 6

## Breathing Drills

1. Bracket and Leg Float, Side Breathing ___ out of 5
2. Floating and Breathing With Kickboard ___ out of 7
3. Kick and Breathe for Distance ___ out of 5
4. Pulling and Breathing With Deep-Leg Support ___ out of 8
5. Fine-Tune Your Timing ___ out of 6
6. Pull, Kick, and Breathe Without Support ___ out of 3
7. Swim, Breathe, and Turn Without Support ___ out of 10
8. Deep-Water Pull, Kick, Breathe, and Turn ___ out of 5

## Crawl Stroke Coordination Drills

1. Crawl Stroke With Kickboard, Mask, Fins, and Snorkel ___ out of 9
2. Crawl Stroke Without a Kickboard ___ out of 16
3. Crawl Arm Stroke and Breathing, No Kick ___ out of 5
4. Fully Coordinated Crawl Stroke With Goggles Only ___ out of 10
5. Discover Your Natural Coordination Preference ___ out of 4

## Crawl Stroke Open Turn Drills

1. Open Crawl Turn, Push, and Glide ___ out of 4
2. Approaching the Open Crawl Turn ___ out of 5
3. Open Crawl Turn With Free Pivot ___ out of 8
4. Open Turns on a Flat Wall ___ out of 8

## Total ___ out of 145

# Breaststroke

The breaststroke is often used as a slow, strength-saving stroke for long-distance swimming. For swimming in open water with waves, it should be the stroke of choice.

The breaststroke has roots traceable to biblical times. In his 1977 Ohio State doctoral dissertation titled *The History and Development of Men's Intercollegiate Swimming in the United States From 1897 to 1970,* D.F. Robertson stated, "That some form of breaststroke swimming was used by the Hebrews may be inferred from the following passage of Isaiah in the Bible: And he shall spread forth his hands in the midst of them as he that swimmeth spreadeth forth his hands to swim" (page 12).

The breaststroke is recognized today as one of the four strokes used in international swimming competition. The breaststroke is subject to more restrictions and qualifying rules for competition than any other stroke and is defined very precisely in the rule books.

Despite its precise definition, the breaststroke is easy and comfortable to swim. When properly executed, the breaststroke requires rhythmic breathing with the face submerged during the glide. However, it adapts very easily to a semi-vertical position with the head held up to allow the swimmer to see, breathe, and converse with others. It is, therefore, often called the *social* or the *conversational* stroke.

## BREASTSTROKE KICK

It is often much easier to learn the breaststroke kick in the inverted position because it is easier to see the foot and leg movements when you're on your back. The breaststroke kick is a completely unique motion. You should avoid vigorous practice of the kick until your muscles have had time to adjust. Its efficiency depends on the flexibility of your knees and ankles.

In the introduction, The Sport of Swimming, I mentioned that swimmers can use any combination of movements that will get them where they want to go in the water, but that some movements are more efficient and therefore are packaged into recognized strokes. The breaststroke kick is one of the recognized package movements because of its ease and efficiency. It is efficient not for its use of energy, but for its *conservation* of energy. We have minimized the importance of the kick in some of the strokes introduced to this point, but in strokes that use the breaststroke kick, the kick produces as much propulsion as the arms.

Learn the breaststroke kick in the inverted position. Assume a back-float position with your arms above your head. Keep your hips straight, but drop your heels down behind you as far as you can. Hook your ankles sharply, and turn your feet so that the toes point out (figure 5.1a). Move your feet out, press back on the water with the insides of your ankles, and squeeze until your feet come together with legs fully stretched. Point your toes, streamline your body, and glide (figure 5.1b).

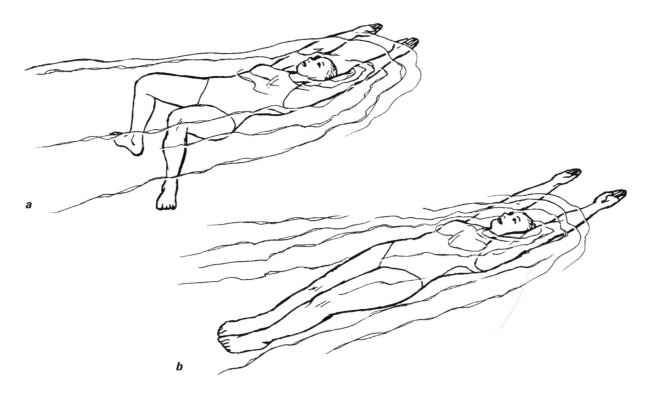

**Figure 5.1** Breaststroke kick from an inverted position: *(a)* hook ankles, pointing toes out; *(b)* squeeze feet together and glide.

**Misstep**
One foot turns in and you engage the water with the top of the foot.
**Correction**
Kicking this way is illegal. Practice hooking the foot and turning the toes out.

# Breaststroke Kick Drill 1. *Inverted Breaststroke Kick*

In shallow water, place your back against the pool wall. Reach back and out to place your arms and elbows on the edge of the pool. Bend 90 degrees at the waist and hold your feet out in front of you. With knees about 4 inches apart, stay bent at the hips but bend your knees and drop both heels toward the bottom of the pool. Hook your ankles as your heels drop. Keep your ankles hooked and turn your toes out as far as they will go. Catch the water with the insides of your feet and push it in a circle—out, around, back, and together—as your knees straighten. Point your toes at the very last moment and try to put the soles of your feet together. Try to prolong the kick with your toes and the soles of your feet. Your feet must move outward *before* your knees at the beginning of the kick. Make 10 kicks that tend to push you against the wall.

**To Increase Difficulty**

- Let your feet lead your knees out and around.
- Make 20 kicks, but not too hard (go easy on your groin muscles).

**To Decrease Difficulty**

- If your pool has a high edge, use the overflow trough or a ladder at water level.

## *Success Check*

- Keep your back against the wall and legs straight out in front, and hook your ankles.
- Drop your heels straight down behind you.
- Keep your knees close and turn your toes out.
- Move your feet out, parting the knees.
- Thrust directly back with the insides of your ankles.
- Squeeze with the knees straight and toes pointed.

## *Score Your Success*

Score 2 points if your instructor says, "You've got it." Score 2 more points if it is still correct after 20 kicks.

Your score ___

# Breaststroke Kick Drill 2. *Inverted Breaststroke Kick Against Pressure*

Repeat breaststroke kick drill 1. Ask your instructor to stand in front of you and place one hand against the inside of each foot, fingers under the arch. Press out, around, and squeeze in against the hands (figure 5.2).

**CAUTION** **Press very lightly—these are weak muscles! This should give you the feeling of pressing against the water. Three trials should be enough.**

**To Increase Difficulty**

- Ask your instructor to increase the pressure gradually.
- After the drill, let go of the side of the pool, drop your heels slowly, then kick quickly against the water.

**Figure 5.2** Inverted breaststroke kick against pressure.

## Success Check

- Follow the instructions for breaststroke kick drill 1.
- Point the toes as you squeeze.

Knees are close when heels drop = 1 point

Feet are hooked and turned out = 1 point

Toes are pointed at end of kick = 1 point

Your score ___

## Breaststroke Kick Drill 3.

## Inverted Breaststroke Kick With Kickboard

Hold a kickboard fairly close to your chest in shallow water. Float on your back with hips elevated and straight. Keep your knees about 4 inches apart. Drop your heels back under you as far as you can with the ankles fully hooked. Turn your toes outward (figure 5.3). Make sure your feet lead your knees out and around and then squeeze together, pushing with the sides of your feet. Kick wide, legs separating widely as you straighten your legs and squeeze with toes pointed at the end. Glide to a full stop. Repeat for 15 yards (13.716 meters).

**To Increase Difficulty**

- Use slow recovery and a whip kick.
- Glide 6 feet (1.8288 meters) per kick.

**To Decrease Difficulty**

- Start in slow motion, then build to a whip kick.

## Success Check

- Keep hips straight—do not sit!
- Flex ankles fully, drop heels, and turn toes out.
- Kick wide to full extension, and point toes.

### Score Your Success

Complete 15 yards = 2 points

Complete 15 yards in 8 kicks = 4 additional points

Your score ___

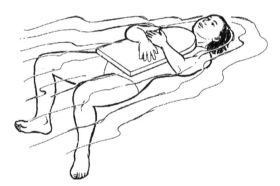

**Figure 5.3** Inverted breaststroke kick with kickboard.

# Breaststroke Kick Drill 4. *Elementary Backstroke*

Without the kickboard, float on your back, arms outstretched and slightly above shoulder level. Hook your ankles, drop your heels, and turn your toes out (figure 5.4a). Begin a full arm pull as in the basic backstroke, then deliver the kick (figure 5.4b). Try to finish the arm stroke and the kick simultaneously (figure 5.4c). Glide until your forward motion slows. Recover for the next stroke by sliding your hands up along your sides and dropping your heels behind you. Do not pull your knees up. Keep your hips straight. As your hands turn out and start to reach up and out, turn your toes out. Then pull and kick together. Do 10 full pulls and kicks or 25 yards (22.86 meters).

**To Increase Difficulty**

- Ride your glide to a complete stop.
- Reach higher for a longer pull.

**To Decrease Difficulty**

- Keep your chin down on the pull, up on the glide.
- Make sure your pull is level.

## Success Check

- Start to pull just before kicking.
- Finish the kick and pull together.
- Use a long glide.
- Recover hands and feet together.

### Score Your Success

Complete 25 yards = 4 points

Complete 25 yards in 10 strokes or fewer = 6 additional points

Your score ___

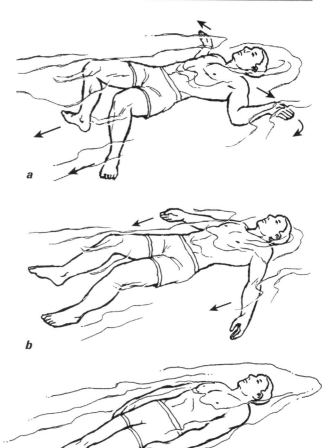

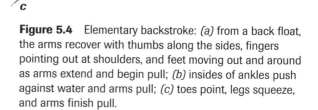

**Figure 5.4** Elementary backstroke: *(a)* from a back float, the arms recover with thumbs along the sides, fingers pointing out at shoulders, and feet moving out and around as arms extend and begin pull; *(b)* insides of ankles push against water and arms pull; *(c)* toes point, legs squeeze, and arms finish pull.

# Breaststroke Kick Drill 5.

## *Prone, Bracketed Breaststroke Kick*

Keep in mind the inverted breaststroke kick. Turn over and grasp the top of the pool edge or overflow trough with one hand. Position the other hand directly below, palm against the wall and fingers pointed to the bottom of the pool. By pulling gently with the top hand and pushing with the lower hand, you can hold a position with your feet near the surface (figure 5.5). This is the bracketed position. If your body swings to one side, move the bottom hand slightly toward that side. When comfortable in the bracketed position, bring both heels up behind you in the breaststroke kick recovery. Allow your legs to sink far enough to keep the heels underwater. The kick is identical to the one in the inverted version. Avoid bringing your knees under you. Keep your thighs in line with your body. Practice the breaststroke kick in the bracket position, concentrating on the backward thrust with the insides of your ankles. Feel the thrust of your kick driving you against the wall. Do 20 kicks.

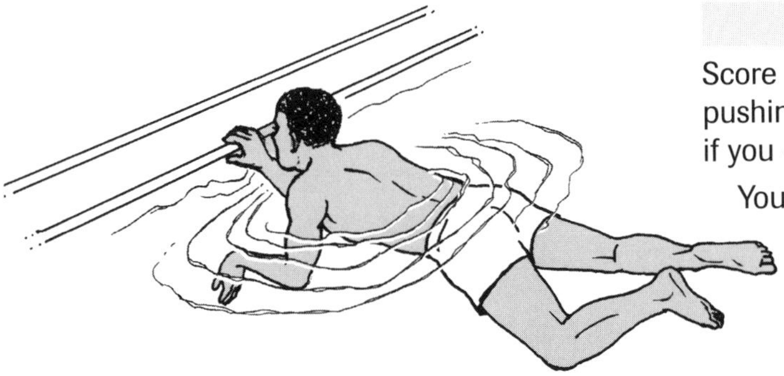

**To Increase Difficulty**

- Float with both hands in front, but don't grasp the edge.
- Keep your face down as you kick. Take a breath between kicks.

**To Decrease Difficulty**

- Wear a mask and snorkel. Keep your head down as you practice.
- Keep both hands on the top edge. Don't press on the wall.

## *Success Check*

- Keep your hips straight.
- Raise your heels.
- Hook your ankles.
- Point toes out.
- Kick out, around, back, and squeeze.
- Point your toes at the end of the kick.

## *Score Your Success*

Score 2 points if you feel thrust from your kick pushing you against the wall. Score 2 more points if you complete 20 kicks.

Your score ___

**Figure 5.5** Breaststroke kick, prone position, bracketed.

## Breaststroke Kick Drill 6.

## Breaststroke Kick With Kickboard

Hold a kickboard at arm's length with both hands and practice the breaststroke kick for propulsion. Keep your chin as low as possible to breathe. Do not bring your knees in under your body on the recovery. Bring your heels up behind you. Your hips should bend only very slightly. Kick across the pool or for 15 yards.

**To Increase Difficulty**

- Discard the kickboard and press with your hands to inhale.

**To Decrease Difficulty**

- Wear a mask and snorkel but inhale on the recovery and exhale on the glide.
- Put your arms on top of the kickboard and grasp the front edge with your fingers.

### Success Check

- Thrust your chin forward to inhale as your legs recover.
- Drop your face into the water and exhale on the glide.
- Drive with the insides of your hooked feet and ankles.

### Score Your Success

Complete 15 yards = 2 points

Complete 15 yards without using a kickboard = 4 points

Your score ___

# BREASTSTROKE ARM PULL

The breaststroke arm pull is a rather short and somewhat ineffective pull that seems contrary to the principle that long, full arm motions are the best. It's necessary to keep this pull short and sharp, however, because of the way it coordinates with the kick.

As the propulsive arm motion of a competitive swimming stroke, the breaststroke arm pull is important, but the breaststroke is a very kick-intensive stroke in which the kick provides as much or more propulsion than the arm pull. The arm pull, then, is not as important for the propulsion it provides as for the role it plays as the basis and support of the kick that follows.

Start in a prone float with arms extended forward. Flex your wrists, point your fingertips down, and lift your elbows into the over-the-barrel position of the crawl stroke. Slightly turn your palms out. Lift your chin as you pull sharply with both hands in a semicircular motion—out, back, and in—with elbows bent at 90 degrees and fingertips pointing directly down (figure

5.6a). Breathe as you finish the pull with elbows out and palms up under your chin.

To recover, drop your face back into the water, bring your elbows in to your sides, but leave your hands at neck or chin level (figure 5.6b). Turn your palms down and push them forward just under the water, fingertips leading, into full arm extension again (figure 5.6c). Normally a kick and long glide would follow, but with no kick to provide propulsion, your glide will be very short. Exhale on the glide.

The pull should feel as if you were digging your fingertips into the water ahead and using them to pull your body through between them. Your elbows must remain as high as you can keep them until they are pulled in to your sides. Propulsion should come from the palms, first pulling out and back and then inward to your chin. The entire pull is completed forward of your shoulders, and your hands should never pull past shoulder level. Each hand moves approximately in a small half-circle from full extension to your chin.

## Figure 5.6 Breaststroke Arm Pull

### PULL

1. Flex wrists, point fingers down
2. Lift elbows and turn palms out
3. Pull with elbows bent
4. Lift chin during pull and inhale

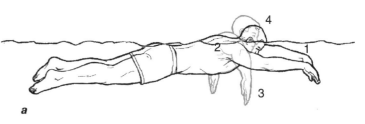

*a*

### RECOVER

1. Bring hands in to chin
2. Turn palms up
3. Bring elbows in
4. Move facedown

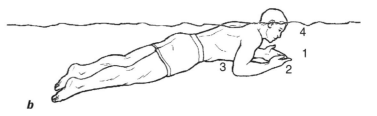

*b*

### GLIDE

1. Extend arms
2. Turn palms down
3. Use a long glide
4. Exhale

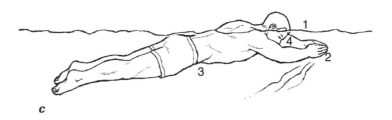

*c*

**Misstep**

Your pull is too wide.

**Correction**

Bend your elbows 90 degrees as your pull moves out. Point hands down, not out.

## Breaststroke Arm Pull Drill 1. *Slow-Motion Breaststroke Pulls*

In shallow water, attach the deep-float leg float to one ankle. Put on your mask and snorkel. This will allow you to concentrate more on the arm stroke without worrying about breathing.

Start from a prone float with your arms extended. Flex your wrists, point your fingertips down, and lift your elbows into the over-the-barrel position of the crawl stroke. Turn your hands to a slightly palm-out position. Tilt your head to look straight forward as you pull slowly in a semicircular motion—out, back, and in—with elbows bent at 90 degrees and fingertips pointing directly down.

Inhale as you finish the pull with elbows out and palms up under your chin.

To recover, bring your elbows in to your sides, but leave your hands at chin or neck level. Turn your hands palms down. Push them forward just under the water, fingertips leading, into full extension again. Exhale. Do not raise your head. Move your arms in very slow motion without thought of propulsion. Concentrate on correct arm and hand position as you float (review figure 5.6). Do 20 slow-motion arm strokes as you float.

## To Increase Difficulty

- Gradually increase the speed of the pull for some forward motion.
- Breathe in correct coordination.

## To Decrease Difficulty

- Use a pull-buoy float.
- Breathe at will, not in correct coordination.

## Success Check

- Use your snorkel to inhale near the end of your pull. Exhale in glide position.
- Pull very slowly. Concentrate on arm and hand positions.

### Score Your Success

Pull with correct arm and hand positions
 = 1 point

Pull while breathing in correct coordination
 = 2 additional points

Your score ___

# Breaststroke Arm Pull Drill 2.

# One-Arm Breaststroke Pulls

Hold a kickboard in one hand and wear a deep-leg support float and your mask and snorkel. Float facedown. (Do not raise your head during this exercise.) Move one arm through the breaststroke arm pull pattern in slow motion. Emphasize the high-elbow position. The forearm and hand should move in a semicircle, hanging down from a high, bent elbow. Keep your palm facing the direction of motion as it circles. After 30 practice pulls, shift the kickboard to the other hand and repeat.

## To Increase Difficulty

- Eliminate the kickboard.
- Breathe in coordination.

## To Decrease Difficulty

- Use a pull-buoy leg float.
- Breathe at will, not in coordination.

## Success Check

- Simply float. Do not try for propulsion.
- Concentrate on hand and arm positions.

### Score Your Success

Complete 30 pulls with correct arm motions
 = 1 point for each arm

Complete 30 pulls while breathing in coordination = 1 additional point for each arm

Your score ___

## Breaststroke Arm Pull Drill 3.

## *Breaststroke Pulls for Propulsion*

Use a leg float of your choice, but eliminate the mask and snorkel. Change the emphasis on practice pulls to gain propulsion. Dig in forcefully with your fingertips and thrust your chin forward. Pull sharply and quickly with the forearms and hands to a position under your chin and inhale. Bring your elbows in, drop your face into the water, and thrust your hands forward easily. Stop and glide. Exhale. Repeat 30 times.

**To Increase Difficulty**

- Eliminate the leg float.

**To Decrease Difficulty**

- Wear a mask and snorkel, but thrust your chin forward and breathe in coordination.

### *Success Check*

- Pull hard; recover easily.
- Inhale at the end of the pull.
- Exhale on the glide.
- Thrust your chin forward, but do not raise your head.

### *Score Your Success*

Pull and breathe in coordination for 30 pulls = 1 point

Perform the drill without a mask and snorkel = 2 additional points

Your score ___

# BREASTSTROKE COORDINATION

The classic breaststroke coordination requires bringing together the same three elements you encountered in coordinating the crawl stroke: kicking, pulling, and breathing. Breaststroke coordination is somewhat easier because arms and legs move in paired movements as opposed to the individual leg beats in the crawl kick.

The breaststroke can be used for several purposes, each requiring a somewhat different coordination. Swimming in rough water or so-called social swimming requires your face to be out of the water most of the time. In this form, no coordination of stroke and breathing is necessary, and your kick will be much deeper. You may still wish to exhale occasionally with your face down to relieve tension in your neck. In breaststroke competition, minor adjustments to the coordination are necessary for shortening the glide and achieving a continuous (but tiring) propulsive force. We are interested in the coordination for the classic breaststroke. If you learn that, the adaptations for the other styles will come without effort.

Start in a prone float, facedown with arms extended forward (figure 5.7a). Exhale and begin to thrust your chin forward on the first stroke. Inhale as you pull for propulsion and lift your heels behind you. Hook your feet and turn your toes out as the pull finishes (figure 5.7b). Move your feet out as your elbows squeeze in to your sides. Drop your face into the water as your hands come in under your chin (figure 5.7c), and thrust out, around, and back with your legs as your arms extend forward, palms down. Exhale after the leg thrust as you glide in the stretched position (figure 5.7d). Glide until forward motion begins to slow, then thrust your chin forward and inhale as you pull for the next stroke.

## Figure 5.7     Classic Breaststroke Coordination

### PRONE POSITION

1. Glide in prone position
2. Arms extend forward

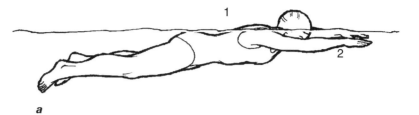

a

### PULL

1. Pull with arms
2. Raise head
3. Bring heels up and hook feet
4. Turn toes outward

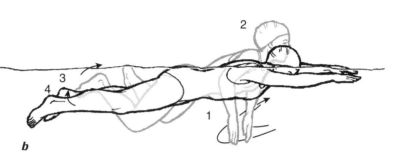

b

### THRUST

1. Bring hands under chin
2. Move feet out
3. Drop head
4. Thrust with legs and extend arms

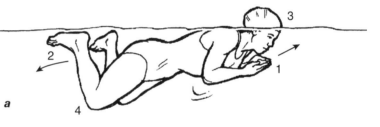

a

### GLIDE

1. Use a long glide
2. Exhale

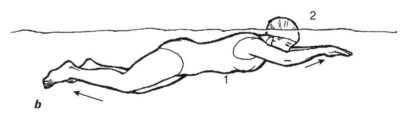

b

**Misstep**

Coordination is lost.

**Correction**

Think *pull, kick, glide,* not *kick, pull, glide.*

# Breaststroke Coordination Drill 1. Breaststroke Coordination With Mask and Snorkel

Float on the surface, facedown, with mask and snorkel. With absolutely no thought of propulsion, work on the coordination of arms and legs. Start lifting your heels as the pull begins. Hook your feet and turn them out as the pull finishes. Move your feet out while your elbows squeeze in to your sides. Thrust out, around, and back with your legs as your arms extend forward, palms down. Do this drill in *very* slow motion while floating. Make 40 slow-motion strokes.

**To Increase Difficulty**

- Gradually add propulsive power after 10 strokes.
- Try for one body-length glide.

**To Decrease Difficulty**

- Wear a float belt.
- Take only 25 strokes.

## Success Check

- Pull and inhale while your legs recover.
- Kick while your arms thrust forward.
- Hold still for a glide. Exhale.

## Score Your Success

Perform 25 good strokes = 1 point

Perform 40 good strokes = 2 points

Achieve a full body-length glide
  = 1 additional point

Your score ___

# Breaststroke Coordination Drill 2. Breaststroke Coordination Without Aids

Begin in a stretched prone float. Exhale and thrust your chin forward to get your mouth clear. Pull for propulsion and inhale as you raise your heels and turn out your hooked toes. Drop your face back into the water as your hands come in under your chin. Thrust with your legs and extend your arms forward (kick your arms forward). Exhale as you glide. Do one stroke at a time and ride your glide while you concentrate on the beginning movements of the next stroke. Continue for 25 yards with coordinated breathing.

**To Increase Difficulty**

- Pull and kick for power. Try for one body length per stroke.
- Continue for 50 yards (45.72 meters).

**To Decrease Difficulty**

- Wear a float belt.
- Wear goggles.

## Success Check

- Exhale in float position.
- Thrust the chin forward and inhale during the pull.
- Drop head and kick arms forward. Glide. Exhale.

## Score Your Success

Swim for 25 yards correctly coordinated
  = 5 points

You achieve full body length on most strokes
  = 2 additional points

Your score ___

## Breaststroke Coordination Drill 3.

## *Breaststroke in Deep Water*

With a lifeguard watching you, start at the deep end of the pool. Push off in a prone glide and swim a fully coordinated breaststroke to the shallow end of the pool, or 25 yards. Note: The objective of this drill is to swim in deep water. If the pool is 15 yards wide, swim across the pool to score 2 points for swimming 15 yards in deep water. If you swim the length of the pool, you will be in deep water for only part of the way, probably around 10 yards.

### To Increase Difficulty

- Push off the side of the deep end. Turn and swim to shallow water.
- Swim to the shallow end. Turn and swim back to the deep end.

### To Decrease Difficulty

- Wear a float belt and goggles.
- Swim slowly near the edge of the pool.

### *Success Check*

- Push off and exhale during the glide.
- Pull, inhale, and lift your heels.
- Kick your arms forward, glide, and exhale.

### *Score Your Success*

Swim in deep water for 15 yards = 2 points

Swim two pool lengths, or 50 yards
  = 4 points

Your score ___

## Breaststroke Coordination Drill 4.

## *Breaststroke for Distance*

With a lifeguard watching you, start at the shallow end of the pool. Swim breaststroke to the deep end. When you get to the wall, place your feet against the wall and push off. Swim to the shallow end and repeat. Continue swimming breaststroke for 100 yards (91.44 meters).

### To Increase Difficulty

- Shorten your glide to emulate the competitive style and have someone time you for 50 yards (45.72 meters).
- Swim and glide easily for 200 yards (182.88 meters).

### To Decrease Difficulty

- Wear goggles and a float belt.
- Rest at each end.
- Have a friend swim with you.

### *Success Check*

- Maintain steady rhythm with a long glide.
- Exhale during your glide off each wall.

### *Score Your Success*

Swim 100 yards nonstop = 4 points

Swim 200 yards nonstop = 6 points

Your score ___

## Breaststroke Coordination Drill 5.

## *Breaststroke Adaptation*

Swim the breaststroke with your head above water and chin constantly at water level. Allow your feet and legs to drop into a near-vertical position; do not try to glide at all. Constantly alternate leg kicks and arm strokes to maintain your position, but don't try to rise above chin level. Breathe whenever you wish. Make forward progress slowly. This conversational adaptation of the breaststroke is one of its nicest features. Try 5 minutes of conversational breaststroke.

### To Increase Difficulty

- Use wide, sweeping arm motions instead of the breaststroke arm pull.

### To Decrease Difficulty

- Wear a float belt and goggles.

### *Success Check*

- Use a short kick. Stop your kick just short of full extension.
- Use a short arm pull. Start another arm pull just before full-arm extension.
- Keep your face clear of the water.

### *Score Your Success*

Swim for 1 to 4 minutes in semivertical position = 1 point

Swim for 5 minutes or more in semivertical position = 2 points

Your score ____

# BREASTSTROKE TURN

All breaststroke turns are open turns. Competitive breaststroke turns differ only in that competitive swimmers remain underwater for a full stroke and glide after the turn. Recreational swimmers usually surface for a breath after a short glide. Consult a competitive swimming rule book for instructions on doing competitive turns.

In a closed course, it may seem a nuisance to have to break your stroke to turn at each end of the pool. However, turning smoothly also increases your speed. You should turn smoothly with consistent, reliable efficiency and lack of stress. The breaststroke turn allows such ease.

To turn easily when swimming for recreation, swim breaststroke toward the wall, gliding after each kick. When your head passes over the turn warning line or when it comes within 5 feet of the wall, complete the stroke then in progress with a kick and a glide. Streamline your body to glide with minimum loss of speed and touch the wall at water level with both hands simultaneously (figure 5.8a). At the touch, bend your elbows until your head is close to the wall. If the edge of the pool has a handhold, grasp it and pull in quickly. Tuck your knees tightly and turn sideways to the pool wall, pulling one hand away over the water and pressing down with the other as your feet come in under you sideways to the wall (figure 5.8b). Lift your head sideways, grab a breath, release the wall as or before your feet make contact, and place your face in the water facing the other direction. Put both hands under your chest, palms down and elbows in, and push off strongly, extending your arms to glide at or just under the surface (figure 5.8c). As the speed of the glide slows to swimming speed, resume swimming the breaststroke.

## Figure 5.8    Breaststroke Turn

### PULL IN

1. Touch wall with both hands simultaneously
2. Bend elbows
3. Pull in to wall

### TUCK AND TURN

1. Tuck knees
2. Turn sideways to wall
3. Press down on one hand
4. Inhale

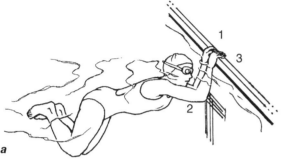

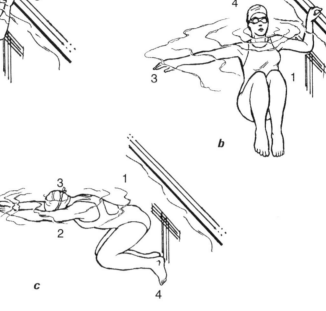

### PUSH OFF

1. Pivot
2. Bring arms in
3. Turn your face down
4. Push off

**Misstep**
You are too far from the wall for a good push-off.
**Correction**
Pull in tight to the wall as you turn your body sideways to the wall.

## Breaststroke Turn Drill 1.

## Judging Distance for Breaststroke Turns

Wear goggles. Start swimming breaststroke at moderate speed toward the end of the pool from about 20 feet (6.096 meters) out. Watch for the line turn target on the bottom of the pool, or judge a distance of 5 feet (1.524 meters) from the wall. As your head passes the turn target or the spot you picked, finish the arm stroke in progress, then kick exceptionally hard and streamline your body for a glide. Touch the wall with both hands simultaneously.

If you find that you slowed down perceptibly before touching, you must get a little closer for your last pull. Do that in one of two ways: Either glide a little longer on the next-to-last stroke or take an extra, very short arm stroke after your head passes the mark. Practice the approach until you can judge your position consistently to allow a final glide of 2 feet (0.6096 meters) or less. Make 5 consecutive approaches with a glide of 2 feet or less.

**To Increase Difficulty**

- Come in at full speed.

**To Decrease Difficulty**

- Moderate your speed to fit your ability.

### Success Check

- Take an extra, short, circular arm stroke if needed.

### Score Your Success

Complete 3 successful approaches
  = 2 points
Complete 5 successful approaches
  = 4 points
Your score ___

## Breaststroke Turn Drill 2.

## Completing the Breaststroke Turn

Wear goggles and start about 20 feet from the end wall. Make your approach as in breaststroke turn drill 1. When your head passes over the turn warning line or when it comes within 5 feet of the wall, complete the stroke in progress with a kick and a glide. Streamline your body to glide with minimum loss of speed and touch the wall at water level with both hands simultaneously.

At the touch, allow your elbows to bend until your head is close to the wall. If the edge of the pool has a handhold, grasp it and pull in quickly. Tuck your knees tightly and turn sideways to the pool wall, pulling one hand away over the water and pressing down with the other as your feet come in under you sideways to the wall. Lift your head sideways, grab a breath, release the wall as or before your feet make contact, and place your face in the water facing the other direction. Put both hands under your chest, palms down and elbows in, and push off strongly, extending your arms to glide at or just under the surface. Resume your stroke after a short glide. Do the turn in a slow, easy fashion without regard for speed. Do 5 left turns and 5 right turns smoothly and easily.

**To Increase Difficulty**

- Use a flat-wall turn. Do not grasp the end wall, but push sideways on it.

**To Decrease Difficulty**

- Slow down and float through the drill in slow motion.

### Success Check

- Glide, touch, pull in, tuck and turn, face in, push, glide.
- Turn slowly and smoothly, almost in cadence.

### Score Your Success

Score 3 points for 3 good, smooth turns to the right and to the left. Score 2 additional points for 5 good turns each way.

Your score ___

# SUCCESS SUMMARY OF BREASTSTROKE

Mastery of the breaststroke is a very real accomplishment. The kick must be exactly correct under the competitive rules. Any deviation from the rules will disqualify you from a competition. Ask your instructor or swim coach to examine your stroke if you wish to make sure you are swimming it within the narrow definitions established by the competitive swimming rule book. Recreational swimmers may, and often do, deviate from the technical definition of the stroke, but good swimmers try to stay within the definition in the competitive rule book.

You have made satisfactory progress if you have scored at least 36 points in this step. A score of 37 to 54 points shows great aptitude for swimming. If you scored 55 points or more, you can really be proud of your stroke and turn.

---

### Breaststroke Kick Drills

1. Inverted Breaststroke Kick ___ out of 4
2. Inverted Breaststroke Kick Against Pressure ___ out of 3
3. Inverted Breaststroke Kick With Kickboard ___ out of 6
4. Elementary Backstroke ___ out of 10
5. Prone, Bracketed Breaststroke Kick ___ out of 4
6. Breaststroke Kick With Kickboard ___ out of 4

### Breaststroke Arm Pull Drills

1. Slow-Motion Breaststroke Pulls ___ out of 3
2. One-Arm Breaststroke Pulls ___ out of 4
3. Breaststroke Pulls for Propulsion ___ out of 3

### Breaststroke Coordination Drills

1. Breaststroke Coordination With Mask and Snorkel ___ out of 3
2. Breaststroke Coordination Without Aids ___ out of 7
3. Breaststroke in Deep Water ___ out of 4
4. Breaststroke for Distance ___ out of 6
5. Breaststroke Adaptation ___ out of 2

### Breaststroke Turn Drills

1. Judging Distance for Breaststroke Turns ___ out of 4
2. Completing the Breaststroke Turn ___ out of 5

*Total* ___ *out of 72*

---

# Sidestroke

Swimmers in ancient times discovered that swimming the breaststroke with the head out of water was literally a pain in the neck. In an effort to ease the strain, they began to turn their heads to one side and put one ear on the water. Turning the head led to dropping one shoulder, and a new stroke gradually developed, using the same paired motions of arms and legs but rolling the body onto the side. The lateral motion of the legs when turned on the side became the forward-and-back motion of the scissors kick. Thus was born the sidestroke, the second stroke in the evolution of swimming strokes.

The sidestroke has a colorful history. In 1886 H. Kenworthy wrote in *A Treatise on the Utility of Swimming,* "Until within the last few years it was generally supposed that Breast or Belly swimming was the swiftest process, but this opinion has proved fallacious. The sidestroke is now universally acknowledged as the superior method and young swimmers would do well to practice it accordingly."

Today we recognize the sidestroke not as the swiftest but as the most powerful swimming stroke. The sidestroke is the lifesaving stroke. A lifeguard attempting a rescue without equipment must carry the weight of a victim and give up the use of one arm while swimming back to shore. The sidestroke is the stroke of choice when such power is needed. It employs a scissors kick to supply the power.

The sidestroke was *the* competitive swimming stroke when it was proven to be faster than belly swimming (breaststroke). It, too, ultimately lost its place in competition, but it has never lost its reputation for being the workhorse of swimming strokes. It is the strongest stroke known for lifeguard training.

## SCISSORS KICK

Swimmers perform the scissors kick in the side position. Since this is the position you learned for rolling your shoulders to breathe in the crawl stroke, it should be easy to attain, and it will be comforting to know that you can breathe whenever you wish.

The scissors kick is very powerful. It provides a longer glide and rest than any other kick and is easy to learn because it uses the forward-and-back motion that we use for walking.

Hold a kickboard under one ear. Glide on your side with your lower arm under the kickboard and upper arm at your side. Bend at the knees and hips to bring both feet in a direct line toward your body (figure 6.1a). When your knees are fully bent (hips at 90 degrees), hook the top foot and step forward as if to step up onto a high step. At the same time, point the toes of your lower foot and step back as far as you can, as if to lay your toes on top of a large step behind you (figure 6.1b). Now step forward and back as far as you can as your legs thrust and squeeze. Straighten legs to full extension (figure 6.1c). Point the toes of both feet during the thrust. Finish with feet together and streamlined. Turn your toes in slightly so that they catch on each other at the finish. Glide. Your legs must be very close together laterally during the kick, as a pair of scissors must have tight blades to cut. As your glide slows, bend your knees and hips in preparation for the next kick.

## Figure 6.1　　**Scissors Kick**

### SIDE GLIDE POSITION

1. Get in side glide position
2. Hold kickboard under ear with one hand
3. Tuck legs and hips at 90-degree angles
4. Keep feet in line with body

### SEPARATE LEGS

1. Hook top foot
2. Point lower foot
3. Bring top foot forward
4. Move lower foot back

### KICK

1. Step wide, drive, and squeeze
2. Point toes
3. Streamline body
4. Use a long glide

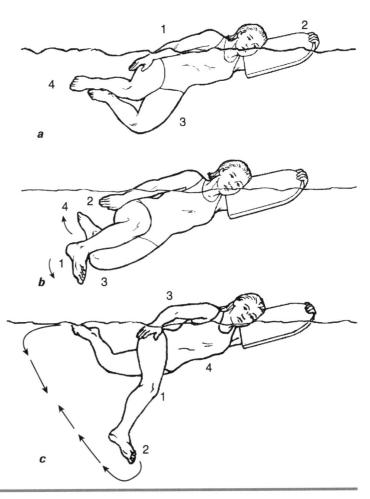

**Misstep**

Your lower thigh still points forward after you step out.

**Correction**

Step back farther with your lower leg.

72

# Scissors Kick Drill 1.  *Scissors Kick Land Drill*

Lie on your side on a mat, one arm stretched forward under your ear, the other along your side. Bring your knees up, but keep your feet back in line with your body. Check the position of your feet. Point the toes of your lower foot and hook the upper foot at the ankle. Step forward with the top foot and back with the bottom foot in as big a step as possible without rolling your hips forward (figure 6.2a). Stop and check to see if the lower leg is as far back as it will go (lower thigh straight with body). Carefully move the feet out and around, then down together in a circular motion (figure 6.2b). Streamline your legs and toes as for a glide. Repeat slowly 10 times.

**To Increase Difficulty**

- Gradually increase speed and smoothness.
- Ask a critical expert to correct you.

**To Decrease Difficulty**

- Move slowly. Stop and check each position.
- Place top hand on mat for balance.

## Success Check

- Bend knees and hips at 90-degree angles.
- Keep feet in line with body. Point lower toes, hook upper foot.
- Step forward and back, around and down. Streamline.

### Score Your Success

Score 2 points for passing scrutiny of an expert.

Your score ___

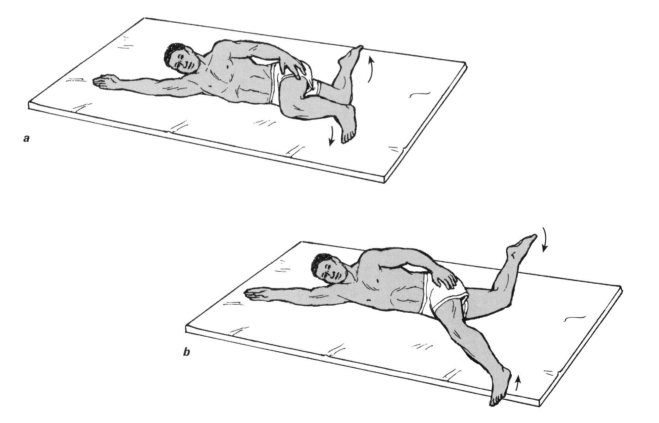

**Figure 6.2** Scissors kick land drill: *(a)* step forward with top leg and back with lower leg; *(b)* move feet out, around, and down in circular motion.

## Scissors Kick Drill 2. *Scissors Kick Bracket Drill*

In shallow water at the side of the pool, turn your side to the wall. Lay your cheek on the water with your head toward the wall. Grasp the edge of the pool with your top hand. Place the bottom hand against the wall about 18 inches (45.72 centimeters) down, palm against the wall with fingertips pointing down (bracket position). The lower hand must be directly under the top hand. Pull slightly with the top hand and push slightly with the bottom hand to bring your feet off the bottom in a side float position (figure 6.3a). If your body moves to the side, move your lower hand slightly in the same direction until you can hold the side position comfortably. Keep your ear underwater. Recover your legs slowly, as in the land drill. Hook the top foot; point the lower foot; step out *slowly* (top foot forward, lower foot back); then drive out, around, and down with vigor (figure 6.3b). Stop in the glide position. Do not let your feet pass each other. Repeat 30 times.

**To Increase Difficulty**

- Bend elbows slightly as the kick drives you into the wall.

**To Decrease Difficulty**

- Achieve a steady, balanced bracket position before beginning.
- Start slowly and build vigor gradually.

### Success Check

- Keep knees at 90-degree angle, feet in line with buttocks.
- Keep hips vertical. Step out wide.
- Kick with vigor. Streamline.

### Score Your Success

Complete 10 successful kicks = 2 points

Your score ___

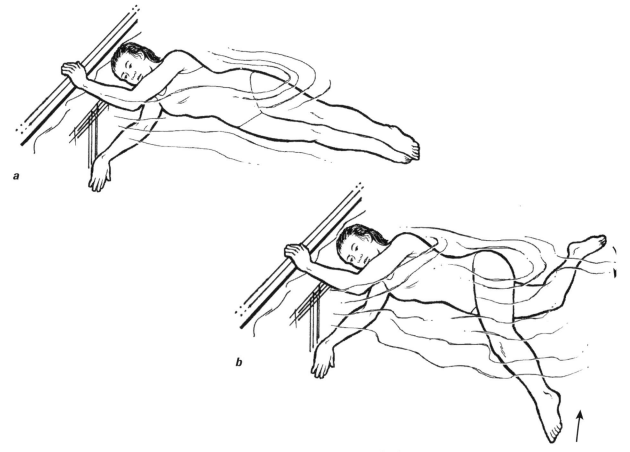

**Figure 6.3** Scissors kick bracket drill: *(a)* side float position; *(b)* step out slowly.

## Scissors Kick Drill 3. *Scissors Kick With Kickboard*

Get in side float position, lower arm extended under your head, upper arm along your side. Hold a kickboard lengthwise under your upper arm, fairly close to your hip. Use the scissors kick across the pool or for 15 yards (13.716 meters). Glide.

**To Increase Difficulty**

- Try kicking on the other side.
- Try top leg back, bottom leg forward.

**To Decrease Difficulty**

- Move the kickboard slightly forward or back to help maintain balance.
- Use a float belt along with the kickboard.

### Success Check

- Step way back. Keep hips vertical.
- Hold streamlined position for long glide.

### Score Your Success

Complete 15 yards correctly = 2 points

Complete 15 yards correctly in five kicks or fewer = 4 points

Your score ___

## Scissors Kick Drill 4. *Distance Per Scissors Kick*

Assume a side glide position. Hold a kickboard lengthwise in your forward arm under your head. Keep your ear tightly pressed against the board. Grasp the lower corner of the kickboard with the fingertips of your other hand. Push off the bottom into a side glide and begin the scissors kick. Make the kick as wide as you can, and try for distance on the glide. Remember to balance on your side for the glide by bending slightly at the hips to prevent rolling onto your back. Arch slightly to prevent rolling onto your front. Kick across the pool or for 15 yards. Your goal is 10 feet (3.048 meters) per kick.

**To Increase Difficulty**

- Push water with your top hand as your top leg kicks.
- Hold the kickboard at arm's length.

**To Decrease Difficulty**

- Use a float belt and a kickboard.

### Success Check

- After glide, slowly draw your knees up.
- Step out wide and thrust hard.
- Streamline. Ride a balanced glide.

### Score Your Success

Average 8 feet per kick = 1 point

Average 10 feet per kick = 3 points

Your score ___

## Scissors Kick Drill 5. *Continuous Kick for Distance*

Using a kickboard either under your ear or on your top hip, kick across the pool. Turn immediately, push off, and kick back again. Continue without stopping to rest on the turns until you have completed 4 pool widths or about 180 feet (54.864 meters).

**To Increase Difficulty**

- Eliminate the kickboard. Use your hands for balance.

**To Decrease Difficulty**

- Inhale quickly on the kick. Exhale slowly on the glide.
- Cut your distance to about 45 yards (41.148 meters).

### Success Check

- Try to glide 10 feet per stroke.
- Streamline, step wide, kick hard.

### Score Your Success

Complete 45 yards = 1 point

Complete 60 yards = 3 points

Your score ___

# SIDESTROKE ARM STROKES

The sidestroke arm motion is sometimes likened to picking apples and putting them into a basket while lying on your side. Think of reaching over your head with one hand to pick an apple, then bringing the apple down to your chin. The other hand then takes the apple and carries it down to your knee to put it in the basket. As the lower hand puts the apple in the basket, the upper hand reaches for another apple. Substitute a good handful of water for the apple, and you have the sidestroke arm motion. The arms move in opposite directions in the sidestroke. The upper, back arm pushes simultaneously with the thrust of the kick, and the lower, forward arm pulls as the legs and back arm recover.

The sidestroke arm motion is not a powerful arm stroke, but it is essential to the most powerful stroke we know. Only one arm pattern fits the sidestroke. It is unique in that it is the only arm stroke that allows the use of one arm to carry something or someone while the other arm continues to pull.

Start in a side glide position, with the lower arm extended under your head and upper arm along your side (figure 6.4a). Flex your forward wrist to put the hand in position to pull back horizontally. Start the pull of the forward arm by bending your elbow and pulling back with your hand and forearm. Allow your hand and forearm to assume a horizontal position, elbow bent to 90 degrees, as you begin to pull from the shoulder. Pull as though you were gathering an armful of water and pulling it to your chest (figure 6.4b). When your forward elbow points straight down, bring your hand up under your ear, turning it palm up. Squeeze your elbow to your side and point your fingertips forward (figure 6.4c). Fully extend your arm, palm up just under the surface. Turn the palm down when your arm reaches full extension. Glide until ready for the next stroke.

## Figure 6.4  Sidestroke Arm Pull

### SIDE GLIDE POSITION
1. Extend forward arm under head
2. Hold rear arm along side
3. Flex wrist of forward arm

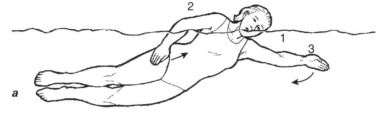

### PULL
1. Bend elbow and pull back with forward hand
2. Bend elbow to 90 degrees
3. Pull armful of water to chest

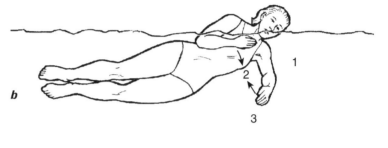

### SQUEEZE
1. Forward elbow points down
2. Raise hand, palm up
3. Squeeze elbow to side
4. Point fingertips forward

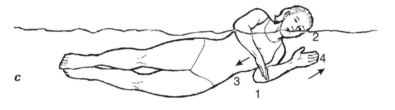

**Misstep**
Your forward arm pulls too far.
**Correction**
Don't pull past the shoulder. Bring hand up to ear.

Your upper, back arm moves in opposition to your forward arm. As the forward arm begins to pull, press the elbow of your top arm into your side. Bend the elbow, bringing the top hand to your chin. Leave the palm down and keep the hand flat under the water as it moves (figure 6.4b). As your forward hand turns palm up under your lower ear, bring your top arm forward to shoulder height and plunge your hand deep into the water in front of your face. Your top arm is now extended straight out from your shoulder; the elbow is bent at 90 degrees with the fingers pointed straight down at the bottom of the pool (figure 6.4c). As your forward arm extends to the starting position, your top arm pushes water with the forearm and hand directly back toward your feet until it rests once again along your side. This returns your body to a streamlined position for the glide and preparation for the next stroke. Figure 6.4 shows both forward (lower) and rear (upper) arm motions.

## Sidestroke Arm Stroke Drill 1.
## Sidestroke Forward-Arm Pull With Support

Attach the deep-float leg support to one ankle and assume a side glide position with lower arm extended overhead. Hold a kickboard under your upper arm. Keep it fairly close to your armpit to support your upper body. Keep your ear on the water.

Flex the forward (lower) wrist to put your hand in position to pull back horizontally. Start the pull of the forward arm by bending your elbow and pulling back with your hand and forearm. Allow your hand and forearm to assume a horizontal position, elbow bent at 90 degrees, as you begin to pull from the shoulder. Pull as though you were gathering an armful of water and pulling it to your chest. When the forward elbow points straight down, bring your hand up under your ear and turn it palm up. Squeeze your elbow to your side, point your fingers forward, and extend your arm (palm up) just under the surface to full extension. Turn the palm down as you reach full extension. Hold the glide for a moment, then repeat the pull.

Pull in very slow motion as you float so that you can study the arm motion. Do not try for propulsion or distance at first. As you become accustomed to the motion, quickly complete the pull and sneak the hand forward again, slowly, with the least possible resistance. Stop in the glide position, but do not expect to glide very far. Inhale as you pull; exhale as you glide. Review figure 6.4. Complete 40 pulls with breathing.

**To Increase Difficulty**

- Turn over and try the pull with the other arm.

**To Decrease Difficulty**

- Move the kickboard forward or back for balance.
- Wear a float belt instead of using a kickboard.

### Success Check

- Pull only to shoulder level.
- Bring your hand to your ear, palm up.
- Reach hand forward to full extension, turning palm down.

### Score Your Success

Complete 40 correct pulls with one arm = 1 point

Complete 40 correct pulls with both arms, one arm at a time = 3 points

Your score ___

## Sidestroke Arm Stroke Drill 2.
## Sidestroke Upper-Arm Push With Support

Using the deep-float leg support, hold a kickboard under your chin in a side glide position. Start the motion by recovering the upper arm from its position on your thigh. Keep your hand flat on the water and your wrist straight. Keep your elbow close to your side as it bends, bringing your hand to your chin. As you dig down into the water with your hand, allow your elbow to move forward until it is straight out in front of your shoulder. Keep a 90-degree bend in the elbow, fingertips pointing directly at the bottom of the pool. Now push water toward your feet with the forearm and hand until your arm is straight and resting on your thigh again. Glide. Inhale on the recovery; exhale on the glide. Make 40 upper-arm thrusts with breathing and glide.

**To Increase Difficulty**

- Try the drill on the other side.

**To Decrease Difficulty**

- Hold the board at arm's length in front.
- Wear a float belt instead of using a kickboard.

## Success Check

- Slice the flat palm edgewise through the water to your chin.
- Bring elbow to shoulder height, bent at 90 degrees.
- Push with hand and forearm toward feet to full extension.

## Score Your Success

Complete 40 correct strokes with one arm = 1 point

Complete 40 correct strokes with both arms, one arm at a time = 3 points

Your score ___

# SIDESTROKE COORDINATION

Once again, coordination of the sidestroke follows the pattern of coordination of previously learned strokes: bringing together the timing of the arms, legs, and breath. Timing the movement of the upper arm with the leg kick should be very easy because they work together almost as though they were tied with a short line.

An uncoordinated sidestroke is like a boat without a rudder. All the power of the strongest leg kick is undirected. An uncoordinated sidestroke results in swimming in an erratic circle. In a coordinated sidestroke, the forward arm establishes the direction of the kick and upper arm aids in the power of the thrust.

To correctly coordinate the sidestroke, begin in a side glide position with the lower arm fully extended beyond your head and upper arm lying extended along your thigh (figure 6.5a). Pull with your forward arm and inhale as your legs and top arm move into position to deliver a powerful thrust (figure 6.5b). Scissors-kick with your legs and push back with your top arm as your forward arm moves to your face and extends forward (figure 6.5c). Keep your ear on the water throughout the stroke. Remember that your top hand and legs move together in the same direction and at the same time. The powerful stroke ends in a streamlined side glide position for a long glide (figure 6.5d). Exhale on the glide.

# Figure 6.5 Sidestroke Coordination

## SIDE GLIDE POSITION

1. Assume an easy, relaxed side glide
2. Extend lower arm above head
3. Extend upper arm along thigh

## PULL

1. Draw knees up
2. Bring upper hand to chin
3. Pull lower hand to shoulder
4. Inhale

## KICK

1. Step feet out and kick strongly
2. Dig in with upper hand
3. Bring lower elbow in
4. Point fingers forward

## GLIDE

1. Extend lower arm, palm down
2. Use a long glide
3. Exhale

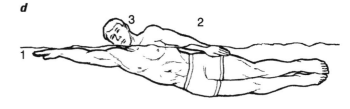

**Misstep**

You move diagonally or in a long curve.

**Correction**

Step back farther with your lower leg.

# Sidestroke Coordination Drill 1.

## *Top-Arm and Kick Coordination With Kickboard*

Hold a kickboard under your chin with your lower hand. Place your upper hand on the front of the thigh of your top leg. As your legs recover for a scissors kick, allow the top hand to remain on the front of your thigh, elbow bending as necessary. During the thrust of your legs, push with the hand on the front of your thigh as if to help the leg push against the water. After the third or fourth kick, gradually move your hand back from your thigh, but continue to make the same movement pattern with your hand 3 to 6 inches above your thigh. Keep the same hand–leg coordination, but move your hand farther away from your thigh on each stroke until your hand is slicing to your chin and digging in to push water in the correct sidestroke motion. Stroke and kick for 45 feet (13.716 meters).

### To Increase Difficulty

- Discard the kickboard and hold the lower arm straight.

### To Decrease Difficulty

- Use a float belt instead of a kickboard.
- Hold the kickboard at arm's length in front.

### Success Check

- Push on your leg during the kick for 4 kicks.
- Push water 6 inches above your leg for 4 kicks.
- Move your hand forward to your chin and push water back simultaneously with the kick.

### Score Your Success

Complete 45 feet correctly = 1 point

Complete 45 feet correctly without a kickboard = 3 points

Your score ___

# Sidestroke Coordination Drill 2.

## *Forward-Arm and Kick Coordination With Kickboard*

In sidestroke position, hold a kickboard under your upper arm near your hip. From a glide position, pull with your forward arm and recover your legs for a scissors kick. Stop momentarily when your feet are ready to drive and your hand is under your ear. Check that everything is ready for a simultaneous leg thrust and arm extension to glide position. Keep your ear on the water as you kick and reach into a long glide. Continue to hesitate at the coordination checkpoint for a few strokes, then eliminate the hesitation and swim the stroke smoothly with a long glide for at least 40 strokes.

### To Increase Difficulty

- Use no flotation help. Rest top hand on thigh while kicking.

### To Decrease Difficulty

- Use a float belt instead of a kickboard. Use top hand for balance.

### Success Check

- Pull with forward arm while bringing knees up and stepping out.
- Stop, check position, drive legs back, and bring hand forward. Glide.

### Score Your Success

Complete 40 correct strokes = 2 points

Complete 40 correct strokes without a kickboard = 4 points

Your score ___

## Sidestroke Coordination Drill 3.
## *Fully Coordinated Sidestroke*

Push off from the side of the pool and swim a fully coordinated sidestroke across the shallow end of the pool. Keep your ear underwater. Kick with power. Streamline and ride your glide. Inhale on the forward arm pull. Exhale on the glide. Turn, push off, and swim back again. Continue to swim widths for at least 50 yards (45.72 meters). Concentrate on timing, smoothness, and length of glide.

**To Increase Difficulty**

- Stretch and hold glide longer.
- Swim for 100 yards.

**To Decrease Difficulty**

- Lay your head down, ear underwater.
- Take a deep breath on the forward-arm pull. Hold it until the glide.

### *Success Check*

- Pull with the forward arm while the legs and top arm recover. Inhale.
- Extend the forward arm as you kick. Ear stays on the water.
- Glide at least one body length. Exhale.

### *Score Your Success*

Complete 50 yards correctly = 2 points

Complete 50 yards correctly in 25 strokes = 4 points

Your score ___

## Sidestroke Coordination Drill 4.
## *Deep-Water Sidestroke*

With a skilled swimmer watching you, start at the deep end of the pool. Push off and swim side-stroke to the shallow end. Count your strokes. Try to average 6 feet (1.8288 meters) or more per stroke. Swim at least 25 yards (22.86 meters).

**To Increase Difficulty**

- Try to do 25 yards in 10 strokes.

**To Decrease Difficulty**

- Stay close to the edge of the pool.
- Wear a float belt.
- Have a skilled swimmer carry a rescue tube and swim with you.

### *Success Check*

- Use a smooth, fully coordinated stroke.
- Keep your ear in the water and streamline your body for the glide.

### *Score Your Success*

Complete 25 yards = 2 points

Complete 25 yards in 10 strokes = 3 points

Your score ___

## Sidestroke Coordination Drill 5.

## *Lifesaving Sidestroke*

Swim the sidestroke across the pool using only your legs and forward arm. With your top arm, carry a 10-pound diving brick or item of similar weight on top of your hip (figure 6.6). Do not try to glide, but alternate stroking and kicking continuously. Try for one pool width or 15 yards (13.716 meters).

**To Increase Difficulty**

- Carry 15 pounds.
- See how much you can carry.

**To Decrease Difficulty**

- Carry only 5 pounds.
- Tow a large floating object instead.

### *Success Check*

- Use a quick, powerful pull of your forward arm.
- Alternate kick and pull with no glide.

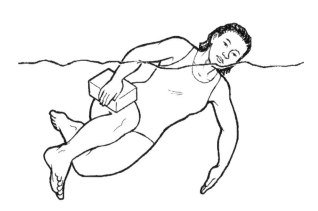

**Figure 6.6**   Lifesaving sidestroke.

### *Score Your Success*

Complete 15 yards while carrying less than 10 pounds = 1 point

Complete 15 yards while carrying 10 pounds = 2 points

Complete 15 yards while carrying more than 10 pounds = 3 points

Your score ___

# OVERARM SIDESTROKE

The sidestroke was the fastest stroke known in the late 1800s, yet competition sparked a search for even faster strokes with less negative motion. Recovering the top arm over the water reduced the negative motion of the sidestroke.

In his book *Swimming* (1909), Archibald Sinclair said that ". . . the adoption by racing men of the style of progression known as the sidestroke ultimately led to the English side-overarm method of swimming" (page 92). The overarm sidestroke is presented here as the third in the evolutionary series leading to the present-day crawl stroke.

Begin by swimming an easy, relaxed sidestroke. Notice that your upper arm pushes forward underwater on the recovery, resisting your body's forward movement. Pull through a stroke and glide. Now lift your upper arm just above the water, keeping your elbow close to

your side (figure 6.7a). Bend the elbow and slice your hand over the water, palm down, toward your face. As your hand reaches shoulder level, lift your elbow and bring the forearm in front of your face with your elbow bent at a right angle (figure 6.7b). As your hand reaches the level of your eyebrows, let your upper arm continue to come forward, but drop your forearm and hand to point vertically downward in front of your forehead (figure 6.7c). Your forearm, straight wrist, and hand should enter the water vertically and begin to push back toward your feet (figure 6.7d). Push with the kick exactly as you would for a conventional sidestroke. The timing and coordination also remain the same. The only change from the conventional sidestroke is that one arm recovers over the water. Continue the overarm sidestroke with your upper arm entering the water at eyebrow level.

## Figure 6.7 — Overarm Sidestroke

### LIFT UPPER ARM

1. Glide
2. Lift upper arm about 8 inches above the water

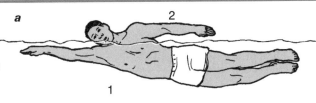

### BEND ELBOW

1. Keep hand flat and wrist straight
2. Bend and lift upper elbow

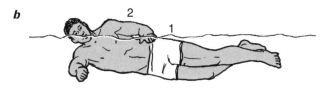

### BRING ARM OVER

1. Move forearm to vertical in front of forehead
2. Forearm and hand point down

### RECOVER

1. Dig hand and forearm in
2. Push toward feet

**Misstep**

Your upper hand pulls too far from your body.

**Correction**

Keep your upper elbow tight to your body until your hand reaches shoulder level.

## Overarm Sidestroke Drill.

Swim a normal sidestroke. Pay particular attention to coordination and glide. Note that your upper arm causes considerable resistance on the recovery even though the hand slices sideways. From a standpoint of efficiency, a longer stroke and less resistance are desirable. Now lift your upper arm over the water and reach forward to your forehead before placing your hand in the water for a push. Swim the overarm sidestroke, but don't change the coordination. Note the increase in speed and efficiency. Swim at least 25 yards (22.86 meters).

### To Increase Difficulty

- Swim overarm sidestroke on the other side.

## Overarm Sidestroke

### To Decrease Difficulty

- Swim in slow motion while wearing a float belt.

### Success Check

- Maintain sidestroke coordination.
- Upper arm enters at eyebrow level.
- A longer push should result in a longer glide.

### Score Your Success

Complete 25 yards with correct form
  = 2 points

Complete 50 yards with correct form
  = 3 points

Your score ___

# SUCCESS SUMMARY OF SIDESTROKE

You now know the power of the sidestroke, but it doesn't have to be a power stroke all the time. You can also use it as an easy stroke to cover great distances. Let your head float comfortably on the water with your mouth clear to breathe, and take long restful glides to swim over long distances

The sidestroke lends itself to the quantitative assessment of power through measurements of weight and distance. That still doesn't measure confidence, relaxation, and fluid dynamics, which can only be measured qualitatively. If you do not recognize an increase in efficiency when using the overarm sidestroke, perhaps your technique is faulty. Ask an expert to evaluate your sidestroke and your overarm sidestroke according to the success checks.

If you have scored at least 20 points in this step, your swimming is satisfactory. Try to raise your scores. A score in the range of 21 to 30 is good, and a score of 31 points or more is excellent.

### Scissors Kick Drills

1. Scissors Kick Land Drill      ___ out of 2
2. Scissors Kick Bracket Drill      ___ out of 2
3. Scissors Kick With Kickboard      ___ out of 4
4. Distance Per Scissors Kick      ___ out of 3
5. Continuous Kick for Distance      ___ out of 3

### Sidestroke Arm Stroke Drills

1. Sidestroke Forward-Arm Pull With Support      ___ out of 3
2. Sidestroke Upper-Arm Push With Support      ___ out of 3

### Sidestroke Coordination Drills

1. Top-Arm and Kick Coordination With Kickboard      ___ out of 3
2. Forward-Arm and Kick Coordination With Kickboard      ___ out of 4
3. Fully Coordinated Sidestroke      ___ out of 4
4. Deep-Water Sidestroke      ___ out of 3
5. Lifesaving Sidestroke      ___ out of 3

### Overarm Sidestroke Drills

1. Overarm Sidestroke      ___ out of 3

**Total**      ___ *out of 40*

# Back Crawl Stroke

You learned a basic backstroke in step 2. It may someday save your life because it is easy and relaxing to do for long distances. Competitive swimmers, however, are not as interested in *conserving* energy as they are in *using* energy efficiently. No swimming course would be complete without presenting the way to use energy most efficiently while swimming on the back. The back crawl stroke is the fastest way yet discovered to move through the water on your back. You have already learned the leg motion used in the back crawl stroke. Refine it a bit and coordinate it with a new arm stroke, and you will have learned the back crawl stroke.

The back crawl arm stroke is like no other stroke. It only vaguely resembles the crawl arm motion in that it uses an alternate, overarm recovery. In every other respect it is completely different.

The back crawl arm stroke is a major component of one of the standard competitive swimming strokes. It also adds a new concept to the swimmer's repertoire by being the only alternating arm stroke used while swimming on the back.

Start with a glide on your back, with both arms extended overhead with palms facing out. Roll slightly onto one side and drop one shoulder deeper in the water. Rotate your lower arm out from the shoulder so that your palm is turned down, as if you were reaching behind you to grasp the edge of the pool (figure 7.1a). Now bend your wrist forward sharply to put your palm in position to press directly back toward your feet. Leave your elbow high as far forward as possible while you begin to pull with your hand and forearm. Bend your elbow to bring your forearm into position to press directly back toward your feet.

As your forearm attains pulling position perpendicular to your body, straighten your wrist again. At this point, the forearm and hand should be about 12 inches (30.48 centimeters) underwater and parallel to the surface. Your elbow should be bent at about 90 degrees, and your upper arm should have moved very little from the shoulder (figure 7.1b).

You are now in position to exert maximum force directly back against the water. Leave your elbow bent as you pull directly toward your feet with your entire arm. Your hand and forearm should rise slightly toward the surface as you pull, with your hand about 4 inches (10.16 centimeters) deep as it passes your shoulder. As your arm passes your shoulder, begin to straighten your elbow and relax your wrist. The pressure of the water will begin to bend your hand back at the wrist. Keep your hand perpendicular to the line of thrust for as long as possible (figure 7.1c).

As your arm nears full extension, rotate the entire arm from the shoulder to a palm-down position and press down, flipping your hand down as it passes your thigh. Use this downward hand pressure to help you roll away from that side and elevate that shoulder above the water for the arm recovery (figure 7.1d). Keep your elbow straight and relax your wrist as you lift your arm from the water, palm down. If your wrist is totally relaxed, your hand will flop forward to a position at approximately a right angle to your arm (figure 7.1e). Raise your straight arm through a vertical position. As your arm passes shoulder height on its recovery, rotate your entire arm out from the shoulder so that your fingertips point away from your body. Stretch your arm as far forward as possible as you roll onto that side again and place your hand in the water palm down to start the next pull (figure 7.1f).

## Figure 7.1    Back Crawl Arm Stroke

### BACK GLIDE

1. Glide on your back
2. Extend arms overhead
3. Rotate right arm out, palm down

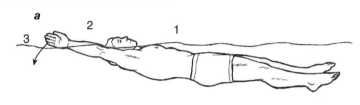

### PULL

1. Pull with hand
2. Keep elbow high, bent at 90 degrees
3. Pull with bent arm; straighten wrist

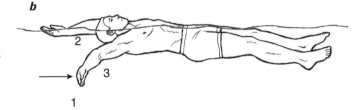

### PRESS

1. Straighten elbow
2. Bend wrist back
3. Press down with hand
4. Roll away

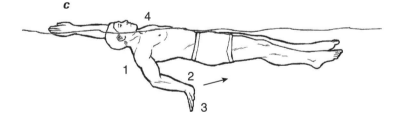

### RECOVER

1. Recover arm straight
2. Turn palm down

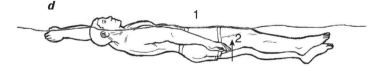

## ROTATE

1. Relax wrist
2. Rotate arm out

## ROLL

1. Reach forward
2. Roll
3. Begin pull phase again

The opposite arm follows the same pattern, beginning to pull as you roll toward that side to effect the recovery of the first arm. Your arms should be in direct opposition to each other at all times—when one arm is in midpull, the other should be in midrecovery; when one arm is finishing a pull, the other should be entering the water (figure 7.1).

Keep your hips up and your head back so that both ears remain underwater. Do not allow your head to roll as your shoulders roll. Look steadily and directly at the ceiling.

**Misstep**

Your pulling arm is too deep.

**Correction**

Your elbow should be bent at 90 degrees while pulling.

**Misstep**

One hand stays at the hip until the other hand reaches the hip also.

**Correction**

Concentrate on keeping arms in direct opposition to each other.

# Back Crawl Stroke Arm Drill 1. *Mental Imaging Drill*

This drill is directed toward achieving the correct high-elbow arm-and-hand position at the start of the back crawl arm stroke pull. Close your eyes and imagine yourself standing in a ditch with your arms at your sides. The ditch is only slightly wider than your body, and the sides rise above the top of your head. Your challenge is to get your shoulders and torso above the sides of the ditch by placing your hands over the top on both sides and pressing yourself up.

With your eyes still closed, stretch your arms above your head and imagine yourself trying to get out in two ways, first by keeping your elbows pointed down and pulling (figure 7.2a) and second by pressing with your elbows bent at 90 degrees, forearms and hands pointing forward, elbows as high as possible to get them above your hands as soon as possible (figure 7.2b). Which method would be more successful? If you pick the second, you are correct.

**Figure 7.2**   Mental imaging drill: *(a)* elbows down, hands pull; *(b)* elbows bent at 90 degrees and pressing.

Now think back to the moment you first began to press, elbows high, forearms and hands pointing forward. Imagine yourself floating on the water, rolled slightly to one side, reaching forward with one arm to catch the water and press it back toward your feet. Your arm should be in the same position as when you started to lift yourself from the ditch—elbow high and bent 90 degrees (see fig 7.1b, page 88). Ask a coach or a good back crawl swimmer to show you the correct position.

## Success Check

- Place your arm and hand in correct position for the back crawl pull.

### Score Your Success

Correctly place each arm = 2 points
Your score ___

# Back Crawl Stroke Arm Drill 2. *Supported Tether Drill*

In water 4 feet (1.2192 meters) deep, wear a high-buoyancy float belt. Tie a slipknot in the end of a 6- to 8-foot (1.8288- to 2.4384-meter) piece of surgical tubing, shock cord, or any line. Tie the other end of the cord to a pool ladder, a lane line anchor, or another stable object. Put the slipknot around one ankle so that you float on your back, tethered a few feet from the wall.

Keep your feet together and go through the motions of the back crawl arm stroke in very slow motion. Do not pull hard, but study arm, hand, and body position at each point in the arm stroke. Pull and study the motion for 10 minutes.

**To Increase Difficulty**

- Remove the tether and hold a pull buoy between your knees.

**To Decrease Difficulty**

- Keep the hips up; do not bend at the waist.
- Keep the chin up and the ears under.

## Success Check

- Roll your body toward the pulling arm.
- Bend elbow at 90 degrees on pull; straighten arm on recovery.
- Move arms exactly in opposition.

### Score Your Success

Successfully complete 10 minutes at a slow, easy pace = 2 points

Successfully complete 10 minutes while using a pull buoy = 3 points

Your score ___

# Back Crawl Stroke Arm Drill 3. *Touch-and-Go Back Crawl Arm Drill*

Use a pull-buoy leg float between your knees. Float on your back with both arms stretched overhead. Roll partially onto your right side and pull your right arm through a backstroke arm motion. Leave your left arm stretched overhead as you roll partially onto your left side to recover your right arm. When both arms are again stretched overhead, glide for a moment in back glide position. Roll partially onto your left side and pull through with your left arm. Roll to the right to allow recovery of the left arm while your right arm remains stretched overhead. Continue alternating arm pulls, completing each arm pull and gliding before beginning the next arm pull. In effect, one arm must touch the other overhead before it can go (thus *touch-and-go* back crawl). Concentrate on the correct arm position during each pull. Swim touch-and-go for 50 yards (45.72 meters).

**To Increase Difficulty**

- Drop the float and kick during the glide.

**To Decrease Difficulty**

- Wear a float belt.
- Wear goggles and a nose clip.

## Success Check

- Keep your head steady and your ears underwater.
- Keep hips up; do not bend at the waist.

### Score Your Success

Complete 50 yards correctly = 2 points

Complete 50 yards by just kicking, no float = 3 points

Your score ___

## Back Crawl Stroke Arm Drill 4.
### Pull-and-Glide Back Crawl Arm Drill

Put a leg float between your knees and stretch into a back glide position, arms overhead. Roll onto your right side and pull through a backstroke arm pull with your right arm. As you finish the pull, stop with your right hand resting on your thigh (figure 7.3). Glide with your left arm overhead for a count of 4, then roll to your left, pull through with the left arm as you recover the right, and stop with your left hand resting on your thigh for a count of 4. Roll right and repeat, letting each hand rest on your thigh for 4 counts. Keep your arms in direct opposition to each other. Swim for 50 yards.

**To Increase Difficulty**

- Drop the float and kick steadily.

**To Decrease Difficulty**

- Wear a float belt.
- Wear goggles and a nose clip.

### Success Check

- Keep arms in opposition at all times.
- Straighten arm to recover.
- Bend arm on the pull.

### Score Your Success

Master the pull-and-glide stroke = 2 points

Pull and glide without the float = 3 points

Your score ___

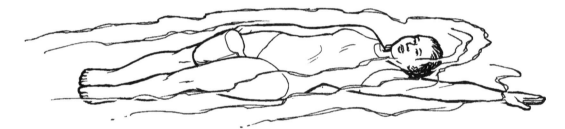

**Figure 7.3**  Pull-and-glide back crawl arm drill.

## Back Crawl Stroke Arm Drill 5.
### Counting Back Crawl Arm Pull

Place a leg float between your knees and start in a back glide position, arms stretched overhead. Begin a steady, rhythmic back crawl arm stroke with no glide or hesitation. Keep your arms directly opposite each other throughout the stroke.

After two or three strokes, begin counting in a six-beat rhythm. Say "one" as your right hand strikes the water on its overhead entry, and say "two" and "three" as it pulls. Say "four" as your left hand strikes the water on entry, and say "five" and "six" as it pulls. Continue counting the six-beat rhythm as you swim. Remember, hands strike the water on counts 1 and 4. If you get off count, stop, slow down, and begin again. Swim and count for 50 yards.

**To Increase Difficulty**

- Discard the float and kick to the count.

**To Decrease Difficulty**

- Wear a float belt.
- Wear goggles and a nose clip.

### Success Check

- Start slowly.
- Hands hit the water on counts 1 and 4.
- Keep head steady and hips up.

### Score Your Success

Complete 50 yards without losing count
  = 2 points

Complete 50 yards without losing count while
  kicking = 4 points

Your score ___

## Back Crawl Stroke Arm Drill 6. *Back Crawl Head Position Drill*

Use a leg float between your knees. From a back glide position, begin a steady back crawl arm stroke. Concentrate on holding your head absolutely still as your shoulders rotate from side to side. Imagine that your nose is tied with a string to a track in the ceiling and cannot turn to the side. Use your head as an anchor to steady the entire back crawl arm stroke. Turn your head only if you need to look back to find the pool end wall for safety. Otherwise gauge your distance from the wall by using backstroke turn flags or the color change in the competitive lane line floats. Coast in when you think you are close. Swim 100 yards (91.44 meters) with your head steady.

**To Increase Difficulty**

- Discard the float and kick.

**To Decrease Difficulty**

- Wear a float belt.
- Wear goggles or a nose clip.

### Success Check

- Shoulders roll with the stroke, but the head stays still, looking straight up.
- Look for a ceiling beam, tile seam, or pipe to follow. Fasten your gaze on it.

### Score Your Success

Score 1 point for trying. Score 3 points if you feel you have succeeded.

Your score ___

# BACK CRAWL STROKE COORDINATION

The back crawl kick and the back crawl arm stroke must be finely coordinated to produce the back crawl stroke. This stroke is so named because it resembles the crawl stroke in its alternating overarm recovery and alternating vertical kicking movements. In competitive swimming circles, it is often referred to as simply the *backstroke,* but this can be misleading because there are two other backstrokes: the basic backstroke and the elementary backstroke.

The back crawl stroke is one of the four competitive swimming strokes recognized by all of the governing bodies of competitive swimming. In competitive swimming the term *backstroke* describes any swimming motion performed in the supine position. Because the back crawl is the fastest of these, it is the stroke that is universally used. The rules of competitive swimming have only one rule governing the execution of the backstroke: "Swimmers shall push off on the back and, except when turning, must continue swimming on the back throughout the race" (National Collegiate Athletic Association 2005). That definition allows considerable leeway in execution, and coaches often disagree on the exact execution of the correct (read *fastest)*

backstroke. The specific stroke in this text has led one swimmer to two national championship performances.

One advantage of swimming the back crawl stroke is that your nose and mouth are free at all times, allowing you to breathe at will. Its biggest disadvantage is that you cannot see where you are going.

Begin the back crawl stroke in a back glide position with right arm stretched overhead, palm turned out, and left arm along your side. Keep your hips up as you begin the back crawl kick. Starting with your left foot, count the upthrust of each foot in a series of six-beat cycles (figure 7.4). Hold your head in normal alignment with your body, chin up and both ears submerged. Do not allow your head to roll from side to side as you swim.

On the third count of 1, roll to the right and extend your right arm to catch the water for a pull. Use the arm stroke exactly as described in back crawl stroke arm drill 5, pulling through on the kick counts of 2, 3, and 4 as you recover your left arm. As you finish the pull on 4, roll to the left and extend your left arm for the left arm catch. Pull with your left arm on counts 5 and 6 as you recover your right arm through the vertical. Finish the pull of your left arm on count 1 as you roll to the right and your right arm enters the water for the next catch.

Keep your arms in diametrically opposed positions as you pull with one and recover the other. Continue the cycle rhythmically. Be sure your right hand enters the water exactly on the 1 count and your left hand enters exactly on the 4 count. Keep your head steady and your hips up. Though your nose and mouth are free to breathe at any time, develop the habit of exhaling through your nose during one arm pull and inhaling through your mouth during the other.

## Figure 7.4    Back Crawl Stroke

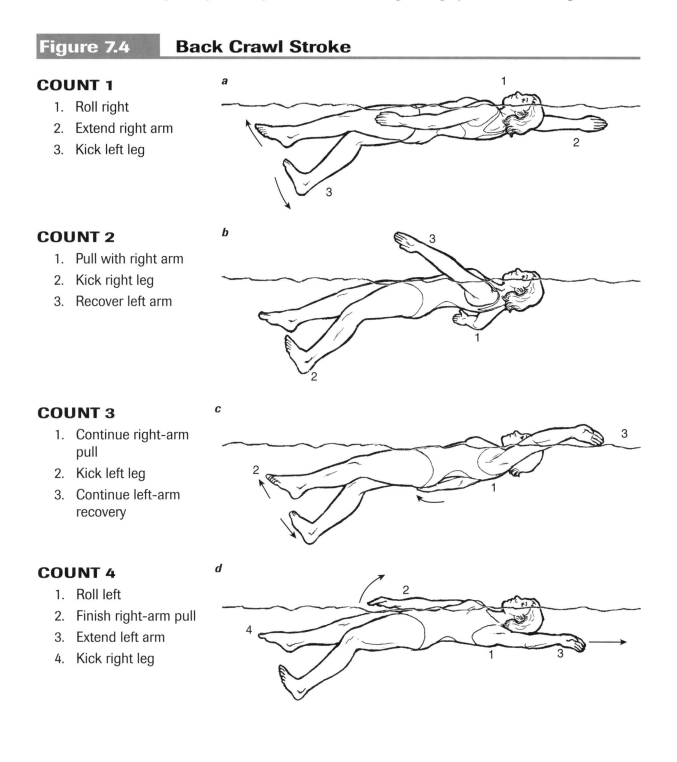

### COUNT 1

1. Roll right
2. Extend right arm
3. Kick left leg

### COUNT 2

1. Pull with right arm
2. Kick right leg
3. Recover left arm

### COUNT 3

1. Continue right-arm pull
2. Kick left leg
3. Continue left-arm recovery

### COUNT 4

1. Roll left
2. Finish right-arm pull
3. Extend left arm
4. Kick right leg

## COUNT 5

1. Start recovery of right arm
2. Pull left arm
3. Kick left leg

## COUNT 6

1. Recover right arm through vertical
2. Pull left arm
3. Kick right leg

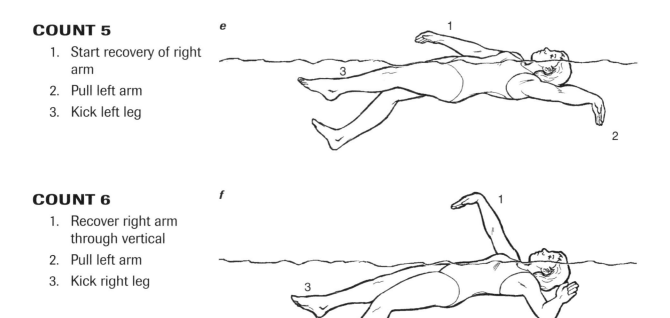

# Back Crawl Stroke Coordination Drill 1. *One-Arm Drill*

In back-glide position, start kicking with your right foot on the count of 1. Count kicks in six-beat cycles with your arms stretched overhead. On the third count of 1, roll slightly to the right, reach forward with your right arm, and catch the water by bending your wrist. Pull through on counts 2 and 3. On count 4, press down with your right hand, roll to the left, and lift your right shoulder. Leave your left arm stretched overhead as you recover your right arm on counts 5 and 6. Roll strongly to the right side as your right hand strikes the water on count 1. Continue to pull with your right arm only, leaving your left arm stretched overhead. Make at least 10 right-arm strokes. Repeat the drill, pulling with your left arm only, leaving your right arm stretched overhead. Make your left hand strike the water on count 4, and roll your left shoulder up on count 1. Make at least 10 strokes with the left arm only.

**To Increase Difficulty**

- Swim 50 yards on each side using the one-arm stroke.

**To Decrease Difficulty**

- Start very slowly.

## Success Check

- Right arm strikes water on count 1, pulls until count 4.
- Left arm strikes water on count 4, pulls until count 1.

### Score Your Success

Try the drill = 1 point

Complete the drill with correct coordination = 3 points for each arm

Your score ___

## Back Crawl Stroke Coordination Drill 2. *Slow-Motion Drill*

Wear a float belt near your hips for this drill. Swim the back crawl stroke very slowly, counting the kicks at about one per second. Swim using both arms, but concentrate on the full cycle of one arm for several strokes, then shift your concentration to the other arm for a few strokes. Finally, concentrate on the coordination between arms and legs for a few strokes. Keep the pace very slow. Avoid the tendency to speed up. Swim 100 yards in slow-motion backstroke.

### To Increase Difficulty

- Discard the float belt.
- Swim for 200 yards (182.88 meters).

### To Decrease Difficulty

- Wearing goggles or a nose clip might help.

### Success Check

- Arms strike the water on counts 1 and 4.
- Roll your shoulders, not your head.

### Score Your Success

Swim 100 yards with correct coordination
  = 2 points
Swim 200 yards with correct coordination
  = 4 points
Your score ___

## Back Crawl Stroke Coordination Drill 3. *Normal Back Crawl Stroke*

Always be alert to judge your distance from the end of the pool. Use lane float color changes or backstroke turn flags to prevent injury. If your pool does not have turn flags or lane floats, place chairs or other markers at the sides of the pool 15 feet (4.572 meters) from each end of the pool.

Swim an easy, relaxed back crawl stroke at a speed you estimate to be about half as fast as you can swim. Keeping it smooth and rhythmic, swim continuously (except for turns) for 200 yards. Concentrate alternately on each arm, on your kick, and on coordination of the stroke as you swim.

### To Decrease Difficulty

- Slow down and think about the stroke.
- Wear goggles or a nose clip.

### Success Check

- Keep chin up and head steady.
- Hands strike the water on counts 1 and 4.
- Keep hips up; don't bend at the hips.

### Score Your Success

Swim 200 yards, but hips bend and head
  turns while swimming = 2 points
Swim 200 yards correctly = 6 points
Your score ___

# BACK CRAWL STROKE OPEN TURN

There are two turns to use while swimming backstroke—the open turn and the tumble turn. You may use the open turn for either the elementary backstroke or the back crawl stroke. It will be described here as used with the back crawl stroke. The open turn is so named because your head remains above water, allowing you to take a breath during the turn. It is not used in competitive swimming. The tumble turn is a closed turn (that is, your head remains underwater during the turn with no opportunity to breathe). The tumble turn is designed solely for high speed, so competitive swimmers use the tumble turn during backstroke races. You can learn about the back tumble turn in any of the many texts on competitive swimming.

It's easy to misjudge your distance from the end of the pool when swimming on your back. Dangerous head injuries could result from failure to execute a turn properly. Therefore you must be able to use a simple and safe method for changing direction in a pool. The open backstroke turn is the easiest of the backstroke turns. You may use the open turn for any stroke on the back, whereas you may use the tumble turn only with the back crawl stroke.

To help judge your distance, use backstroke turn flags, colored lane line floats, or a marker you have placed at the side of the pool 15 feet from the end. Swim the back crawl toward the end of the pool. When your head passes the flag, colored floats, or marker, finish the pull and take two more.

As you finish the second pull, roll completely onto your side on the outstretched forward arm, streamline your body, and glide into the wall (figure 7.5a). As your hand touches the wall, grasp the edge of the pool and pull. Tuck your knees quickly and bring both feet under you as you turn to face the wall (figure 7.5b). Take a big breath, release the wall as you float through the pivot, and lay your head back. Place both feet against the wall just under the surface, place both hands palms up by your ears, and push off just under the surface (figure 7.5c). Extend your arms as you push off, streamline your body, and exhale slowly through your nose as you glide under the surface (figure 7.5d). When your speed slows to swimming speed, kick to the surface and resume swimming the back crawl.

If your pool has a flat end wall with no place to grasp, place your palm flat against the wall, bend your elbow until your head is close to the wall, then press down with your hand to initiate the pivot in a tuck position. Try to stay as close to the wall as possible to ensure a good push off the wall.

| Figure 7.5 | **Backstroke Open Turn** |

## APPROACH WALL

1. Roll onto forward arm
2. Glide to the wall

*a*

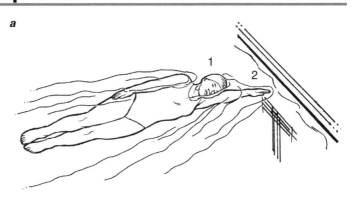

*(continued)*

**97**

## Figure 7.5 *(continued)*

### TUCK AND TURN

1. Grasp the wall and pull
2. Tuck knees
3. Pivot to face the wall

*b*

### PUSH OFF

1. Release the wall, bringing hands to ears
2. Inhale and tilt head back
3. Plant feet
4. Push off

*c*

### GLIDE

1. Glide underwater
2. Streamline your body
3. Exhale

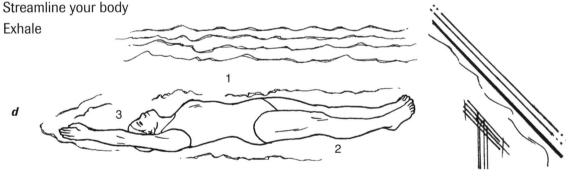

*d*

**Misstep**

You roll your shoulders past the vertical before you touch the wall.

**Correction**

Keep the trailing arm slightly back behind you.

## Open Backstroke Turn Drill 1.

## *Open Backstroke Turn Push-Off With Nose Clip*

Carefully position a nose clip on your nose. It should be relatively comfortable and should block your nose completely. Goggles are optional, but you may have trouble keeping them in place.

From a prone position in the water, facing the end wall, grasp the edge of the pool overflow trough with both hands. (Note: You may grasp the edge of the pool coping if it is not more than 4 inches above the water surface. If no handhold is within 4 inches of the water surface, place both palms flat against the wall at water level and keep them there by kicking in the prone position.) Pull with both hands as you tuck your legs and bring them under your body to place both feet against the wall, toes about 4 inches beneath the surface. (Note: With no handhold, press down on the water with both hands to bring your tightly tucked legs under you and into the wall.) Lay your head back until your face is about 3 inches (7.62 centimeters) underwater. Stay tucked as you bring your hands quickly underwater to a palm-up position by your ears. Begin exhaling slowly through your mouth as your head sinks under. Push with your feet and extend your arms overhead as you bring your hips up into a streamlined glide position just under the water. Use your arms and head position to stay submerged for a 5-second glide. Begin the back crawl kick to the surface and pull through with one arm to start the back crawl stroke.

Continue your exhalation steadily throughout the underwater glide. Some practice in breath control will be necessary for maintaining a steady stream of bubbles until you reach the end of the glide. You will need to learn this breath-control skill before moving to the next drill. Using your voice as you exhale often helps maintain a steady bubble rate. Make 10 push-offs in good position with controlled underwater glide.

**To Increase Difficulty**

- Try it without goggles.

**To Decrease Difficulty**

- Find a spot where you can pull on something at water level to start.

## *Success Check*

- Tuck and pull in.
- Lie back with hands at ears.
- Push off underwater.

### *Score Your Success*

0 to 5 successful push-offs = 1 point

6 to 10 successful push-offs = 4 points

Your score ___

## Open Backstroke Turn Drill 2.

## *Breath Control for the Open Backstroke Turn*

This is the most difficult drill for the open backstroke turn; but if you don't learn it, you will have to wear a nose clip to do the turn. Improper technique here could cause water to enter your nose, causing considerable distress, so practice open backstroke turn drill 1 until you can exhale steadily the entire time your head is underwater. Then remove your nose clip and repeat open backstroke turn drill 1, except you must exhale steadily through your nose. Keep your mouth closed tightly. Do not get discouraged during the first few tries; you can do it with practice. Do 10 push-offs without getting water in your nose.

**To Decrease Difficulty**

- Go back to wearing a nose clip, then try again.

### *Success Check*

- Tuck and pull in.
- Bring the head back.
- Bring hands by ears.
- Push off and exhale on the glide.

### *Score Your Success*

Complete 10 push-offs while wearing a nose clip and exhaling by mouth = 2 points

Complete 10 push-offs without wearing a nose clip and without getting water in your nose = 5 points

Your score ___

## Open Backstroke Turn Drill 3.

## *Side Glide Into Backstroke Open Turn*

Goggles are optional. Do the drill without a nose clip if possible. Start about 15 feet (4.572 meters) from the end of the pool in a back-float position, arms overhead. Take three back crawl pulls, starting with your left arm. As your left arm pulls through the third stroke, roll onto your right side, look at the end wall, and glide with your right arm extended and your left hand resting on your thigh. Do not let your shoulders roll past the vertical as you roll onto your belly until you have touched the wall.

As your right hand reaches the end wall, grasp the gutter, pull, tuck, and turn to face the wall as your feet come under you. Do not bring your left hand to the wall, but place it immediately beside your ear, palm up. Release the wall with your right hand, place your right hand beside your right ear, and push off as in open backstroke turn drill 2.

(If no handhold is available on the end wall, place your right palm flat against the end wall, bend your elbow to get your body in close, and press down with your hand to initiate a pivot in tucked position. As your feet come under you, press back on the water as you bring your right hand up to your ear. This backward press of the right hand will push you into the wall.)

Repeat the drill, but start pulling with your right arm so that you will glide in to the wall on your left side. Make five smooth-flowing turns on each side.

**To Increase Difficulty**

- Do not wear a nose clip.
- Work up to full speed.

**To Decrease Difficulty**

- Wear a nose clip.
- Do all trials slowly.

### *Success Check*

- Pull, roll, glide, touch, tuck, pivot, push off, glide.
- Do not roll past the vertical until after you touch the wall.

### *Score Your Success*

Score 1 point for each correct turn on each side, for a maximum of 10 points.

Your score ___

## Open Backstroke Turn Drill 4.

# *Open Backstroke Turn*

Wear a nose clip only if you have been unsuccessful in controlling your breathing properly in open backstroke turn drills 2 and 3. Goggles are optional. Place a marker 15 feet (4.572 meters) from the end of the pool or use backstroke turn flags if they are available. You may also use competitive lane float markers that are of a contrasting color for the last 15 feet before they attach to the wall.

Start about 40 feet (12.192 meters) from the end of the pool. Swim the back crawl toward the end of the pool until your head is even with the marker. Complete the pull and take two more arm strokes. As you complete the second pull, roll onto your forward arm and leave your trailing hand resting on your thigh. Glide into the wall in side glide position. As your forward arm reaches the wall, perform the turn and the push-off exactly as you did in open backstroke turn drill 3.

After practicing a few times, you may find that when your head passes the marker, you need to take three strokes instead of two to avoid gliding too long. Be careful in determining the correct number of strokes so that you don't strike the wall with your head. Also, vary your strokes during the drill so that you practice turning to both sides. Make 10 smooth and efficient turns to each side.

**To Increase Difficulty**

- Don't wear a nose clip.
- Work up to top speed.

**To Decrease Difficulty**

- Work very slowly.
- Wear a nose clip.

## *Success Check*

- Work carefully on determining the number of strokes you need after the marker.

### *Score Your Success*

Complete 0 to 5 perfect turns on each side = 3 points

Complete 6 to 10 perfect turns on each side = 8 points

Your score ___

# SUCCESS SUMMARY OF BACK CRAWL STROKE

Distance alone will not make you a good back crawl stroke swimmer, but it will help smooth out your stroke. You need someone to watch your stroke and judge it on a qualitative basis. Ask your coach or instructor to evaluate your stroke. Head and hip position, shoulder roll, and timing all play major roles in perfecting this stroke.

If you scored at least 32 points, you have completed the step successfully. If you scored 33 to 48 points, you show real promise. If you scored 49 points or more, your coordination is outstanding.

---

### Back Crawl Stroke Arm Drills

1. Mental Imaging Drill ___ out of 2
2. Supported Tether Drill ___ out of 3
3. Touch-and-Go Back Crawl Arm Drill ___ out of 3
4. Pull-and-Glide Back Crawl Arm Drill ___ out of 3
5. Counting Back Crawl Arm Pull ___ out of 4
6. Back Crawl Head Position Drill ___ out of 3

### Back Crawl Stroke Coordination Drills

1. One-Arm Drill ___ out of 6
2. Slow-Motion Drill ___ out of 4
3. Normal Back Crawl Stroke ___ out of 6

### Open Backstroke Turn Drills

1. Open Backstroke Turn Push-Off With Nose Clip ___ out of 4
2. Breath Control for the Open Backstroke Turn ___ out of 5
3. Side Glide Into Backstroke Open Turn ___ out of 10
4. Open Backstroke Turn ___ out of 8

*Total* ___ *out of 61*

---

# Butterfly Stroke

The butterfly stroke is the fourth of the internationally recognized competitive swimming strokes. It was developed in an effort to find a faster way to swim the breaststroke. Changes in the arm and leg movements became so different from those of the traditional breaststroke that the governing bodies of the competitive swimming world made it a new, fourth style of competitive swimming. It has gained popularity and is now considered a significant part of any swimming instruction book.

As many as 20 different combinations of propulsive movements have been recognized as distinct swimming strokes (some of which are included in this text), but only four have been chosen for use in competition. One of those is the butterfly stroke.

The butterfly stroke employs a dolphin kick and a unique double overarm motion not employed in any other stroke. It's important to learn these propulsive motions separately before trying to coordinate them into a cohesive stroking pattern.

## DOLPHIN KICK

The dolphin kick is humankind's attempt to emulate the powerful swimming motions of the creatures of the sea. The gentle, sleek bottlenose dolphin was one model selected for imitation in our search for more efficient modes of locomotion in the aquatic medium. The dolphin kick is sometimes called the *fishtail kick,* but its vertical plane of motion more closely resembles that of sea mammals.

The dolphin kick is powerful and great fun. It has considerable versatility in its application and is a step in attaining true mastery of the water. To date, however, its greatest use has been for competitive swimming. It can be used in several strokes but has been used primarily in the butterfly stroke. It is described here as the first step in learning that stroke. Later in this text we explore its use in other situations.

We must think of the dolphin kick not so much as a leg kick but as an undulation of the whole body culminating in a whipping motion of the feet. Keep the picture of a dolphin in mind all the time you do this kick.

Begin the kick in a prone-float position with both arms stretched in front of you. Hold your breath and keep your face in the water as you do this kick. Think of your body as a perfectly flexible rubber cylinder floating on the waves. As an imaginary wave approaches, flex your wrists to guide your hands up, over, and down the other side of the wave (figure 8.1a to figure 8.1d). Your arms, shoulders, chest, waist, hips, and knees flex in turn to follow the passage of the wave under you. As your legs pass over the top of the wave, your hands turn up to ride over the next wave. As the wave passes under you, your body curls slightly forward and then arches into the trough as your legs rise behind you. Leave your ankles perfectly relaxed as

you lift your legs and as your hips drop (figure 8.1e). As the crest of the wave passes your feet, press down and back with the tops of your feet, ankles extended.

Continue to undulate, but focus on your legs. As your legs move down, bend your knees. The downward motion will cause your floppy ankles to extend and your toes to point. Forcibly straighten your legs and flip the water down and back with your floppy feet. As your legs start up, straighten your knees. Continue the rhythmic undulation of your body, alternately lifting and pressing with floppy ankles. Keep your legs close together and move them simultaneously in a vertical plane. Emphasize the vertical thrust and flipping action of the lower legs and feet.

## Figure 8.1    Dolphin Kick

**UP**
1. Point fingertips up
2. Arch back
3. Lift legs

**OVER**
1. Curl hands and arms
2. Ride "over the top of the wave"

**DOWN**
1. Begin to press legs down
2. Bend knees
3. Raise hips

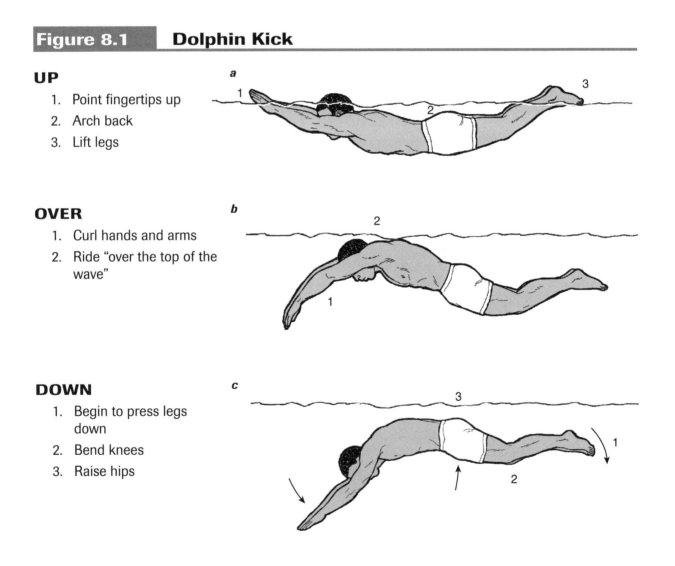

## DIG

1. Dig deep with hands and arms
2. Flip down
3. Lower legs and feet

*d*

## RECOVER

1. Turn up hands and arms
2. Lift legs as hips drop

*e*

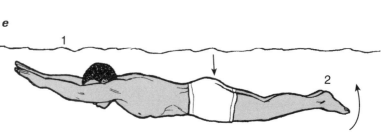

**Misstep**

You bend too deeply at the hips.

**Correction**

Make the downward kick shallow.

# Dolphin Kick Drill 1. *Sideways Fishtail*

Goggles are recommended. You may also wear a nose clip if desired. At the end of the pool, take a breath and submerge on your side. Push off from the wall underwater on your side, arms stretched overhead. Remain on your side with feet together as you begin an undulating body motion, culminating in a lower-leg kick and a flip of your relaxed feet. Pretend you are a fish; imitate the way you think a fish moves. Start fairly deep and try to stay underwater as you kick. Go as far as you can on one breath before surfacing. Remember to kick both back and forth with your feet. Take a new breath and continue for 30 feet (9.144 meters).

**To Increase Difficulty**

- Try to rise, take a breath, and continue.

**To Decrease Difficulty**

- Start slowly and gradually increase speed.

## Success Check

- Your entire body undulates.
- Flip your floppy feet.

### Score Your Success

Swim 30 feet in two breaths = 2 points

Swim 30 feet in one breath = 4 points

Your score ___

## Dolphin Kick Drill 2. *Fishtail Kick With Fins*

Put on socks or boots and swim fins. Wear goggles. Repeat dolphin kick drill 1 with fins. Keep both arms overhead for safety. You will move so fast that you may run into the wall before you realize it. Stop and breathe when necessary. Swim 60 feet (18.288 meters) by fishtailing with fins.

**To Increase Difficulty**

• Go 45 feet (13.716 meters) on one breath.

**To Decrease Difficulty**

• Use a nose clip.

• Start slowly and increase speed.

### Success Check

• Undulate your whole body, not just your legs.

### Score Your Success

Swim 60 feet on three breaths = 2 points

Swim 60 feet on two breaths = 4 points

Your score ___

## Dolphin Kick Drill 3. *Fishtail, Roll to Dolphin Kick*

Repeat dolphin kick drill 2, but after starting on your side (figure 8.2a), continue to kick as you roll into a facedown position (figure 8.2b). Try to stay underwater on the same breath to finish a 60-foot (18.288 meter) kick. Then do the drill again, starting in the prone position and remaining on your belly throughout. Stay deep and try for 60 feet on one breath.

**To Increase Difficulty**

• Stay underwater for the full 60 feet.

**To Decrease Difficulty**

• Wear a mask and snorkel, but try to stay underwater.

### Success Check

• Hands turn up and down to lead undulation.

• Kick up as well as down.

### Score Your Success

Swim 30 feet underwater = 1 point

Swim 60 feet underwater = 3 points

Your score ___

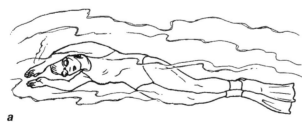

a

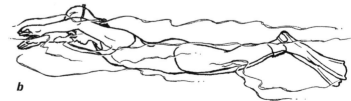

b

**Figure 8.2** Fishtail, roll to dolphin kick: *(a)* begin on one side; *(b)* roll to prone position.

## Dolphin Kick Drill 4. *Dolphin Kick With Kickboard*

Wear goggles. Put on socks or boots and swim fins. Hold a kickboard at arm's length in front of you. Keep your arms stretched out in front of you as you push off from the wall on your belly. Begin a small undulation from your hips, culminating in a small downward flip of both fins. Do not emphasize the upward lift of your fins, but allow them to rise as a result of your hips dropping while your body undulates. Keep your ankles completely relaxed. Continue to flip your fins down against the water. Try to keep the fins underwater by pressing on the kickboard and raising your chin. Exhale with your face in the water and thrust your chin forward to the surface to inhale. Exhale during two kicks, inhale during one. Kick slowly and easily for 100 yards (91.44 meters). Do not try for speed.

**To Increase Difficulty**

- Try 200 yards (182.88 meters). Practice makes perfect.

**To Decrease Difficulty**

- Wear a mask and snorkel, but breathe correctly.

### Success Check

- Kick with your legs and body, not your feet.
- Let your fins flop.

### Score Your Success

Swim 100 yards = 2 points

Swim 200 yards = 4 points

Your score ___

## Dolphin Kick Drill 5. *Underwater Dolphin Kick, No Fins*

Goggles are recommended. Push off in prone position underwater from the end of the pool. Flex your wrists to turn your fingertips up as you arch your back and bend your knees slightly, raising your heels and preparing to start your kick. Remain underwater as you start to kick down and back with floppy ankles. Guide your hands over an imaginary underwater wave, then down to dig deeply into the water ahead. As you kick down, the rest of your body should follow the path of your hands, undulating up and over the imaginary wave and sliding down the other side. Dig your hands into the water and lift with the backs of your hands against the water as you raise your heels again for a second kick. Try to stay underwater for 30 feet (9.144 meters).

**To Increase Difficulty**

- Work on form. Don't increase the distance.

**To Decrease Difficulty**

- Try for good form for 20 feet (6.096 meters).

### Success Check

- Undulate from fingertips to toes.
- Start deep and stay underwater.

### Score Your Success

Swim for 20 feet with correct form = 1 point

Swim for 30 feet with correct form = 3 points

Your score ___

## Dolphin Kick Drill 6. *Variation on the Underwater Kick*

Repeat dolphin kick drill 5, but leave your arms relaxed at your sides as you kick underwater. Wear goggles so that you can see where you're going. Be careful not to kick into the wall. Some people find it much easier to kick with their arms down. Kick 30 feet underwater with your arms down.

**To Increase Difficulty**

• Stay at least 3 feet deep.

**To Decrease Difficulty**

• Kick for 20 feet.

### Success Check

• Use full-body undulation.
• Flip feet down with relaxed ankles.

### Score Your Success

Kick underwater for 20 feet = 1 point
Kick underwater for 30 feet = 3 points
Your score ___

## Dolphin Kick Drill 7. *Dolphin Kick With Kickboard, No Fins*

Wear goggles and hold a kickboard at arm's length in front with both hands. Do a dolphin kick on the surface. Leave your face in the water while you exhale for two or more kicks. Press on the kickboard to help you raise your head when you want a breath. Kick mostly with your legs from the knees down. Bend your knees as you drop them under, then flip your relaxed feet down and back against the water. Keep the kick small and kick slowly. Feel the undulation in your torso as your hips move up and down. Work slowly into a full-body undulation as you kick. Swim 50 yards (45.72 meters) of slow dolphin kick.

**To Increase Difficulty**

• Reach full undulation within 25 yards (22.86 meters).

**To Decrease Difficulty**

• Do 50 yards with legs only (no full-body undulation).

### Success Check

• Start with lower legs only.
• Work into full undulation.

### Score Your Success

Swim 50 yards with legs only = 1 point
Swim 50 yards with full-body undulation = 3 points
Your score ___

## Dolphin Kick Drill 8. *Paired Dolphin Kicks*

Use goggles and a kickboard. Prepare to do a small dolphin kick with your face in the water. Do two downward kicks in rapid succession, then stop. Slowly raise your feet in preparation for the next kick. Kick downward twice in rapid succession, then stop again while you raise your legs slowly. Exhale during the two kicks; raise your chin to breathe when you stop.

Start to count while you kick. As your legs kick down, count "one." As your legs lift, count "and." On the second downward kick, count "two." During the stop, count a very slow and drawn-out "a-a-n-d" as you raise your legs for the next pair of kicks. Thus, for two rapid kicks and a stop, the count is "one, and, two, a-a-n-d." Continue to kick and count with paired kicks for 50 yards.

**To Increase Difficulty**

- Gradually work some undulation into the kick.

**To Decrease Difficulty**

- Do 25 yards, stop, and start over.

### Success Check

- Inhale on "a-a-n-d."
- Kick with legs only.

### Score Your Success

Kick and count for 25 yards = 2 points

Kick and count for 50 yards without stopping = 4 points

Your score ___

# BUTTERFLY STROKE ARM PULL

The butterfly stroke is often said to be the most difficult of the swimming strokes because both arms recover over the water simultaneously. For some swimmers who have exceptionally tight shoulder joints, the arm stroke may be bothersome, but most swimmers can learn to do it with an easy, relaxed motion. The arm stroke cannot be hurried; it must be long and full, with a relaxed recovery.

The butterfly arm pull is a major component of a competitive swimming stroke. As such, it is a step in the learning progression for the stroke. Also, butterfly is the only swimming stroke performed in the prone position in which the arms recover simultaneously over the water.

The underwater propulsive portions of this stroke and of the crawl stroke are nearly identical. Review the crawl stroke arm pull in step 4. Both this stroke and the crawl stroke arm motion start in a prone-float position with both arms extended overhead in line with your shoulders (figure 8.3a). To do the butterfly arm pull, pull with both arms simultaneously. Flex both wrists to point your fingertips down and, by bending your elbows slightly, turn your palms slightly out (figure 8.3b).

Begin the pull by slicing (sculling) your hands out, around, and in, bending your elbows and turning your palms to facilitate the sculling action, as if you were trying to draw a large circle with your fingertips on the bottom of the pool (figure 8.3c). Leave your elbows as far forward as you can during the first half of the circle, pulling with your hands and forearms. Bring your shoulder muscles into play by beginning to pull with your upper arms as your hands and forearms pass your ears. With elbows bent at 90 degrees, press back and in toward the centerline of your body until your hands complete the circle, nearly touching under your chest. Begin to bend back your wrists to keep the palms perpendicular to the line of effort. (They will be forced into that position if you simply relax them slowly as you push.) Push straight back toward your feet, extending your elbows and separating your hands enough for them to pass, palms up, outside your thighs.

Keep your elbows straight as you lift both arms free of the water (figure 8.3d). Begin to bring both arms forward over the water with palms facing up until your arms are nearly at shoulder level. At that point, turn your palms down and continue to bring both arms over the water to enter as far forward as you can reach, in line with your shoulders (figure 8.3e). Keep your elbows high on the entry, as though you were reaching over a wave with both arms. Allow your head, hands, and upper torso to dive "over a wave" to about a foot beneath the water (figure 8.3f), then bend your wrists back to turn the fingertips up and glide toward the surface (figure 8.3g). As soon as your hands return to the

surface, flex your wrists to drop your fingertips in preparation for the next stroke.

Do not begin the next stroke as your hands enter the water. Allow time to dive, reach, and glide to the surface before starting the next stroke. The whole stroke resembles drawing a keyhole in the water with your hands: A circle at the top followed by a straight push from your chest to your thighs circumscribes a keyhole shape. Simply do a crawl stroke with both arms simultaneously.

## Figure 8.3    Butterfly Stroke Arm Pull

### GLIDE POSITION

1. Begin in prone glide position
2. Extend arms overhead

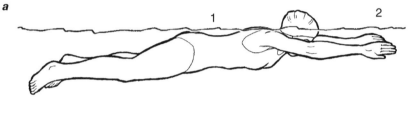

### FLEX

1. Flex wrists
2. Turn palms out slightly

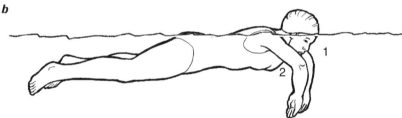

### SCULL

1. Scull out, around, and back to chest
2. Press straight back
3. Bend wrists back

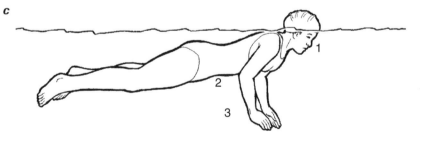

### LIFT

1. Lift arms
2. Keep elbows straight
3. Turn palms up

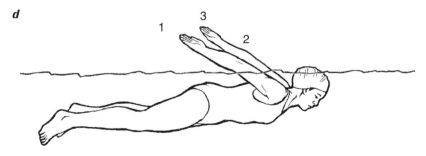

## RECOVER

*e*

1. Bring arms over
2. Turn palms down

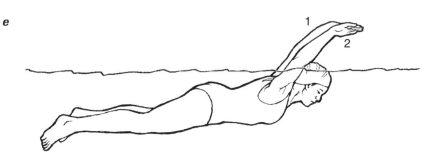

## DIVE

*f*

1. Go "over a wave"
2. Keep elbows high

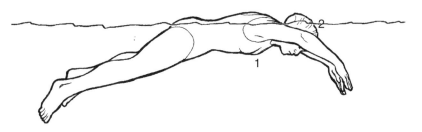

## SURFACE

*g*

1. Dig in
2. Turn up
3. Come to the surface

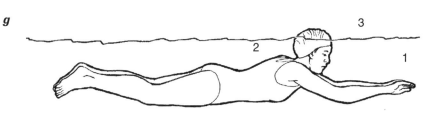

**Misstep**

You pull too wide.

**Correction**

Keep elbows bent at 90 degrees.

**Misstep**

You pull straight through.

**Correction**

Make your hands draw a keyhole.

## Butterfly Stroke Arm Pull Drill 1.

# Slow-Motion Drill With Mask, Snorkel, and Float Belt

Wear a float belt near your hips, put on a mask and snorkel, and float facedown. Breathe through the snorkel as you move your arms *very* slowly through the motions of the butterfly arm pull. Stop frequently to study each new position critically. Watch your arms and hands through the mask as they move slowly. Outline a keyhole with your hands as they pull and push. You will sink deeper in the water as your arms begin to lift for the arm recovery. Keep them moving slowly, nevertheless, and go through the motions of the recovery with your shoulders and upper arms partially submerged. Have someone read the how-to section to you as you try to follow the pattern. Study figure 8.3 again and continue to practice in slow motion. Do not try to get propulsion; just float and move through the pattern. Do at least 25 *very* slow-motion strokes.

### To Increase Difficulty

- After 25 slow-motion pulls, try for some propulsion.

### To Decrease Difficulty

- If you are still too fast, slow down.

## Success Check

- Make keyhole patterns.
- Scull out, around, and back to the chest.
- Push straight back past thighs.

### Score Your Success

Complete at least 10 correct strokes out of 25 attempts = 2 points

Complete 25 correct strokes out of 25 attempts = 3 additional points

Your score ___

## Butterfly Stroke Arm Pull Drill 2.

# Hesitation Butterfly Stroke With Equipment

Put on a mask, snorkel, and a float belt at your hips. Float facedown, breathing through your snorkel. Pull through a butterfly arm stroke at moderate speed, but stop at the end of the underwater pull with your arms along your sides. Hold still and glide for a count of 3 (about 3 seconds). Quickly bring your arms forward over the water in a butterfly stroke recovery—elbows straight, palms turned up. Stop again and glide as your hands enter the water. Prepare your hands and arms carefully for the next stroke, then pull again and glide with your arms at your sides.

Continue to pull, stop, recover, stop. Pull strongly for distance and try to get your arms as high as possible on the recovery. Your shoulders and upper arms will still be partially submerged. Pull 50 yards of hesitation butterfly stroke.

### To Increase Difficulty

- Inhale during the pull and exhale while arms are overhead.

### To Decrease Difficulty

- Wear two float belts, one at your hips and one under your armpits.

## Success Check

- Glide *at least* 3 seconds at each stop point.
- Straighten your arms for the recovery, palms up.
- Make a keyhole stroke pattern.

### Score Your Success

Swim 50 yards using two float belts = 1 point

Swim 50 yards with only one float belt = 2 points

Swim 50 yards with only one float belt, inhaling during the pull and exhaling when arms are overhead = 4 points

Your score ___

## Butterfly Stroke Arm Pull Drill 3.
## Hesitation Butterfly Stroke With Breathing

Use a pull-buoy leg float between your thighs. Wear goggles, but no mask or snorkel. Start in a prone position with arms extended overhead. Prepare to do a butterfly stroke, then exhale just before you begin. As you pull, tilt your head back and thrust your chin forward until it is at water level. Open your mouth and inhale during the pull. Stop and glide. Drop your face into the water again, but hold your breath while your arms are at your sides and while you recover them over the water. Stop and glide, then exhale just before the next pull. Make your stops short—only about 2 seconds. Swim 50 yards, breathing on each pull.

### To Increase Difficulty

- Try the drill without the float.

### To Decrease Difficulty

- Use a nose clip.
- Add a float belt.

## Success Check

- Make a short stop before and after every pull.
- Thrust chin forward to clear mouth.
- Inhale on pull; exhale on glide with arms overhead.

### Score Your Success

Swim 50 yards with your breathing sometimes uncoordinated = 1 point

Swim 50 yards while taking a breath on every pull = 3 points

Your score ___

## Butterfly Stroke Arm Pull Drill 4.
## Full Butterfly Arm Stroke and Glide

Repeat butterfly stroke arm pull drill 3, but pull through and recover your arms with no hesitation in the arms-back position. Stop and glide for a full 3 seconds after each complete pull and recovery with your arms overhead. Inhale during the pull and exhale during the glide. Do not shorten your arm pull. Pull all the way through on each stroke. Rise only enough to thrust your chin forward to the surface for air. Swim 25 yards, breathing on every pull.

### To Increase Difficulty

- Drop the leg float.

### To Decrease Difficulty

- Wear a mask and snorkel, but breathe properly.

## Success Check

- Pull through, thumbs touch thighs in passing.
- Stop only with arms overhead.
- Glide for 3 seconds.

### Score Your Success

Swim 25 yards while breathing properly while wearing the mask = 2 points

Swim 25 yards while breathing properly without wearing the mask = 4 points

Your score ___

## Butterfly Stroke Arm Pull Drill 5.

## Butterfly Stroke Arm Pull With Counting

The counting pattern aids in the coordination of the arms and legs. Use a leg float between your knees. Goggles are recommended.

Start in the prone-float position with arms stretched overhead. Start a butterfly stroke arm pull. Count "one" at the midpoint of the pull and take a breath. Count "and" as your arms recover. Count "two" as your hands strike the water at the completion of the recovery. Count a very long "a-a-n-d" as you glide, exhale, and get ready for the next stroke. Thus, the count will be "one, and, two, a-a-n-d, one, and, two, a-a-n-d." The glide (a-a-n-d) should be about 2 seconds, but every other count will be only one second. Swim 25 yards, then repeat until you've covered 100 yards with correct counting rhythm.

**To Increase Difficulty**

- Take off the leg float and let your body undulate.

**To Decrease Difficulty**

- Wear a mask and snorkel.

### Success Check

- As you pull and recover, count "one, and, two," then pause for "a-a-n-d."
- Inhale on "one," exhale on "a-a-n-d."

### Score Your Success

Swim 100 yards with correct rhythm while wearing a mask = 2 points

Swim 100 yards with correct rhythm without wearing a mask = 4 points

Your score ___

# BUTTERFLY STROKE COORDINATION

This unique stroke gets its name from the simultaneous overwater recovery of the arms. As water drips from the trailing edge of the hands and arms, the swimmer looks like a butterfly flying over the water. The butterfly stroke has the reputation of being difficult to do because those who have not learned to do it properly try to rise too high and go too fast. It requires only moderate effort if done slowly and easily.

The butterfly stroke is faster than any stroke except the crawl. It's used for competitive swimming and as another step on the ladder of aquatic mastery. It's not used for lifesaving, or as a resting stroke, or for distance swimming, or for recreation. The butterfly stroke is sometimes used for its showmanship value as part of a synchronized swimming routine.

You have learned the dolphin kick and the butterfly stroke arm pull. Putting these together in the proper sequence and adding the breathing and rhythm constitute the butterfly stroke. For exact detail on the movements of the legs

and arms, refer back to figures 8.1 and 8.3, respectively.

Start the stroke by kicking the dolphin kick slowly, arms stretched overhead. Time the first arm pull to coincide with a downward kick of the legs. Thrust your chin forward and inhale as you pull (figure 8.4a). Recover your arms over the water while your legs are lifting (figure 8.4b). Kick down again as your head, hands, and arms dive into the water (figure 8.4c). That is the end of one butterfly stroke. Exhale and, as your legs lift into position to kick again, prepare your hands and arms for another pull (figure 8.4d). Thus, one arm stroke, two downward kicks, and a breath constitute one stroke, but you must take time between strokes to prepare.

You can easily master the coordination once you understand that the arms complete a cycle in 3 counts (pull, recover, enter), whereas the legs take 4 counts per cycle (down, up, down, up). Your arms must wait and prepare for the next stroke while your legs finish the last count. The arms must glide while your legs rise on count

**114**

4 (count a long "a-a-n-d") to be ready for the next kick. This fact is the greatest cause of consternation among those who are trying to learn the stroke. The pause in the arm stroke may be called a glide, a catch, a rest, or a lift, but it must be there. Do not begin to pull again as soon as your hands enter the water. Wait until your legs rise and are ready to kick down again.

## Figure 8.4    Butterfly Stroke Coordination

### COUNT "ONE"

1. Drive legs down
2. Pull with arms
3. Lift chin forward and inhale

### COUNT "AND"

1. Raise legs
2. Lift arms forward over the water

### COUNT "TWO"

1. Drive legs down
2. Arms and head enter water

### COUNT "A-A-N-D"

1. Raise legs
2. Glide with arms forward
3. Flex wrists
4. Exhale

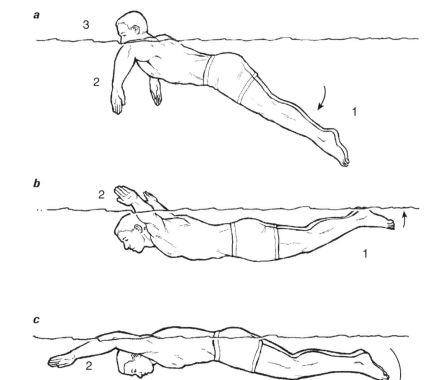

---

**Misstep**

Head and chest rise too high.

**Correction**

Pull back, not down.

**Misstep**

Your head is too deep on entry.

**Correction**

Guide your body upward with your hands.

## Butterfly Stroke Coordination Drill 1.

## *Paired Kick Drill With Fins*

Goggles are optional, but put on socks or boots and fins. Hold a kickboard in front of you with both hands. Begin kicking with the dolphin kick, but stop after two downward kicks. Glide and slowly raise your feet and legs in preparation for the next pair of downward kicks. Continue to kick in pairs. Kick downward twice and stop.

Begin to count downward kicks, saying "one, and, two" as your legs alternately kick down, up, and down. Then as you glide and your legs rise to prepare for the next pair, say a long, drawn-out "a-a-n-d." Thus the count is "one, and, two, a-a-n-d." Exhale and inhale during the long "a-a-n-d" count. Swim 50 yards using paired dolphin kicks.

### To Increase Difficulty

- Swim without the kickboard.

### To Decrease Difficulty

- Wear a mask and snorkel, but exhale and then inhale on the glide.

### *Success Check*

- Kick from the hips, keeping ankles floppy.
- Kick down, up, down, and stop.
- Do a slow leg lift.

### *Score Your Success*

Swim 50 yards with mask and snorkel = 1 point

Swim 50 yards without mask and snorkel = 3 points

Your score ___

## Butterfly Stroke Coordination Drill 2.

## *One-Arm Butterfly Stroke With Fins*

Wear fins; goggles are optional. Hold a kickboard at arm's length in front of you and keep your face in the water. Start kicking and counting as in butterfly stroke coordination drill 1. During the glide at the end of the second pair of kicks, shift the kickboard to one hand and exhale (figure 8.5). Pull with the free arm, raise your head, and inhale. Start the pull slightly before you count "one" so that the kick and inhalation come at midpull. Recover your arm over the water on the count of "and." Return your hand to the kickboard exactly on the count of "two." Leave both hands on the board during the long "a-a-n-d" count and exhale. Continue to stroke with one arm only, inhaling on the pull, for 50 yards. Then change hands on the kickboard and pull 50 yards with the other arm.

### To Increase Difficulty

- Discard the kickboard, but hold that arm steady.

### To Decrease Difficulty

- Use a mask and snorkel, but inhale on the pull and exhale on the glide.

### *Success Check*

- Start slowly and gradually increase speed.
- Use keyhole arm pattern.

### *Score Your Success*

Swim 25 yards with each arm = 1 point each arm

Swim 50 yards with each arm, breathing correctly while wearing a mask = 2 points each arm

Swim 50 yards with each arm, breathing correctly, no mask = 4 points each arm

Your score ___

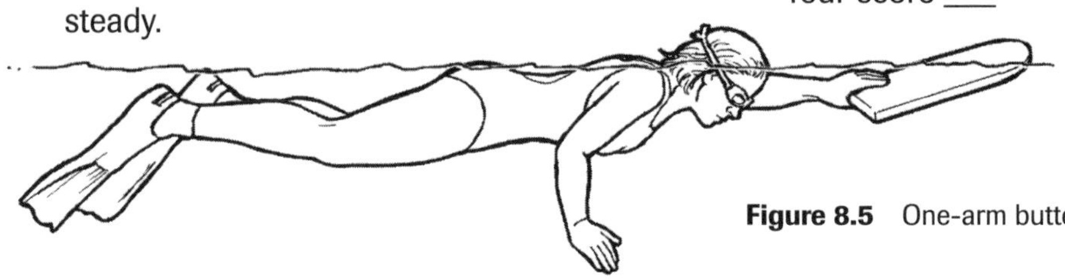

**Figure 8.5** One-arm butterfly stroke with fins.

## Butterfly Stroke Coordination Drill 3.
## *Butterfly Stroke With Fins, No Breathing*

Put on fins and goggles. Do not use a kickboard. Start in a prone-float position with arms extended overhead. Take a deep breath and hold it as you put your face in the water and raise your feet, ready for a dolphin kick. Pull with both arms on the first kick (count "one"). Recover your arms over the water as your legs rise again (count "and"). Make your arms enter the water exactly on the second downward leg kick (count "two"). Glide. Hold your arms steady as your legs rise for the next stroke. Keep your face in the water and hold your breath as you swim two more strokes. Stop, take a couple of breaths, and begin again. Continue to swim three strokes at a time with your face in the water. Swim five sets of three nonbreathing strokes with correct coordination.

**To Increase Difficulty**

- Discard the fins.

**To Decrease Difficulty**

- Wear a mask and snorkel, but try to breathe every three strokes.

### *Success Check*

- Hold your breath.
- Concentrate on arm–leg coordination.
- Do not pull as soon as your hands hit the water.

### *Score Your Success*

Swim five sets of three nonbreathing strokes while wearing a mask and snorkel = 2 points

Swim five sets of three nonbreathing strokes without mask and snorkel = 3 points

Your score ___

## Butterfly Stroke Coordination Drill 4.
## *Butterfly Stroke With Fins, Alternate Breathing*

Wear goggles and swim fins. Start in a prone-float position with arms extended overhead. Raise your feet in preparation for a dolphin kick. Leave your face in the water and exhale as you kick twice and complete the first stroke. On the second pull, tilt your head back, thrust your chin forward, open your mouth, and take a breath. Drop your face into the water and exhale during the third stroke. Take a breath on the fourth pull. Continue to slowly swim the butterfly stroke, breathing on every second pull. Maintain your short glide ("a-a-n-d") as your legs lift for the next stroke. Be careful not to pull immediately as your hands hit the water. Swim 50 yards correctly coordinated, breathing on every second stroke.

**To Increase Difficulty**

- Swim without fins.

**To Decrease Difficulty**

- Use a mask and snorkel, but breathe on every second pull.

### *Success Check*

- Don't be in a hurry.
- Exhale throughout the first stroke. Inhale on the pull of the second.
- Glide on the "a-a-n-d" count.

### *Score Your Success*

Swim 50 yards correctly coordinated while wearing a mask and snorkel = 2 points

Swim 50 yards correctly coordinated without mask and snorkel = 4 points

Your score ___

## Butterfly Stroke Coordination Drill 5. *Butterfly Stroke, Single Breathing*

Use swim fins and goggles. Swim butterfly stroke and take a breath at midpull on every stroke. Be careful not to lift your body and chest too high when you inhale. Stay as low as you can, pulling horizontally with a minimum of downward force. Tilt your head—don't lift it. Thrust your chin forward, not up, to get a breath. Remember to lift your legs during the long "a-a-n-d" count. Swim 50 yards of correct butterfly stroke, breathing on every stroke.

**To Increase Difficulty**

- Swim without fins.

**To Decrease Difficulty**

- Use a mask *only* if you must.

### Success Check

- Inhale at midpull, exhale on "a-a-n-d."
- Lift your fingertips to point up on "a-a-n-d."

### Score Your Success

Swim 50 yards of correct butterfly stroke while wearing a mask = 2 points

Swim 50 yards of correct butterfly stroke without a mask = 3 points

Your score ___

## Butterfly Stroke Coordination Drill 6. *Butterfly Stroke Without Fins*

Use goggles, but no fins. Swim the butterfly stroke. Swim slowly to get used to the lack of fins; it will seem strange, but persevere. Breathe on every stroke or every other stroke, as you wish. Avoid rising too high. Try to keep your chin at water level. Be sure to maintain the glide with your arms as your feet rise for the next kick. Swim 50 yards without fins.

**To Increase Difficulty**

- Increase your speed—go all out.

**To Decrease Difficulty**

- Wear a mask and snorkel, but breathe on the pull.

### Success Check

- Kick with your whole body.
- Count "one, and, two, a-a-n-d."

### Score Your Success

Swim 50 yards of correct butterfly stroke while wearing a mask = 2 points

Swim 50 yards of correct butterfly stroke without a mask = 4 points

Your score ___

## Butterfly Stroke Coordination Drill 7. Refining the Rhythm of the Butterfly Stroke

Swim the butterfly stroke while wearing goggles. Shorten the long "a-a-n-d" count to a simple "and" count, but be sure that your arms continue to stretch forward, not pull, during that count. Use that count to turn your fingertips up and raise your hands to the surface before pulling on the next stroke. Make the rhythm of the kick steady: "one, and, two, and, one, and, two, and." Make the rhythm of the arm stroke "one, and, two, reach, one, and, two, reach." Swim slowly, pulling all the way through. Swim 50 yards of butterfly stroke with steady, even rhythm.

**To Increase Difficulty**

- Increase speed.

### Success Check

- Breathe on the pull and exhale on the reach.
- Kick with your whole body.

### Score Your Success

Score 5 points for learning the stroke. You deserve it.

Your score ___

# BUTTERFLY STROKE TURN

Because the butterfly stroke is used almost exclusively for competition, we will examine a butterfly stroke turn that is compatible with the competitive rules. The only rule governing the butterfly stroke turn states that both hands must touch the end wall simultaneously and that the shoulders must be on a level plane for the first arm stroke after the turn. You may, however, kick underwater for a distance of 15 meters after a turn before surfacing for your first arm stroke. Since we are interested in recreational swimming, we will not try for distance underwater after a turn.

Many a race has been lost because of a poor turn. Because they incorporate a vigorous push from the wall, turns actually add to the speed at which a given distance can be covered. Turns are so important that competitors spend many practice hours sharpening their turning techniques. Noncompetitors benefit from competitive turns as well because the turns allow changing directions in a closed course with the greatest efficiency and the least disruption of the rhythm and fluidity of the stroke.

Swim the butterfly stroke toward the end of the pool. Watch for the turn warning lines on the bottom of the pool and spot the end wall as you raise your head for a breath. Finish the stroke in progress as your head passes the turn line, bring your arms over the water on the recovery, and glide into the wall. *Use great care to avoid hitting your head on the wall.*

Touch the wall with both hands simultaneously (figure 8.6a). Tuck your knees tightly as you turn sideways to the wall. Press with one hand on the wall to help bring your tucked legs under you as you raise your head and pivot (figure 8.6b), removing your other hand from the wall. Return your free hand over the water to point toward the other end (figure 8.6c). As your feet move vertically under you to the wall, bring your pressing hand over the water, begin to roll onto your belly, take a breath, and put your face into the water (figure 8.6d). As your feet touch the wall, push vigorously and extend your ankles to glide away in streamlined prone glide position under the water (figure 8.6e). Glide underwater until your speed decreases to top swimming speed, then begin to use the dolphin kick to get to the surface. As your head is about to break the surface, resume the butterfly stroke, but do not breathe until the second stroke to avoid interrupting the rhythm of the stroke.

## Figure 8.6 Butterfly Turn

### TOUCH THE WALL
1. Glide into the wall
2. Touch the wall with both hands simultaneously

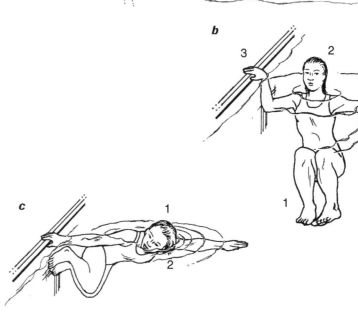

### PIVOT
1. Tuck knees
2. Turn sideways
3. Press with one hand
4. Bring one hand over the water

### INHALE
1. Lift head
2. Inhale

### REACH
1. Bring other hand over the water
2. Move feet to wall
3. Put face in water

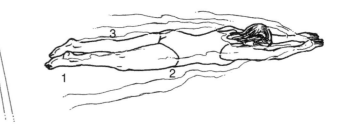

### PUSH OFF
1. Push off underwater
2. Streamline and glide
3. Dolphin-kick to the surface

**Misstep**
You misjudge your distance from the wall and come up short.
**Correction**
Use a short pull or glide and kick into the wall.

# Butterfly Turn
## Drill 1.
## *Judging Distance*

This aspect of the turn is vital to your safety. Learn it well. As you approach the end of the pool, you must make a decision to take one more pull or hold your glide and kick to the wall.

Wear goggles for this drill. Face the end of the pool about 20 feet (6.096 meters) from the pool wall. Assume a prone glide position. Start the butterfly stroke. As your head passes over the turn target (a mark that is 5 feet [1.524 meters] from the end of the pool), complete the butterfly pull in progress and stretch your arms in front for a glide to the wall. If you find that you are still too far away from the wall to glide in without losing momentum, continue to kick until your hands reach the wall. If you think you have room for another arm stroke before reaching the wall, try *cautiously* to take a small, quick, shortened stroke without pulling all the way through, then glide to the wall. Your glide should be about 2 feet. Practice judging your distance and your approach to the wall until you can approach at full speed with confidence and safety. Make 10 consecutive full-speed approaches safely and with confidence.

### To Increase Difficulty

- Practice at full speed.

### To Decrease Difficulty

- Start slowly and increase speed gradually.

## *Success Check*

- As your head passes the turn target, make a decision to glide, kick in, or take one short pull.
- When in doubt, keep hands in front of head.

### Score Your Success

Score 5 points when you can make a safe, confident approach.

Your score ___

# Butterfly Turn
## Drill 2.
## *Choosing the Direction of Your Turn*

Put on your goggles and make a slow butterfly approach to the end of the pool. As your hands reach the end of the pool, grasp the edge with both hands and pull in toward the wall as you tuck your legs and bring them in under you. Release the wall with your left hand and turn to your left, bringing your right side to the wall. Throw your left arm back over the water to point at the other end of the pool. Push with your right hand to lift your head and start it going the other way. Grab a quick breath and release the wall as your tucked legs glide in under you to the wall. Bring your right arm over the water beside your left arm and turn your face into the water as you turn onto your belly and drop underwater.

As your feet touch the end wall with your legs tucked, push strongly and streamline for a glide underwater. Count to 3 while gliding, then start your dolphin kick to the surface. Resume stroking when you reach the surface. Do not breathe on the first arm pull.

Do this drill five times, then repeat it five times while turning to the right, bringing your right hand away quickly and pushing with the left hand. Determine which direction you prefer. Adopt that direction for all future butterfly stroke turns.

### To Increase Difficulty

- Practice turning to the weak side.

### To Decrease Difficulty

- Start slowly and gradually build speed.

## *Success Check*

- Use caution on the approach.
- Approach, touch, hand away, tuck, turn, push, face in, arm over, push off, glide.

### Score Your Success

Score 4 points for selecting a favorite direction for the turn.

Your score ___

**121**

## Butterfly Turn Drill 3.

### Flat-Wall Turns

In the previous butterfly turn drill, you were instructed to grasp the edge of the pool and pull yourself into the wall. However, some pools have flat walls at the ends, with no edge to grasp. Practice making the turn with your palms touching flat against the end wall at water level. Bend your elbows as you glide in close to the wall. Press sideways with your palms to initiate the turn. The rest of the turn is the same. Try the turn five times, turning to your preferred side.

**To Increase Difficulty**

* Try it at top speed.

**To Decrease Difficulty**

* Go very slowly.

### Success Check

* Press sideways first, then withdraw one arm as you turn.

### Score Your Success

Score 1 point for each successful turn, up to 5.
Your score ___

# SUCCESS SUMMARY OF BUTTERFLY STROKE

You cannot assess steadiness of rhythm, fluidity of stroke pattern, and degree of rise and fall in the butterfly stroke by counting the number of lengths you swim. Each drill in the learning process has a reason for inclusion. Experience dictates the importance of taking small steps to success. Don't skip any of them.

An observer who knows what to look for must be the judge of your ability. Ask your coach or instructor to evaluate your success. If you scored at least 46 points in this step, you have learned the stroke. If you scored 47 to 79 points, you are to be commended. If you scored 80 points or more, you are outstanding!

### Dolphin Kick Drills

1. Sideways Fishtail           ___ out of 4
2. Fishtail Kick With Fins           ___ out of 4
3. Fishtail, Roll to Dolphin Kick           ___ out of 3
4. Dolphin Kick With Kickboard           ___ out of 4
5. Underwater Dolphin Kick, No Fins           ___ out of 3
6. Variation on the Underwater Kick           ___ out of 3
7. Dolphin Kick With Kickboard, No Fins           ___ out of 3
8. Paired Dolphin Kicks           ___ out of 4

### Butterfly Stroke Arm Pull Drills

1. Slow-Motion Drill With Mask, Snorkel, and Float Belt           ___ out of 5
2. Hesitation Butterfly Stroke With Equipment           ___ out of 4
3. Hesitation Butterfly Stroke With Breathing           ___ out of 3
4. Full Butterfly Arm Stroke and Glide           ___ out of 4
5. Butterfly Stroke Arm Pull With Counting           ___ out of 4

### Butterfly Stroke Coordination Drills

1. Paired Kick Drill With Fins           ___ out of 3
2. One-Arm Butterfly Stroke With Fins           ___ out of 8
3. Butterfly Stroke With Fins, No Breathing           ___ out of 3
4. Butterfly Stroke With Fins, Alternate Breathing           ___ out of 4
5. Butterfly Stroke, Single Breathing           ___ out of 3
6. Butterfly Stroke Without Fins           ___ out of 4
7. Refining the Rhythm of the Butterfly Stroke           ___ out of 5

### Butterfly Turn Drills

1. Judging Distance           ___ out of 5
2. Choosing the Direction of Your Turn           ___ out of 4
3. Flat-Wall Turns           ___ out of 5

### Total           ___ out of 92

# Trudgen Strokes

The search for increased efficiency and speed that led to the overarm sidestroke led to the next three strokes in the evolutionary process, variations of efforts to eliminate water resistance by recovering both arms over the water. In his 1934 book *How to Teach Swimming and Diving*, T.K. Cureton Jr. wrote that "[John] Trudgen demonstrated the principle of recovering both arms free of the water, and greatly increased the interest in competitive swimming" (page 94). The three strokes that bear his name are the trudgen stroke, the double trudgen, and the trudgen crawl. You will learn all three in this step.

## TRUDGEN STROKE

The trudgen stroke is a key link in the evolution of strokes from the breaststroke to the crawl. It is swum by many swimmers today who think they are doing the crawl. It is an easy, restful version of the overhand stroke, but it is still three evolutionary steps from the crawl.

The trudgen stroke consists of a crawl arm stroke with a single scissors kick. Start in a prone-float position with both arms overhead. Begin a normal crawl stroke with your breathing-side arm and roll your head to take a breath. As your arm begins to pull, roll your hips to face toward the pulling arm and recover your legs for a standard (top leg forward) scissors kick (figure 9.1a). As your hand reaches waist level, begin the power phase of the kick and inhale. Make your arm stroke and scissors kick finish together. Allow your legs to relax, but keep your feet together as you turn your face into the water and recover your breathing-side arm (figure 9.1b). Exhale while your other arm makes a full crawl arm stroke and recovery, legs resting (figure 9.1c). Thus, you recover your legs and deliver a scissors kick while pulling with one arm, then allow your legs to relax and rest during the other arm pull and recovery (figure 9.1d). Use normal crawl stroke coordination of the arms. One arm starts when the other is about to enter the water. The delivery of power is uneven, and the stroke will appear somewhat jerky. You surge ahead while breathing and kicking, and slow somewhat while the second arm pulls. Continue to repeat the sequence, breathing with the kick.

## Figure 9.1 | Trudgen Stroke

### PULL AND ROLL

1. Pull
2. Roll for breath
3. Recover legs for scissors kick

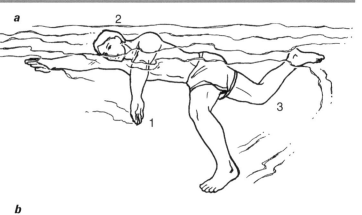

### RECOVER

1. Finish kick and pull together
2. Recover arm
3. Put face in the water

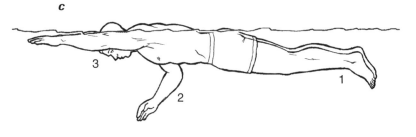

### PULL OTHER ARM

1. Drag feet along while relaxing legs
2. Pull with opposite arm
3. Exhale

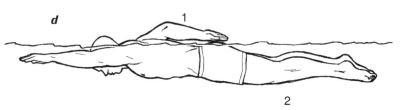

### RECOVER OTHER ARM

1. Recover opposite arm
2. Continue to relax legs

**Misstep**

You breathe on the wrong side.

**Correction**

Always breathe on the kick.

**Misstep**

You invert the scissors kick.

**Correction**

Always move the top leg forward.

# Trudgen Stroke Drill 1.

## Overarm Sidestroke, Overreaching

If a longer pull in the overarm sidestroke contributed to greater efficiency, then an even longer stroke might make it even more efficient.

Wear goggles if you wish. Swim an overarm sidestroke. Maintain the same coordination and glide after each stroke. Begin slowly, bit by bit, to reach farther forward with your upper arm. Place your upper hand in the water near the top of your head, then reach a little farther on the next stroke. Continue until you are reaching just as far for the entry as you do on a crawl stroke entry. As your reach and pull grow longer, you will find that you must roll more onto your belly for the entry. As you reach farther forward, the pull will take longer and your kick will not fit the coordination pattern as well. Delay the recovery of your legs until your upper arm begins to pull. Thus, you will not bring your legs up until the end of your lower-arm pull and the beginning of your upper-arm pull. Because your legs must now recover and kick on one arm stroke, you have to narrow the kick somewhat to speed it up. Recover your legs and kick on the upper-arm pull as your lower arm moves forward for the glide.

Swim 25 yards (22.86 meters) of overarm sidestroke with the upper hand reaching as far forward as a crawl stroke entry.

### To Increase Difficulty

- Make the lower-arm pull all the way to your thigh.

### To Decrease Difficulty

- Glide longer, and think about what's coming next.

## Success Check

- Maintain your glide.
- Inhale on the kick and upper-arm pull.

### Score Your Success

Score 2 points for swimming 25 yards while using a long-reaching overarm sidestroke. If you lengthened the lower-arm pull as well, give yourself an extra point.

Your score ___

# Trudgen Stroke Drill 2.

## Overarm Sidestroke, Extended Lower-Arm Pull

Wear goggles if you wish. Swim overarm sidestroke, overreaching to the full extent with your upper arm and both recovering and kicking your legs on the pull of your breathing-side arm. As you swim, also begin to pull farther with your lower arm on each stroke. Continue to recover and kick your legs as your breathing-side arm pulls and the lower arm shoots forward for the glide. Because you delay the leg recovery, your legs do absolutely nothing but rest and drift during the lower-arm pull.

When you reach the stage at which your lower arm is pulling all the way through to your thigh, you will find that you must roll completely onto your belly during the pull of your lower arm while your breathing-side arm recovers. Because you are already on your belly when your lower arm finishes, it would be easy to lift your lower arm over the water as in a crawl stroke recovery. Do it. Delay the pull of your breathing-side arm until your lower arm has nearly finished its recovery. Your legs will continue to drag because they do not start to recover until your breathing-side arm starts to pull.

Now the stroke should begin to look like a crawl stroke, but everything happens on one side. While your breathing-side arm pulls, breathe, recover, and kick your legs. As your other arm pulls and recovers, your legs remain still and rest. Do a sidestroke on one side and a crawl stroke with the other arm.

Swim 25 yards (22.86 meters) using a crawl stroke arm motion with a single scissors kick with one arm only. That's the trudgen stroke.

**To Increase Difficulty**

- Lift your head and look forward as you inhale and kick.

**To Decrease Difficulty**

- Wear a mask and snorkel, and keep your head down until you get the arm–leg coordination.

## Success Check

- Breathe and kick on the last half of one-arm pull.
- Exhale on the pull of the other arm.

### Score Your Success

Swim with correct coordination while wearing a mask and snorkel = 1 point

Swim with correct coordination without a mask = 2 points

Your score ___

## Trudgen Stroke Drill 3.   *Scissors Kick Crawl*

Wear goggles if you wish. Swim the crawl stroke without kicking your feet. Let your legs relax and drag. Do two strokes with each arm. As you begin to pull with your breathing-side arm, turn your hips slightly to that side. During the first half of the arm pull, recover your legs in preparation for a narrow standard scissors kick (top leg forward). During the second half of the pull, deliver the narrow scissors kick. Allow your legs to drag as you recover that arm and pull and recover the other arm. Swim a crawl stroke with a scissors kick on the breathing side. This is the trudgen stroke, refined from the stroke introduced in England by John Trudgen in the early 1900s. Swim 100 yards (91.44 meters) of correctly coordinated trudgen stroke.

**To Increase Difficulty**

- Breathe on every second breathing-side arm pull.

**To Decrease Difficulty**

- Swim only 50 yards (45.72 meters).

## Success Check

- Use a standard (top leg forward) scissors kick.
- Kick and breathe on the last half of the pull.

### Score Your Success

Swim the trudgen stroke correctly for 50 yards = 1 point

Swim the trudgen stroke correctly for 100 yards = 2 points

Your score ___

# DOUBLE TRUDGEN STROKE

John Trudgen followed the development of competitive swimming strokes after inventing the stroke named for him. Other swimmers began to copy his stroke and sought to improve it to gain more speed. Using the same reasoning Trudgen applied to using arm and leg motion more efficiently, someone noticed that the swimmer's feet dragged during one arm stroke and wondered why the feet were not used for propulsion during that time. He added a kick in place of the leg rest and called it the double trudgen.

The double trudgen stroke is the most powerful of all the overhand strokes. It is used in lifesaving situations when the swimmer must move as quickly as possible to a drowning victim without losing sight of the victim.

The double kick employed in this stroke allows you to keep your head above water at all times. The crawl stroke is faster, but it's very difficult to swim with your head up. Keeping your head above water may also useful when swimming in surf where waves obscure your vision. So the stroke that was meant to increase

speed became significant for entirely different reasons.

Begin swimming the trudgen stroke. Notice the dead space in the leg kick during the pull of your nonbreathing-side arm. After delivering a kick and stroke on your breathing side, immediately rotate your hips and recover your legs on the opposite side for a scissors kick with your other arm stroke (figure 9.2a). The kick must also be a standard scissors kick (top leg forward), so your opposite leg must step forward. Deliver the kick during the last half of that arm pull. In summary, pull with your left arm as you deliver a scissors kick facing to the left with your left leg forward. Next, pull with your right arm as you deliver a scissors kick facing to the right with your right leg forward. In effect, you are doing a sidestroke, rolling and alternating sides for each stroke. Breathe only on one side, exhale on the other (figure 9.2b). Each kick is powerful, and you will surge through the water with each stroke. You will find that you can carry your head out of water better with this stroke than with any other.

---

## Figure 9.2    Double Trudgen Stroke

### STROKE AND KICK

1. Complete trudgen kick and stroke
2. Rotate hips to opposite side on arm recovery
3. Recover legs
4. Scissors-kick with opposite arm pull

### ROTATE AND BREATHE

1. Rotate hips for next trudgen stroke on arm recovery
2. Breathe on one side only

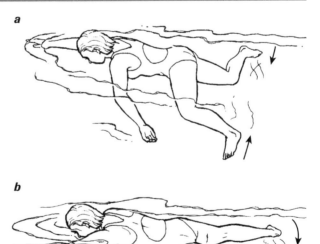

a

b

---

**Misstep**

You try to kick with the same leg forward on every stroke.

**Correction**

Change the forward leg on every stroke.

## Double Trudgen Stroke Drill 1.

## *Double Trudgen Kick Drill*

Start in a prone-float position with a kickboard in both hands at arm's length. Do scissors kicks, alternating sides. Be sure that your top leg moves forward on each side. Your right leg leads when you face the right (figure 9.3a), and your left leg leads when you face the left (figure 9.3b). Inhale on one kick. Leave your face in the water and exhale on the other kick. Kick 50 yards with smooth transition from one side position to the other.

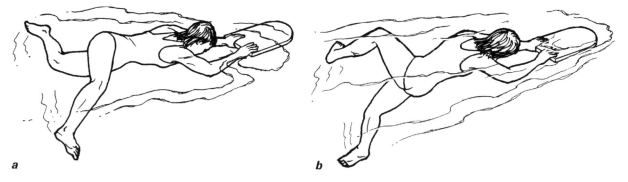

a                                                                          b

**Figure 9.3**    Double trudgen kick drill: *(a)* right leg leads when facing right; *(b)* left leg leads when facing left.

**To Increase Difficulty**

- Keep your head up and your chin at water level.

**To Decrease Difficulty**

- Wear a mask and snorkel and keep your head down, but breathe properly.

### *Success Check*

- Roll your hips from side to side.
- Make your kick slightly smaller than a usual scissors kick.

### *Score Your Success*

Swim 50 yards while wearing a mask = 1 point

Swim 50 yards while inhaling on one kick, exhaling on the other = 3 points

Your score ___

## Double Trudgen Stroke Drill 2.

## *Double Trudgen Kick, Single-Arm Pull*

Start double trudgen kicks while holding a kickboard with both hands. After two sets of kicks, start pulling with one arm while your legs recover for a kick. Deliver the kick during the last half of the arm pull, then return that hand to the board. Leave both hands on the kickboard while you kick on the other side. Then pull again with the same arm on the next kick. Continue with only one arm for 25 yards, then shift to pull with the other arm on the other side with the other kick. Slow down enough so that you can be sure the kick comes during the last half of the arm pull. Swim 25 yards on that side with one arm only.

### To Increase Difficulty

- Discard the kickboard.

### To Decrease Difficulty

- Use a mask and snorkel, but inhale only while the one arm is pulling.

### *Success Check*

- Inhale with the arm pull.
- Exhale on the kick-only side.

### *Score Your Success*

Swim 25 yards on the right side and 25 yards on the left side while wearing a mask = 1 point

Swim 25 yards on the right side and 25 yards on the left side without a mask = 3 points

Your score ___

## Double Trudgen Stroke Drill 3.

## *Double Trudgen Stroke With Kickboard*

Hold a kickboard in both hands at arm's length. Begin alternate-side scissors kicks. Pull with your left arm during a left-side kick, then return your hand to the kickboard and glide. Next pull with your right arm during a right-side kick, then return that hand to the kickboard and glide. Continue pulling and kicking alternately on the left and right sides with a glide following each stroke. Swim 50 yards of alternate-side trudgen strokes with a glide after each one.

### To Increase Difficulty

- Keep your head up to see, but breathe at the proper time.

### To Decrease Difficulty

- Swim even slower. Take long glides.

### *Success Check*

- Keep it slow. Think about coordination.
- Breathe on the second half of one-arm pull. Exhale, face down, on the next pull.

### *Score Your Success*

Swim 50 yards, head up or down = 3 points

Your score ___

## Double Trudgen Stroke Drill 4.

## *Double Trudgen Stroke in Rough Water*

Begin in a prone glide. Begin a trudgen stroke pull with a scissors kick on each side, alternating sides continuously. Imagine you are in water with high waves. Cut your glide short and use each kick to lift your head high enough to see over the next wave. Your body will assume a semi-upright position in the water. This is the best stroke for this purpose, though somewhat more tiring. Fix your eyes on an object ahead of you (a drowning victim?) and do not lose sight of it. Swim for 25 yards while watching a fixed point.

### To Increase Difficulty

- Play with pressing and kicking in a nearly vertical position without much forward progress.

### To Decrease Difficulty

- Simply do not rise so high. Work on the stroke until you can rise higher in the water.

### Success Check

- Kick with the last half of the arm pull.
- Press down as you pull back to lift your head and body.

### Score Your Success

Remain in high position for 25 yards
= 3 points
Your score ___

# TRUDGEN CRAWL STROKE

Most people are either right handed or left handed. Likewise, most people prefer to perform a swimming action, such as a scissors kick, to one side or the other. However, the double trudgen stroke requires doing a scissors kick on both sides. It's possible that early swimmers who had trouble mastering the double trudgen stroke for competition because of their kicking-side preference developed a flaw in the stroke, leading to the next step in the evolution of the crawl stroke—the trudgen crawl stroke.

The trudgen crawl stroke employs a kick different from that of the double trudgen. Instead of two scissors kicks, the trudgen crawl stroke employs one scissors kick and three flutter (crawl) kicks.

T.K. Cureton Jr., in his 1934 book *How to Teach Swimming and Diving*, wrote that ". . . some of the American coaches were reluctant to give up the wide scissors kick of the trudgen stroke. [Frank] Sullivan experimented with a stroke which combined the features of the trudgen and the crawl. The stroke became known as the trudgen-crawl and was characterized by a series of flutter kicks added to the wide major kick of the trudgen" (page 97). The trudgen crawl inserts three smaller crawl kicks in place of the second scissors kick of the double trudgen.

Swim a few double trudgen strokes. Think about your leg kicks. Your new leg rhythm will be "slash, beat, beat, b-e-a-t," where "slash" is a scissors kick and the long "b-e-a-t" is the recovery time for the next scissors kick. The slash comes at the end of one arm pull. The other arm pulls occur during the three flutter kicks. Breathe on the scissors kick as with the trudgen stroke. Keep your face in the water and exhale during the pull and flutter kicks. Keep the scissors kick small, not much more than a large flutter kick. In fact, if you narrow the scissors kick to the same size as a flutter kick, it becomes a flutter kick and you would be swimming a four-beat Australian crawl. The trudgen stroke would then have evolved into a crawl stroke. Adding two more leg kicks in the coordination pattern would make it a standard American crawl. That would complete the process of the evolution of the sidestroke into the American crawl.

**Misstep**

You breathe at the wrong time in the stroke.

**Correction**

Breathe during the scissors ("slash") beat.

# Trudgen Crawl Stroke Drill 1.

# *Trudgen Crawl Kick With Kickboard*

Start in a prone-float position, holding a kickboard in both hands at arm's length. Rotate your hips to the left side. Recover your legs—step forward with your left leg and back with your right leg. Execute a scissors kick but allow your feet to pass each other at the end of the kick (count "slash" as you kick). As you deliver the kick, roll back to a prone position. Do three crawl stroke (flutter) kicks, counting "beat, beat, beat" as you kick with the left foot kicking down on the first, right foot kicking down on the second, and left foot kicking down again on the third.

As you begin the third crawl kick, roll again to the left and extend the third beat into a recovery for another scissors kick. If you counted properly, the left foot will move forward on the third beat. Your left foot will lead to the recovery for a scissors kick, as in the first scissors kick. Extending the third beat into a scissors kick recovery will slow the third beat, so the rhythm now becomes "slash, beat, beat, b-e-a-t, slash, beat, beat, b-e-a-t." Keep this kicking rhythm for 25 yards, inhaling on the scissors kick and exhaling with your face in the water on the three flutter kicks.

Change to do the scissors kick facing right instead of left. The right leg now moves forward on the recovery for the scissors kick. Also, you now inhale on the right side during the scissors kick and exhale with your face down on the three flutter

kicks. Continue kicking while facing the right for 25 yards. Choose which side seems most natural for you, but remember that you must breathe on the same side as the scissors kick. Kick 50 yards of trudgen crawl kick on the side you choose and on which you will breathe.

### To Increase Difficulty

- Kick 50 yards of trudgen crawl kick on each side. Narrow the scissors kick somewhat.

### To Decrease Difficulty

- Wear a mask and snorkel if you wish.
- Kick 50 yards only on your favorite side. Breathe correctly.

## *Success Check*

- Remember, "slash (scissors kick), beat, beat, b-e-a-t" into position for the next scissors kick.
- Always inhale on the scissors kick.

## *Score Your Success*

Swim 50 yards on your favorite side only = 2 points

Swim 50 yards on each side = 4 points

Your score ___

## Trudgen Crawl Stroke Drill 2.    *Combined Trudgen and Crawl*

Start in a prone-float position. Goggles are optional. Begin a slow trudgen crawl kick sequence. On the second cycle, begin pulling and breathing on the same side as the scissors kick. Add the second arm stroke with the three flutter kicks. Do the stroke in slow motion, floating along at first, until you establish the rhythm between your arms and legs. Gradually increase the speed to a normal, easy trudgen crawl stroke. Remember, you *must* inhale on the scissors kick and exhale on the flutter kicks. Swim 100 yards of easy, smooth trudgen crawl.

**To Increase Difficulty**

- Practice each side for 50 yards.

**To Decrease Difficulty**

- Using a mask and snorkel allows you to concentrate on coordination before working breathing into the timing.

### Success Check

- Let your feet slide past each other on the scissors kick to be ready for the flutter beat.
- Extend the third flutter kick into a recovery for the scissors kick.

### Score Your Success

Swim for 100 yards, kicking on preferred side = 2 points

Swim for 100 yards, kicking for 50 yards on each side = 4 points

Your score ____

# SUCCESS SUMMARY OF TRUDGEN STROKES

For many years competitive swimming has shaped the progress in the development of swimming strokes. The search for greater speed started with the sidestroke and progressed to the overarm sidestroke, the trudgen stroke, the double trudgen, the trudgen crawl, and finally the Australian (four-beat) crawl and the American (six-beat) crawl strokes. Experiments are still under way, some making use of the dolphin kick to enhance backstroke and crawl. It will be interesting to see what develops.

One of the greatest skills achieved through learning the various strokes is the ability to adapt to intricate coordination of movements and timing. Use this ability to invent your own strokes. Power, speed, and efficiency are the key words.

If you scored at least 16 points in this step, your strokes are satisfactory. If you scored 17 to 23 points, you are doing well in the trudgen strokes. Scoring 24 points or more makes you a master swimmer.

### Trudgen Stroke Drills

1. Overarm Sidestroke, Overreaching     \_\_\_ out of 3
2. Overarm Sidestroke, Extended Lower-Arm Pull     \_\_\_ out of 2
3. Scissors Kick Crawl     \_\_\_ out of 2

### Double Trudgen Stroke Drills

1. Double Trudgen Kick Drill     \_\_\_ out of 3
2. Double Trudgen Kick, Single-Arm Pull     \_\_\_ out of 3
3. Double Trudgen Stroke With Kickboard     \_\_\_ out of 3
4. Double Trudgen Stroke in Rough Water     \_\_\_ out of 3

### Trudgen Crawl Stroke Drills

1. Trudgen Crawl Kick With Kickboard     \_\_\_ out of 4
2. Combined Trudgen and Crawl     \_\_\_ out of 4

### Total     \_\_\_ out of 27

# Surface Dives and Underwater Swimming

Surface dives take you underwater. From that position, you must make your way back to the surface by swimming underwater, but sometimes you will want to swim some distance before surfacing. This step examines how to get underwater efficiently and how to move about while there.

Skin diving, with mask, fins, and snorkel, is a sport that many swimmers enjoy. Neat and efficient surface diving is a prerequisite to enjoying skin diving. Underwater swimming involves the use of swim fins, a mask, and a snorkel as in skin diving, but you must consider the basics before tackling the more advanced sport. Entire books have been devoted to skin diving, which leads naturally into scuba diving. Let's start with getting underwater.

## SURFACE DIVING

Surface diving is diving under the water from a position on the surface. You will choose from three types of surface dives to find one that suits your purpose: the pike surface dive, the tuck surface dive, and the feetfirst surface dive.

**CAUTION** You should not learn surface dives in water less than 8 feet (2.4384 meters) deep. There is a danger of striking your head or toes on the bottom of the pool.

Surface dives are utilitarian skills, tools that allow pleasure seekers and scuba divers to move more efficiently into the depths in pursuit of their goals. We may use surface dives for moving quickly and easily to a position underwater to recover objects, to swim under an obstruction, or to explore. In making a swimming rescue, you need an efficient surface dive.

### Pike Surface Dive

The pike surface dive is the choice of most swimmers. It is smooth and efficient, and it looks better than the others. Begin the pike surface dive from a prone-float position with arms stretched overhead (figure 10.1a). Pull back with a wide sweep of both arms until your arms are at your sides (figure 10.1b). This should impart some forward momentum to your body. Turn your hands palms down at the end of the sweep. Keep both legs straight and together, toes pointed as you bend sharply at the waist (pike), driving your head and torso down to a vertical position (figure 10.1c). Because of your forward momentum, the water will press on your back as you bend, helping you keep your legs horizontal at the surface. Leave your hands palms down at your hips.

Press your arms down against the water as you lift both straight legs, toes pointed, into a vertical position above you (figure 10.1d). The downward press of your arms is essential for providing the counteracting pressure that allows your legs to lift clear of the water. To avoid falling over onto your back, stop the press of the arms when your arms point directly downward. Hold perfectly still in streamlined position to allow the weight of your lifted legs to drive you beneath the surface (figure 10.1e). As your toes go underwater, you may pull horizontally with both arms in a wide-sweeping breaststroke arm motion to pull you deeper or to level off for underwater swimming.

## Figure 10.1   Pike Surface Dive

### FLOAT
1. Float in prone position
2. Stretch arms overhead

### SWEEP
1. Sweep both arms back to sides
2. Turn palms down

### PIKE
1. Drive head down
2. Bend sharply at waist

### PRESS AND LIFT
1. Press with arms
2. Extend legs vertically upward

### DROP
1. Hold stream-lined position
2. Body sub-merges

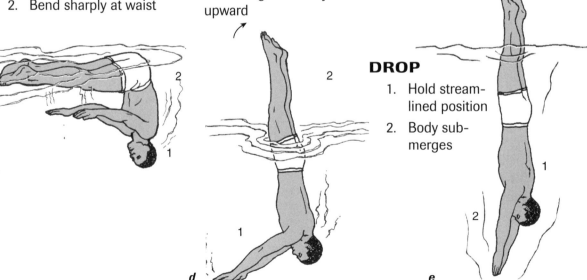

**Misstep**

You lack forward momentum going into the pike.

**Correction**

Sweep your arms longer and harder.

**Misstep**

Your legs come up short or go past the vertical plane.

**Correction**

Make your arm press shorter or longer to adjust.

# Pike Surface Dive Drill 1.    *Sweep and Pike Position Drill*

**CAUTION** Learn all surface drives in water at least 8 feet (2.4384 meters) deep. Be careful not to strike your head or toes on the bottom of the pool.

Wear goggles or a mask and snorkel for this drill. In water at least 8 feet (2.4384 meters) deep, assume a prone-float position with arms stretched overhead. Take a deep breath and hold it. Sweep both arms out to the sides and back just under the surface to start your body moving forward strongly. As you finish the sweep, leave your elbows straight and turn your palms to the bottom of the pool.

Hold still in this position with hands at your hips as you pike forward sharply at the waist, forcing your head down until your body is at a right angle. Your goal is to achieve a position with your legs still straight at the surface, your head pointed directly at the bottom, and your hands palms down beside your hips. Freeze! Hold this position for 5 seconds before coming up. Do not lift your legs above you, and do not press down on the water with your arms. Hold the right-angle position rigidly for 5 seconds. Repeat the drill five times, trying to get enough forward momentum from your arm sweep so that you can attain a pike position without pressing your arms.

**To Increase Difficulty**

- Try lifting your legs without using your arms.

**To Decrease Difficulty**

- Push off the wall before starting the drill.

## *Success Check*

- Keep legs straight and together.
- Keep toes pointed throughout the drill.

### *Score Your Success*

Execute five good pike positions = 2 points

Your score ___

## Pike Surface Dive Drill 2.    *Press and Lift*

In water at least 8 feet (2.4384 meters) deep, wearing goggles or a mask and snorkel, assume a prone-float position with arms stretched overhead. Use the keywords *sweep, bend, press and lift,* and *drop* to guide your actions.

Take a deep breath and hold it. *Sweep* your arms wide at the surface until they are at your sides. Turn your palms to the bottom. *Bend* sharply at the waist to drive your head and upper torso to a head-down vertical position with hands still at your hips. *Press* down strongly with your arms as you *lift* your straight legs behind you to a vertical position, allowing your body to *drop* gracefully beneath the surface. Then level off and return to the surface. Do five perfectly streamlined pike surface dives with legs straight and together and toes pointed.

**To Increase Difficulty**

- Rise as high as you can in the inverted position, but measure your arm press to keep legs from leaning forward or back.

**To Decrease Difficulty**

- Raise your legs slowly to remain lower in the water as your legs rise.

### Success Check

- Sweep, bend, press and lift, drop.
- Keep legs straight and together.
- Keep toes pointed.

### Score Your Success

Go completely underwater five times = 2 points per dive

Submerge in perfectly straight position, legs together, toes pointed = 2 additional points

Your score ___

## Pike Surface Dive Drill 3.    *Pike Surface Dive With Fins*

Wear a mask, fins, and snorkel. Start in water at least 8 feet (2.4384 meters) deep. Assume a prone-float position with arms stretched overhead. Sweep your arms out and around to your hips to gain some forward momentum. Turn your palms down. The fins will add power to the downward press as you bend into pike position, but you will have to press your arms more vigorously to lift the added weight of the fins into the vertical position. Keep your legs straight with fins pointed as you raise them above you. The added weight will give you additional momentum when dropping underwater. Do five pike surface dives with the fins, trying to control the pike, the lift, and the aesthetics of stretched legs and pointed fins.

**To Increase Difficulty**

- Try to drop to the bottom of the pool without swimming down 8, 10, or 12 feet; (2.4384, 3.048, or 3.6576 meters).

**To Decrease Difficulty**

- Practice, practice, practice.

### Success Check

- Pike gently, press strongly, and lift carefully.
- Form counts.

### Score Your Success

Dive and reach a depth of 8 feet = 1 point per dive (5 points maximum)

Attain perfectly vertical position on all five dives = 2 additional points

Your score ___

# Tuck Surface Dive

The tuck surface dive is a variation of the pike surface dive. It does not look as neat and structured as the pike dive, but it serves the same purpose. If you have trouble lifting your legs straight and rigid for the pike dive, the tuck dive will make you look less awkward and will get you underwater efficiently.

Continuous diving with the pike surface dive will tire you. After a strenuous day of skin diving, you may enjoy using less effort on the last few dives of the session. Form is still important, but when you're diving to salvage a sunken artifact or rescue a trapped sea dweller, the tuck surface dive might be a welcome relief.

Dive only in water at least 8 feet (2.4384 meters) deep. Wear goggles. Start from a prone position with your arms stretched overhead. Sweep your arms out and back to gain forward momentum and bring them in to your sides, turning the palms down. Immediately bend sharply at the waist, driving your head and upper torso down to a vertical, head-down position with a 90-degree bend at the hips (figure 10.2).

As you press down with your arms, quickly tuck your knees to your chest and thrust them vertically upward, toes pointed and legs together. The weight of your legs will force you under. Do not press as hard or as long with your arms as required for the pike dive because with your body tucked you will rotate more easily and your leg thrust may go past the vertical and turn you over on your back. You need the weight of your legs above you to force you under. Level off and swim or return to the surface.

**Figure 10.2** Tuck surface dive. Drive head down by bending sharply at the waist. Tuck knees to chest. Press and lift.

**Misstep**

Your legs go past vertical because you press too hard or too long.

**Correction**

Press carefully and slowly until you learn how to apply the correct amount of pressure.

## Tuck Surface Dive Drill 1. Tuck, Press, and Extend

In water at least 8 feet (2.4384 meters) deep, wearing goggles or a mask and snorkel, assume a prone-float position with arms stretched overhead. Use the key words *sweep, bend, tuck, press and extend,* and *drop* to guide you.

Take a deep breath and hold it. *Sweep* your arms wide to your sides and turn your palms down. *Bend* sharply at the waist to a right angle with your head down and your legs horizontal. Immediately after bending, *tuck* your knees up to your chest, *press* your arms down, and *extend* your legs to a vertical position. Keep your legs straight and together with your toes pointed as you *drop* beneath the surface. Pull with your arms to level off and return to the surface. Do five tuck

surface dives with legs vertical and together and toes pointed.

**To Increase Difficulty**

- Try to drop to a depth of 10 feet if that depth is available.

**To Decrease Difficulty**

- Tuck your legs before you press.

## Success Check

- Sweep, bend, tuck, press and extend, drop.
- Press and extend carefully so that your legs don't topple.

## Tuck Surface Dive Drill 2.

## Tuck Surface Dive With Fins

Repeat tuck surface dive drill 1 while wearing fins and a mask and snorkel. Tuck your legs *as you sweep*. (Tucking will take the place of the bend.) Do not pause between the sweep and the arm press. Go right from the sweep into the press, then thrust your legs and fins into a vertical position with fins together and extended (pointed). Drop underwater, level off, and return to the surface. Do five tuck surface dives with fins.

**To Increase Difficulty**

- Alternate tuck and pike surface dives, completing five of each.

**To Decrease Difficulty**

- Practice tuck surface dive drill 1 while wearing fins.

### Success Check

- Sweep and tuck, press and thrust, drop.
- Extend legs straight up or you will not drop.

## Feetfirst Surface Dive

The feetfirst surface dive drives you underwater in an upright position. In addition to its utility, it has an aesthetic dimension. Accomplished swimmers do not lumber about, making awkward splashing motions. They are fluid and smooth in the performance of their strokes and dives. Learn to do this surface dive correctly, and prove that you, too, are an accomplished swimmer.

Rescue crews and scuba divers sometimes find themselves in muddy, murky water. They have little or no knowledge of what lies beneath the surface at the point where they expect to dive. Therefore they should not expose themselves to the possibility of serious injury by going headfirst into sharp or dangerous obstructions. The feetfirst surface dive allows swimmers to submerge in a much safer configuration until they can ascertain the obstacles they face. Once underwater, they are in a much better situation to level off and continue their mission.

To perform the feetfirst surface dive, assume a vertical position in the water with your chin at water level. Position your legs for a powerful scissors kick and spread your arms to the sides at the surface (figure 10.3a). Kick and press with your arms simultaneously to lift your body as high as possible in the water. Your kick should finish with your legs together, and your arm press should finish with your arms tight against your sides (figure 10.3b). Leave them in this streamlined position as you rise and then sink, still upright, beneath the surface (figure 10.3c). When your head is well underwater, turn your palms out and lift strongly against the water to drive yourself deeper (figure 10.3d). Your hands should not break the surface on the arm lift. You may repeat the lift with your arms until you are as deep as you wish to go. Tuck your knees to level off, and swim forward.

## Figure 10.3    Feetfirst Surface Dive

### GO VERTICAL

1. Get in vertical position
2. Place chin at water level
3. Put arms out to sides
4. Legs are apart for scissors kick

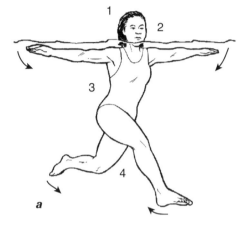

### PRESS AND KICK

1. Press with arms
2. Scissors-kick with legs, ending with legs together
3. Rise as high out of the water as possible

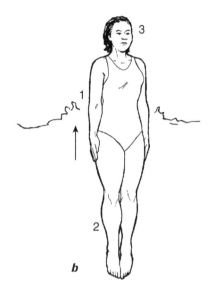

### SINK

1. Hold arms at sides
2. Stretch legs
3. Sink underwater feetfirst

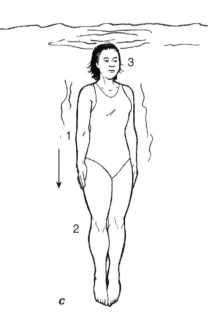

### LIFT

1. Turn palms up
2. Lift on water with wide, outward sweep

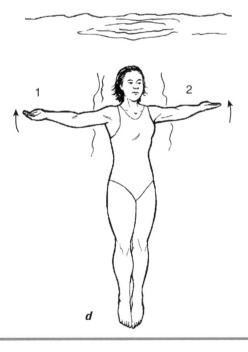

**Misstep**

Your arms come splashing up out of the water as you lift to drive yourself down.

**Correction**

Wait until your head is well underwater before you lift with your arms.

## Feetfirst Surface Dive Drill 1. *Lift and Drop*

Wear goggles or a mask and snorkel for this drill. In water more than 8 feet (2.4384 meters) deep, kick gently to maintain a vertical position with your chin at water level. Take a deep breath and hold it. Extend both arms out to the sides as far as you can reach on the surface. Step forward and back in preparation for a large, powerful scissors kick. Kick powerfully and press on the water with both arms to raise yourself as high as possible out of the water. As your legs finish the kick and your arms finish the press, keep your legs together, your toes pointed, and your arms pressed to your sides as you submerge.

When your head is 8 to 12 inches (20.32 to 30.48 centimeters) underwater, turn your palms out and lift out with your arms strongly to force yourself deeper under water. *Be careful not to drive your pointed toes into the bottom.* Tuck your knees, turn to a level position, and swim forward and up to the surface. Do five consecutive feetfirst surface dives with no splash on submerging and to a depth of at least 5 feet (1.524 meters) when you level off.

**To Increase Difficulty**

- Rise in the water to waist-high depth.
- Wait until downward motion ceases before lifting with arms.

**To Decrease Difficulty**

- Wear goggles instead of a mask. (Goggles are less buoyant.)

### Success Check

- Lift as high as possible, then sink.
- Do not splash with your arms as you lift to force yourself down deeper.

### Score Your Success

Perform five good dives = 2 points

Dive without splashing on any of the five good dives = 1 additional point

Your score ___

## Feetfirst Surface Dive Drill 2. *Feetfirst Surface Dive With Fins*

Wear swim fins and a mask and snorkel. Start in water at least 8 feet (2.4384 meters) deep. Repeat feetfirst surface dive drill 1 while wearing fins. Expect to lift higher because of the added help of the fins; dropping underwater will be a little trickier. If you point your toes while wearing fins, the fins either will catch the water to push your feet back or the water will catch the fin bottoms to force your feet forward. If your feet go back, you will end up on your belly at a very shallow depth. If your feet move forward, you will be on your back at a very shallow depth. If you leave your feet hooked, they will resist your descent. Try to keep your fins pointed straight down to descend to a reasonable depth. This will take a little practice. Do five feetfirst surface dives with fins after you have mastered fin control.

**To Increase Difficulty**

- Try to descend holding your fins flat.

**To Decrease Difficulty**

- Try, try again.

## Success Check

- Allowing your feet to move back will put you in a better position to swim underwater.
- Tuck your knees to turn your head down.

## Score Your Success

Reach 8 feet deep on the fifth feetfirst dive = 2 points

Reach 8 feet deep on all five dives with no splash = 2 additional points

Your score ___

# UNDERWATER SWIMMING

Swimming underwater is fun, safe when properly regulated, and very useful. But there are inherent dangers to consider. It is obvious that unless you are using underwater breathing apparatus, you must hold your breath while swimming underwater. Perhaps the most important aspect of swimming underwater is to set limits on your breath holding to prevent loss of consciousness and, probably, your life. Please read the Be Safe section of this step very carefully.

Underwater swimming is a means of accomplishing rescue and recovery of submerged victims and objects. It's also fun for exploration; you should develop water mastery skills for enjoyment as well as for useful purposes.

The distance you can swim underwater is governed by the efficiency of your stroke and the length of time you can hold your breath. The efficiency of your stroke depends on the exact technical excellence of your propulsive movements, the maximum use of streamlining techniques to reduce drag, and the relaxing of your muscles to the maximum extent consistent with maintaining propulsive movements and streamlining. A relaxed muscle uses oxygen less rapidly than a tense one does.

The most powerful swimming arm motion we know is the butterfly arm stroke. The most powerful kick we know is either the scissors kick or the breaststroke kick, depending on which you do better. By combining these propulsive factors with a long, relaxed glide, you can swim underwater most efficiently.

In clear water with good visibility, wear goggles or a mask and snorkel. Assume a prone-float position with your arms stretched overhead. Take a big breath, do a surface dive, and level off. Start underwater in a horizontal position with arms overhead and body streamlined. Pull back and slightly up with a long, powerful butterfly arm stroke. Streamline your body for a glide with your arms tight to your sides. Your body will tend to rise as you glide because of your buoyancy. Therefore, you must maintain a slightly head-down position and pull up slightly on each stroke, as if you were swimming downhill. While gliding, relax as much as possible while still maintaining a streamlined position. Continue to glide until your forward motion nearly, but not quite, stops. Then, keeping your hands close to your body to minimize drag, bring them under your belly to chest level as you recover your legs into position for a scissors or breaststroke kick (whichever you do better). Kick immediately and powerfully as you thrust your hands forward, fingertips first, into full extension. Glide again in a relaxed and streamlined position until your forward motion nearly stops. Continue this cycle of pull, glide, kick, glide as long as you can hold your breath without undue stress. Then look up, reach up, and return to the surface.

During your glide, relax your abdominal muscles consciously. Most swimmers maintain very tense abdominal muscles during underwater swimming, which rapidly uses oxygen. Some swimmers feel that exhaling a very small amount relieves them of distress. However, any exhalation reduces the amount of oxygen available to you. It's best to retain all of your air while swimming underwater.

## Be Safe

Swimming underwater is subject to two inherent dangers: *limited visibility* and a physiological phenomenon called *underwater blackout,* which is due to prolonged breath holding or hyperventilation.

### Limited Visibility

Wearing goggles or a mask when swimming underwater helps greatly to decrease the danger of underwater swimming. However, the clarity of the water cannot always be controlled, so special precautions are necessary when turbid water restricts visibility. It could ruin your whole day to pull strongly with both arms in water of zero visibility and thrust your head into a battleship you didn't see. In murky water, always take short pulling strokes (within your range of visibility) and glide with your arms in front of you.

### Hyperventilation and Underwater Blackout

Unfortunately, too many people employ hyperventilation to increase their breath-holding ability. This technique consists of breathing deeply and rapidly for 10 to 15 breaths and then trying to hold one's breath for as long as possible.

Physiologically, the practice of hyperventilation is very dangerous. Air taken into the lungs provides the oxygen the body requires to function. Blood carries the oxygen from the lungs to the brain, muscles, and every other part of the body. When muscles use oxygen, they form carbon dioxide, which is carried away from the muscles by blood flow. Thus as oxygen is depleted, there is a corresponding increase in the carbon dioxide content of the blood. The body does not measure the decrease in oxygen but reacts to the increase in carbon dioxide by signaling the breathing center in the brain to take in more air.

It is a common belief that hyperventilation increases the oxygen content of the blood and allows you to hold your breath longer. Hyperventilation does not significantly increase the oxygen content of the blood, but it does tend to purge the bloodstream of carbon dioxide, thus depriving the body of its defensive mechanism that tells the breathing center to cause more breathing. If the bloodstream is deprived of its normal carbon dioxide content, it will take longer to generate the signal to breathe. The body is fooled into thinking that it does not need to take in more air, when in fact the oxygen supply could be seriously depleted. The result of this phenomenon is that you may feel perfectly comfortable holding your breath and may not feel a need to breathe before the oxygen supply to the brain is depleted and you lose consciousness. Despite unconsciousness, the carbon dioxide level would eventually build to the point of triggering your breathing mechanism. You would inhale involuntarily, even if underwater. *Never, never try to extend your breath-holding time by hyperventilating before swimming underwater.* No possible reason for underwater swimming could warrant the risk.

**Misstep**

You use up oxygen unnecessarily by swimming too rapidly.

**Correction**

Swim powerfully but glide relaxed until momentum slows.

Murky water requires modification of the underwater swimming procedure. In unclear water, you will need to take precautions to avoid running into anything. To learn to swim in murky water, begin on the surface in prone-float position with arms stretched overhead. Wear a mask and snorkel and breathe through the snorkel as you float on the surface. Pull with a quick butterfly stroke. Immediately recover your arms under your body with as little resistance as possible, and kick into an extended glide position. Glide. Glide only when your arms are extended in front to protect your head from unseen obstacles. Your key words are *pull, kick, glide*. For very low visibility, shorten the pull. Kick only when your arms are in position to protect your head. In really dark water, pull with only one arm, keeping the other arm in front of you.

## Underwater Swimming Drill 1.   *Glide for Distance*

Wear goggles or a mask. Stand in 4 feet (1.2192 meters) of water at the edge of the pool, with your back to the wall. Take two deep breaths, hold the second one, and sink beneath the surface. Place both feet against the wall behind you, extend both arms ahead, and push off. Streamline your body, keeping your head between your arms and your toes pointed, and hold perfectly still. You will float to the surface. Continue to hold your breath as long as you can, even if it seems that you have stopped moving. When you must breathe, note or mark the distance you glided with an object on the side of the pool.

Try again from the same starting spot, but pay more attention to maintaining a totally streamlined position. Consciously relax your abdominal muscles while gliding. How far can you glide? Note the distance of the second glide.

**To Increase Difficulty**

- Glide in a straight line—no curves.

**To Decrease Difficulty**

- Wear goggles, not a mask. (Goggles produce less drag.)

### Success Check

- Push off hard.
- Stretch.
- Relax.
- Hold still.

### Score Your Success

Score 2 points if your second glide was farther than the first.

Your score ___

**147**

## Underwater Swimming Drill 2.

## *Underwater Swimming Stroke Coordination on Surface*

Use a mask and snorkel for this drill. Float in a prone position, breathing through the snorkel. Stretch both arms overhead. Perform a long, full butterfly pull, but stop when your hands reach your thighs. Streamline and glide for a count of 5 (approximately 5 seconds). Keep your hands close to your body and bring them forward under your chest to your chin.

As your hands recover, bring your legs into position for either a breaststroke kick or a scissors kick, whichever you do better. If you choose a scissors kick, it will be necessary to twist your hips to the side somewhat to keep your feet underwater. When your legs are in position, kick vigorously and drive your arms forward to full extension. Glide for a count of 5 and start the next stroke. Thus, your key timing words will be *pull, glide, kick, glide, pull, glide, kick, glide,* and so on. Swim for 25 yards (22.86 meters) with steady breathing at will.

### To Increase Difficulty

- Breathe only while gliding.

### To Decrease Difficulty

- Glide while relaxed.

### *Success Check*

- Time your glides so that you come nearly to a stop on each.
- Streamline on every glide.

### *Score Your Success*

Count your strokes, counting one pull and one kick as one stroke. Calculate your distance per stroke after 25 yards. Swim 25 yards again the same way, gliding as far as possible on each pull and kick. Calculate your distance per stroke again. If you improved your distance per stroke on the second trial, give yourself 3 points.

Your score ___

## Underwater Swimming Drill 3.

## *Underwater Swimming From a Surface Dive*

Do this drill in clear water of more than 8 feet (2.4384 meters) deep. Wear goggles or a mask and snorkel. Take two deep breaths, hold the second one, and do a surface dive, leveling off at a depth of about 6 feet (1.8288 meters) . Immediately begin swimming underwater. To maintain your depth against the lift of buoyancy, assume a slightly head-down position and be sure to pull up somewhat on the water at the beginning of each pull. If the water is not too deep, it is helpful to follow the contour of the bottom of the pool to judge your depth. Make five swims underwater, refining your form and coordination.

 **CAUTION** Do not force yourself to hold your breath beyond normal comfort limits!

### To Increase Difficulty

- Start from a feetfirst surface dive.

### To Decrease Difficulty

- Use a pike surface dive.

### *Success Check*

- Measure success by form and coordination, not by distance.
- Pull, glide while relaxed, kick, glide while relaxed.
- Streamline.

### *Score Your Success*

Perform five successful underwater swims at 6 feet deep or deeper = 3 points

Your score ___

## Underwater Swimming Drill 4.   *Underwater Swimming in Murky Water*

Do this drill in *clear* water of more than 8 feet (2.4384 meters) deep, wearing goggles or a mask and snorkel. Take two deep breaths, hold the second one, and do a surface dive of any kind. Level off at about 6 feet (1.8288 meters) and immediately begin using the murky water stroke for swimming underwater (see page 147). Do not glide with hands and arms at your sides; glide only when your arms are forward. The rhythm is nearly the same as for breaststroke except the pull is much longer. Do five dives and practice swims.

 **Do not force yourself to hold your breath beyond normal limits of comfort. Concentrate on the stroke, not the distance.**

**To Increase Difficulty**

- Have a buddy swim with you to keep you from running into things, and stuff your mask with cloth as a blindfold. Try two dives.

**To Decrease Difficulty**

- Wear goggles and use pike surface dives.

### Success Check

- Pull, kick your arms forward, glide.
- Close your eyes for a couple of strokes.

### Score Your Success

Complete five dives with correct strokes = 2 points

Your score ___

## Underwater Swimming Drill 5.   *Underwater Swimming With Fins*

Wear a mask, fins, and a snorkel. Swim in *clear* water. You will find that it's too difficult to use a scissors kick or breaststroke kick with fins, so do a surface dive, level off at about 6 feet, and use a crawl kick to swim underwater. You will travel much faster, so beware of obstacles. Note that with fins your kick is much more powerful, your progress is constant (not intermittent), and you don't need to use your arms for propulsion. With fins you can swim underwater in murky water with your arms always fully extended in front of you. Use them as rudders to control your direction and depth. Do five surface dives and underwater swims with fins.

**To Increase Difficulty**

- In clear water, use fins *and* arm pulls.

**To Decrease Difficulty**

- Swim upward gradually so that you are at the surface when you run out of air.

### Success Check

- Do a pike or tuck surface dive.
- Use large, slow crawl kicks.
- Stretch your arms in front of you.

### Score Your Success

Complete five successful underwater swims = 2 points

Your score ___

# SUCCESS SUMMARY OF SURFACE DIVES AND UNDERWATER SWIMMING

Surface diving and swimming underwater are skills that may be more useful to you than any other aquatic skill. They are tools that may well save lives in search-and-rescue missions. Note also that swimming underwater is more fun and much easier when you are wearing swim fins. Fins may not always be available when you need them, so basic underwater skills are necessary for safety.

Add your success score points for this step to determine your progress toward becoming an aquatic expert. If you scored 26 points or fewer, you should consider yourself barely proficient in this skill. If your score is 27 to 34 points, you are well on your way to becoming a skin diver. Scoring 35 points or more makes you a veritable underwater expert.

*Pike Surface Dive Drills*

1. Sweep and Pike Position Drill     ___ out of 2
2. Press and Lift     ___ out of 12
3. Pike Surface Dive With Fins     ___ out of 7

*Tuck Surface Dive Drills*

1. Tuck, Press, and Extend     ___ out of 4
2. Tuck Surface Dive With Fins     ___ out of 8

*Feetfirst Surface Dive Drills*

1. Lift and Drop     ___ out of 3
2. Feetfirst Surface Dive With Fins     ___ out of 4

*Underwater Swimming Drills*

1. Glide for Distance     ___ out of 2
2. Underwater Swimming Stroke Coordination on Surface     ___ out of 3
3. Underwater Swimming From a Surface Dive     ___ out of 3
4. Underwater Swimming in Murky Water     ___ out of 2
5. Underwater Swimming With Fins     ___ out of 2

*Total*     ___ *out of 52*

# Standing and Kneeling Dives

Entering the water is easy—simply go to the edge and fall in. Just how you fall in is the subject under consideration in this step. You can jump feetfirst, fall in flat, or dive gracefully. You can even use a springboard to propel you into the air, but you cannot call yourself an accomplished swimmer until you can do a fully coordinated standing front dive.

**CAUTION** Water depth is critical for all diving skills! You must have a water depth of at least 10 feet (3.048 meters) for safety in this step. Failure to have adequate water depth can result in serious injury, including concussion, broken neck, and quadriplegia.

## KNEELING DIVE

In adequate water depth, this kneeling dive is both safe and easy to learn. It's the first step in learning an easy standing dive. The kneeling dive teaches you how to enter the water smoothly, how to emerge from a dive, and how to do a shallow dive to avoid injury. Don't skip this important step.

Assuming your site has a deck height of 12 inches or less and adequate water depth, stand at the edge of the pool and hook the toes of one foot over the edge. Kneel on the opposite knee. Stretch your arms overhead, intertwine your thumbs, and squeeze your arms against your ears. Keep your ears buried between your arms. Bend over until your hands are slanting down toward the water (figure 11.1a). Rock forward, take a breath and hold it, keep your chin down, and push off with your toes. Lift the rear leg. Push out into the water (figure 11.1b). Hold your breath, arch slightly, point your hands and head up, and rise to the surface.

## Figure 11.1  Kneeling Dive

### KNEEL

1. Toes are over the edge of the pool
2. Kneel on opposite knee
3. Arms are over your ears
4. Lean over
5. Point your hands at the water
6. Take a deep breath and keep chin down

### DIVE

1. Rock forward and push off with toes
2. Lift your rear leg
3. Dive out
4. Under the water, turn head and hands up
5. Glide to the surface

**Misstep**

You hit flat on the water.

**Correction**

Tuck your chin. Lift your trailing leg higher. Keep your ears between your arms.

## Kneeling Dive Drill 1.  *Underwater Glide*

In chest-deep water with your back against the pool wall, stretch your arms overhead to cover your ears. Put one foot against the wall behind you, take a deep breath, put your face down, aim your hands slightly down to dig into the water, and push off. Streamline and glide underwater as far as you can. Try 10 underwater glides.

**To Increase Difficulty**

- Start with both feet against the wall.

**To Decrease Difficulty**

- Wear goggles so that you can see underwater.

### Success Check

- Keep your arms over your ears.
- Aim downhill.
- Stretch.

## Score Your Success

Complete 10 successful glides = 1 point

Glide more than 20 feet (6.096 meters) on at least 5 out of 10 glides = 2 additional points

Your score ___

## Kneeling Dive Drill 2.  *Glide Through the Hoop*

Get a hula hoop that floats. Tie a small weight to it so that it sinks but stands on edge on the bottom of the pool. Set it about 8 feet (2.4384 meters) from the wall about 5 feet (1.524 meters) deep. Standing with your back to the wall, stretch your arms overhead and cover your ears, interlock your thumbs, and squeeze your arms tightly to your ears. Take a big breath, put your face in the water, and tuck both legs. In facedown tucked position, place both feet against the wall, aim downhill toward the hoop, and push off. Glide through the hoop and turn your hands and head up to rise (figure 11.2). Make 10 passes through the hoop.

### To Increase Difficulty

- Move the hoop farther away.
- Kick to maintain forward movement.

### To Decrease Difficulty

- Wear goggles.
- Move the hoop closer.

## Success Check

- Keep your arms over your ears.
- Lift one foot against the wall, then the other. Push.

## Score Your Success

Complete 10 successful passes through the hoop = 1 point

Move the hoop 15 feet (4.572 meters) from the wall and complete 10 successful passes through the hoop by swimming through it = 3 additional points

Your score ___

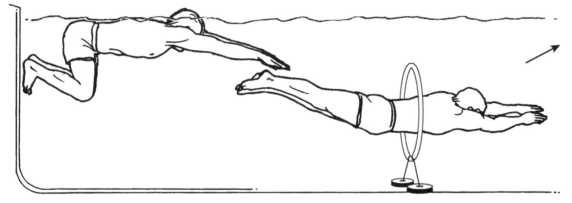

**Figure 11.2**  Glide through the hoop.

## Kneeling Dive Drill 3.  *Dive From One Knee*

Move to an area where the water depth is 10 feet (3.048 meters) or deeper. Stand at the edge of the pool. Hook the toes of one foot over the edge. Kneel on the opposite knee. Stretch your arms overhead, intertwine your thumbs, and squeeze your arms against your ears. Keep your ears buried between your arms. Bend over until your hands slant down toward the water. Rock forward, take a breath and hold it, keep your chin down, and push off with your toes. Lift your rear leg. Push out into the water. Hold your breath, arch slightly, point your hands and head up, and rise to the surface. Do 10 kneeling dives in good form. Review figure 11.1, if necessary.

### To Increase Difficulty

- Dive deeper. Can you touch the bottom?
- Slip in with no splash.

### To Decrease Difficulty

- Do not wear goggles; they will come off.
- Have a friend in the water to guide your entry.

### *Success Check*

- Hook your toes firmly over the edge.
- Keep your chin down and your trailing leg up high.

### *Score Your Success*

Complete 10 good kneeling dives = 3 points

Execute dives with no splashing = 1 additional point

Your score ___

---

# ONE-FOOT DIVE

 **This dive requires a water depth of at least 10 feet (3.048 meters).**

You have learned to do a kneeling dive that carries you out at a shallow angle. Expert divers try to enter the water vertically. A stretched, vertical entry with very little splash is the mark of a good dive. Adequate water depth is required for safety because a vertical entry carries you deeper.

The one-foot dive is a transition from a low position, shallow dive to a stand-up dive that can be done from nearly any height. To gain confidence, you can learn this dive from the deck and then progress to the low diving board for a new experience. This process helps you eliminate painful flat dives that result from skipping progressive steps.

Stand at the edge of the pool at the deep end. The water should be 10 feet (3.048 meters) deep or more. Stand with one foot forward, one back. Grip the edge of the pool with the toes of your forward foot. Extend both arms overhead, covering your ears. Hook your thumbs and squeeze your arms against your ears. Bend forward. Aim at a point only 3 feet (0.9144 meters) from the edge (figure 11.3a). Point the toes of your rear foot. Lift your rear leg high over your head as you rock forward into the water. Keep your forward knee *locked straight* to keep you a safe distance from the pool wall. Enter the water vertically. Keep your hands over your head for protection (figure 11.3b). When submerged, tuck your knees and turn back to the surface. Pull down with both arms to aid you in surfacing.

## Figure 11.3   One-Foot Dive

### STAND AND LEAN

1. Stand at the edge of the pool with one foot forward
2. Hook toes over the edge
3. Press arms overhead, covering ears
4. Bend forward, aiming for a spot 3 feet out
5. Lock the forward knee
6. Point the toes of the rear foot

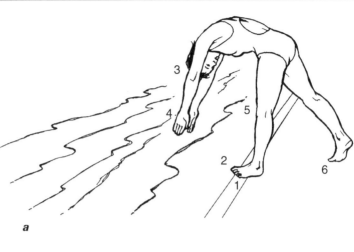

*a*

### DIVE

1. Rock forward
2. Keep chin down
3. Lock the front knee
4. Lift rear leg high

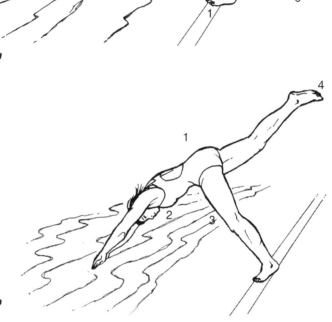

*b*

**Misstep**

Your forward leg bends as you dive, resulting in bruised shins.

**Correction**

Lock that forward knee straight!

# One-Foot Dive Drill 1. *Transition From Kneeling Dive*

In water of at least 10 feet (3.048 meters) deep, do a kneeling dive, then prepare for a second kneeling dive. This time, before you push off, put all your weight on your forward foot and the toes of your rear foot. Raise your rear knee about 6 inches (15.24 centimeters) off the deck so that you're in track-start position (figure 11.4a). As you fall forward, straighten your forward leg and lift your rear leg high over your head (figure 11.4b). Keep your chin down and ears between your arms. Repeat the dive with your knee a little higher. Do three dives with your knee higher each time.

## To Increase Difficulty

- Start with your rear leg straight.
- Stretch both legs together on the entry.

## To Decrease Difficulty

- Have someone on deck lift your leg.
- Don't look at the water; look at your toes.

## Success Check

- Aim down toward the water.
- Raise your knee off the deck. Dive.

## Score Your Success

Dive without hitting flat = 1 point

Correctly straighten forward leg = 1 additional point

Enter vertically = 2 additional points

Your score ___

a

b

**Figure 11.4**   Transition from kneeling dive: *(a)* track-start position; *(b)* dive.

# One-Foot Dive Drill 2. *Correct One-Foot Dive*

At a depth of 10 feet (3.048 meters) or more, stand with one foot forward, one back. Grip the edge with the toes of your forward foot. Extend both arms over your head and cover your ears. Hook your thumbs and squeeze. Bend forward. Aim at a point only 3 feet (0.9144 meters) from the edge. Point the toes of your rear foot. Lift your rear leg high over your head as you rock forward into the water. Keep your forward knee locked straight to keep you a safe distance from the pool wall. Enter the water vertically. Keep your hands over your head for protection. When submerged, tuck your knees and turn back to the surface. Do 10 one-foot dives with vertical entry, pointed toes, and no splash. Review figure 11.3 if necessary.

**To Increase Difficulty**

- Point the toes of the forward leg as they leave the deck.
- Carry the vertical entry to the bottom of the pool.

**To Decrease Difficulty**

- Have someone on the deck hold and lift your rear leg as it leaves the deck.

- Have someone in the water touch your forward knee to remind you to keep it locked.

## *Success Check*

- Keep your forward knee locked.
- Aim in close; kick rear leg way up overhead.

### *Score Your Success*

Correctly lock knee when diving at least 5 out of 10 times = 1 point

Correctly lock knee when diving all 10 times = 2 points

Execute a vertical entry at least 5 out of 10 times = 1 point

Execute a vertical entry all 10 times = 2 points

Point toes while diving at least 5 out of 10 times = 1 point

Point toes while diving all 10 times = 2 points

Your score ____

# One-Foot Dive Drill 3. *Low-Board One-Foot Dive*

Hook the toes of one foot over the end of a one-meter diving board. Don't bounce the board. Bend forward and lift your chin so that you're looking just over your fingertips at a point about 4 feet (1.2192 meters) from the end of the board. Squeeze your arms against your chin. Keep your forward knee rigid. Fall forward and lift your rear leg high. Bring your legs together for the entry. Do five one-foot dives with good form from the springboard.

**To Increase Difficulty**

- Start the board rocking gently and fall on the upward motion.
- Tuck in your chin just before entry.

**To Decrease Difficulty**

- Have someone stand on the board with you to lift your leg as you dive.

- Concentrate on keeping both knees locked straight.

## *Success Check*

- Grip the edge of the board with your toes.
- Look at your fingertips.

### *Score Your Success*

Execute five dives with two straight knees = 1 point

Execute a vertical entry at least three out of five times = 1 point

Make a small splash at least three out of five times = 1 point

Your score ____

# STANDING FRONT DIVE

 **Learn this dive in a water depth of at least 10 feet (3.048 meters).**

A standing front dive is one of the basic skills in aquatic technique. It's a way of entering the water, but it's also a telltale mark of an accomplished swimmer. It allows you to enter the water with grace and precision. The dive is as much aesthetic as utilitarian. In fact, beyond the standing front dive, springboard diving is totally aesthetic. There is no utilitarian need for a full-twisting forward two-and-one-half somersault, but divers work very hard to accomplish the dive, which is then graded purely on its aesthetics.

Diving is a sport separate from swimming but closely related to it. The standing front dive is the elementary technique in a whole series of more complex skills. It's not essential to swimming technique, but it's a skill expected of, and desired by, nearly all swimmers. It might open an entirely new area of interest for you. Try it. You'll like it.

Be sure you have at least 10 feet (3.048 meters) of water depth and no underwater obstructions. Stand with the toes of both feet gripping the edge of the pool, arms at your sides. Swing both arms in a small circle (about 12 inches in diameter): out, back, around, and forward past your hips (figure 11.5a). As your arms circle, bend your knees slightly. As your arms pass your hips, spring upward. Bend fully at the waist, lifting your hips behind you (figure 11.5b). Continue the arm swing until your hands point 4 feet (1.2192 meters) out from the edge. Tuck your head between your arms and lift both legs behind you, straight and stretched. Enter the water vertically (figure 11.5c). Tuck your knees or arch your back and turn your head and arms up to glide to the surface.

## Figure 11.5 Standing Front Dive

### GET READY

1. Grip edge of pool with toes
2. Hold arms at sides
3. Make circles with arms
4. Bend knees

### SPRING

1. Spring upward
2. Lift hips
3. Aim 4 feet from the edge
4. Bend over
5. Tuck chin and lift legs

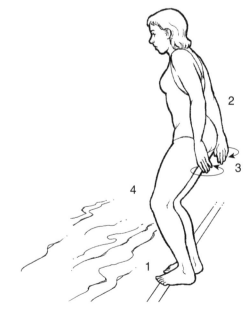

a

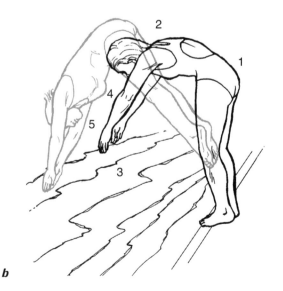

b

## ENTER THE WATER

1. Go for a vertical entry
2. Keep body straight
3. Arch, lift head and arms, and glide to the surface

**Misstep**

You hit the water flat.

**Correction**

Imagine a somersault. A dive is simply half a somersault. Tuck your chin and get your hips up behind you.

**Misstep**

You enter the water too far out.

**Correction**

Jump up, not out. Imagine you are diving over a low fence. Think about jumping into a handstand on the water 3 feet (0.9144 meters) out.

## Standing Front Dive Drill 1. *Standing Fall-In Dive*

This dive may be performed from any low elevation, but it works best from a 12-inch (30.48 centimeter) height. Stand with both feet at the edge of the pool or a platform at the deep end; water should be 10 feet (3.048 meters) deep or more. Grip the edge firmly with the toes of both feet. Extend both arms overhead to cover your ears. Hook your thumbs together. Squeeze your arms against your ears. Bend over until your arms point to the water about 3 feet from the edge (figure 11.6). Do not allow your knees to bend at any time during the dive. Bend your wrists back slightly. Fall into the water. When submerged, lift your chin, turn your arms and hands up, arch your back, and glide out and up. Pull toward the top if you wish to hurry the ascent. Do three or more fall-in dives until you are comfortable with it.

**Figure 11.6** Standing fall-in dive.

**159**

**To Increase Difficulty**

- Lift your legs and point your toes.
- Streamline your body and glide to the bottom of the pool.

**To Decrease Difficulty**

- Have someone kneeling beside you touch your knees to remind you to lock them straight.

## Success Check

- Hook your toes firmly on the edge.
- Keep both knees locked straight.
- Fall. Allow your hips to straighten.

### Score Your Success

Take two practice dives, then score your third dive.

Fall in = 1 point

Fall in with straight legs = 1 point

Fall in with straight hips = 1 point

Fall in with pointed toes = 1 point

Your score ___

## Standing Front Dive *Arms-Down Standing Dive* Drill 2.

Start as for standing front dive drill 1, but leave your arms at your sides. As you bend over and start your fall, bring your hands forward into the dive position, covering your ears. Continue your bend and arm movement right into a forward dive. Do three arms-down dives.

**To Increase Difficulty**

- Stay streamlined all the way to the bottom of the pool.

**To Decrease Difficulty**

- Stand with your arms well behind you. Bring them forward as you bend.

### Success Check

- Keep knees locked straight.
- Point your toes.

### Score Your Success

Score 1 point for each correct dive, up to 3 points maximum.

Your score ___

# Standing Front Dive Drill 3. *Standing Dive With Spring*

Dive into water at least 10 feet (3.048 meters) deep. From any low elevation of about 12 inches (30.48 centimeters) above the water, hook your toes over the edge and stand with your arms at your sides. Bend your knees slightly and keep them bent as you bring your arms forward and start to fall. When you are falling, and are definitely off balance and beyond the point of no return, spring up with your legs and hips and lift them behind you. You will straighten your legs in the process of jumping, so keep them straight with toes pointed for the entry. Do three fall-and-spring dives.

**To Increase Difficulty**

- Try for a splashless vertical entry.

**To Decrease Difficulty**

- To prevent jumping prematurely, have someone yell "jump" at the proper moment.

## Success Check

- Don't jump until you are definitely falling.
- Jump up, not out.

### Score Your Success

Take two practice dives, then score your third dive.

Jump too soon = minus 1 point

Jump at the right time = 2 points

Enter vertically = 1 additional point

Your score ____

# Standing Front Dive Drill 4. *Arm-Swing Dive With Spring*

Stand with your toes gripping the edge of the pool at the deep end; water should be at least 10 feet (3.048 meters) deep. Do not dive, but practice swinging your arms in small circles—out, back, in, and forward past your legs—a few times. Swing them in one-foot circles. Each time they swing back, bend your knees slightly. As your hands come forward past your legs, straighten your knees as if you were jumping.

After several practice swings, think about your fall-and-swing dives. Imagine bending over and falling as you swing your arms forward, and imagine springing directly into a handstand on the top of the water. Imagine it a few times, then do it. Remember, you must be falling *before* you spring. Do five arm-swing spring dives.

**To Increase Difficulty**

- Move to a higher takeoff point.
- Try for a vertical, stretched, toes-pointed entry.

**To Decrease Difficulty**

- Do land-drill arm swings until you are confident.

## Success Check

- Circles go out, back, in, and forward into the dive.
- Fall forward, then spring your hips up.

### Score Your Success

Give yourself 1 point for completing five arm-swing spring dives. On your fifth dive, rate yourself according to the following scoring guide.

Execute the arm-swing spring dive with reasonably correct form = 3 points

Execute the arm-swing spring dive with good form = 4 points

Your score ____

## Standing Front Dive Drill 5. *Fully Coordinated Standing Front Dive*

Be sure you have at least 10 feet (3.048 meters) of water depth and no underwater obstructions. Stand with the toes of both feet gripping the edge of the pool and arms at your sides. Swing both arms in small circles (about 1 foot in diameter) out, back, in, and forward past your hips. As your arms pass your hips, spring up. Bend fully at the waist, lifting your hips behind you. Continue the arm swing until your arms point 4 feet out from the edge. Tuck your head between your arms. Lift both legs behind you, straight and stretched. Enter the water vertically. Tuck your knees or arch your back and turn your head and arms up to glide to the surface. Do 10 fully coordinated standing front dives. Review figure 11.5 if necessary.

**To Increase Difficulty**

- Keep working on vertical, streamlined, no-splash dives.
- Move to a higher takeoff point.

**To Decrease Difficulty**

- Ask a diving coach to watch you and correct your mistakes.
- Practice, practice, practice.

### Success Check

- When off balance, spring up, not out.
- Streamline for a vertical entry.

### Score Your Success

Complete 10 dives and execute at least 1 fair dive = 2 points

On tenth dive, entry is vertical and streamlined = 4 additional points

Your score ___

## Standing Front Dive Drill 6. *Hula Hoop for Height Dive*

Stand in a hula hoop, in position for a standing front dive. Have someone hold the hoop at about shin or knee height so that the hoop is about 1 foot in front of your legs (figure 11.7). (The holder should be at your side so that he or she will not get kicked with your heels.) Dive up and over the hoop, being careful to get your head down for a vertical entry. Keep your entry within 4 feet of the wall. Raise the hoop a little for each dive to see how high you can jump to clear it. Make five or more hoop dives.

**To Increase Difficulty**

- Move the hoop thigh high.
- Make your arm-swing circle outside the hoop.

**To Decrease Difficulty**

- Keep the hoop low.
- Dive over a stick instead of a hula hoop.

### Success Check

- Use a large arm swing.
- Lift your arms in front.
- Spring up, then bend and lift your hips.

**Figure 11.7** Hula hoop for height dive.

162

Use the first four dives for practice, then rate your skill on your fifth dive based on the following scoring.

Execute the fifth dive with the hoop at your shins = 1 point

Execute the fifth dive with the hoop at your knees = 2 points

Execute the fifth dive with the hoop at your thighs = 3 points

Your score ___

## Standing Front Dive Drill 7.

## Standing Front Dive From One-Meter Springboard

Stand on the end of the one-meter diving board with your toes over the edge. Practice some arm circles for a standing front dive. Notice as you practice arm circles that the board bounces. Get your arm circles in rhythm with the board's bounce so that the board rises as your arms move forward and upward (figure 11.8a). As your arms lift upward and the board bounces upward, launch your dive. Use the upward movement of the board to give your dive more height (figure 11.8b). The board will thrust you up and gravity will bring you down, but neither one cares how—that's up to you. Keep your chin up a little more and watch the water. The board will lift your legs. Enter the water vertically (figure 11.8c). Make 10 standing board dives with streamlined vertical entry.

**Figure 11.8** Standing front dive from one-meter springboard: *(a)* stand at edge of board and swing arms; *(b)* dive when arms are moving upward and board is bouncing upward; *(c)* make entry as vertical and splashless as possible.

### To Increase Difficulty

Back up four steps. Take three steps and hop to the end of the board with both feet. Land on the board with your toes about 1 inch from the end. Time your arm swing to move down and forward as you land on the board. Lift your arms and spring up into a high forward dive. Enter the water vertically and streamlined.

### To Decrease Difficulty

- Do a standing dive on the first bounce.
- Keep your whole body stiff for the entry.

## Success Check

- Let the board set the rhythm; match your arm circles to the rhythm of the board.

- Select an upward motion to lift your take-off.
- Dive up, then bend and raise your hips.

## Score Your Success

Try the dive = 2 points

On the ninth dive, dive on the third upswing of the board while using good form = 4 points

On the tenth dive, execute a running front dive (take three steps and hop to the end of the board) = 6 points

Your score ___

---

# SUCCESS SUMMARY OF STANDING AND KNEELING DIVES

Diving requires precise timing, a honed kinesthetic sense, and hours of practice. Consider the fact that the time of each dive is only about 5 seconds from start to entry, and you can see why so much practice is necessary. You cannot do a dive in slow motion to study the proper moves—a dive moves at its own speed. For this reason, it's best to work with an experienced diving coach if you aspire to proficiency. Modern videotape technology enables divers and coaches to study each dive in slow motion. This step gives you the basics on which to build your skills.

Add your drill scores. If you scored at least 30 points, you are destined to be a good diver. If you scored 31 to 42 points, you can show off your diving ability. If you scored 43 to 50 points or more, you may wish to take up springboard diving seriously.

*Kneeling Dive Drills*

 1.  Underwater Glide — ___ out of 3
 2.  Glide Through the Hoop — ___ out of 4
 3.  Dive From One Knee — ___ out of 4

*One-Foot Dive Drills*

 1.  Transition From Kneeling Dive — ___ out of 4
 2.  Correct One-Foot Dive — ___ out of 6
 3.  Low-Board One-Foot Dive — ___ out of 3

*Standing Front Dive Drills*

 1.  Standing Fall-In Dive — ___ out of 4
 2.  Arms-Down Standing Dive — ___ out of 3
 3.  Standing Dive With Spring — ___ out of 3
 4.  Arm-Swing Dive With Spring — ___ out of 5
 5.  Fully Coordinated Standing Front Dive — ___ out of 6
 6.  Hula Hoop for Height Dive — ___ out of 3
 7.  Standing Front Dive From One-Meter Springboard — ___ out of 12

*Total*  ___ *out of 60*

# Universal Sculling

Sculling involves using your hands to apply constant pressure on the water. Your hands, moving in a horizontal plane, can apply pressure vertically.

*Universal sculling* is a term coined for the application of sculling to myriad skills and stunts. You should experiment beyond the descriptions in this text to develop new applications for sculling to prove its universality.

Hand paddles such as those used by competitive swimmers for training and web-fingered gloves as used for water aerobics can be used to multiply the effect of sculling techniques, but their use is discouraged because they distract from the pure skill as experienced with bare hands. They may be suggested here only for those who have trouble with the concepts.

Perhaps no other skill in aquatics is more useful than sculling. It transcends the sport of swimming and is a basic skill for any aquatic sport that requires participants to enter the water. Sculling is a fundamental part of most swimming strokes. It is the basis on which synchronized swimming is built. Lifesaving and nearly all water safety skills employ sculling. Water polo players scull constantly.

How do you do universal sculling? Any way you want to! Here are the fundamentals and some drills that will polish your skills and challenge you to create new uses.

## SCULLING

Sculling to support your body in the water works as you move your hands in a horizontal plane to apply downward pressure. Stand in chin-deep water. Extend your arms in front of you with your hands about 6 inches (15.24 centimeters) under the water, elbows bent at about 90 degrees. Hold your hands flat, palms down, and about 3 feet (0.9144 meters) apart.

Keep your wrists straight, but twist your forearms so that your palms face partly inward at angles of about 45 degrees to the horizontal (figure 12.1a). If you try to move your hands toward each other while at that angle, they tend to rise to follow the line of least resistance toward the edges of your hands. If you move them in an exactly horizontal plane, though, you have to apply downward pressure to keep them from rising. Your hands move horizontally, but you apply force in a vertical, downward direction (figure 12.1b). That force, transmitted through your arms to your body, will support you in the water.

Because of its 45-degree angle, your right hand is applying force not only partly downward but also partly inward. This inward force on the right hand tends to move you to the right, but your left hand is applying an equal force tending to move you to the left, so the two forces cancel each other. The resultant force is downward only.

Continue to move your hands inward until they are almost touching. When they stop, they also stop applying downward force. Now quickly rotate your hands and forearms so that your hands are turned outward at 45-degree angles (figure 12.1c). Immediately start to move them apart. Now the force on your right hand is downward and outward. The downward force tends to support you, again, and the outward force tends to move you to the left. However, your left hand also applies an outward force that cancels the right hand's outward push; once again the residual force is a supporting force downward

(figure 12.1d). When your hands reach the outer limits, turn them and bring them inward again (figure 12.1e). By continually moving your hands inward and outward on a horizontal plane, you can support yourself to keep your head above the water.

At each extreme of your sculling motion, while you are in the process of rotating your hands, you apply no downward force, leaving a dead spot, so to speak. However, if you press directly downward on the water during the time you are in the process of rotating your hands, you can maintain a downward force even then. Your hands are now lower in the water than before, and you cannot continue to press them deeper at each end of the sculling motion.

Solve this problem by sculling slightly uphill. Scull inward and slightly up until your hands are nearly touching. Then press downward as you rotate your arms. Scull outward and slightly upward to the outer end of your sculling motion, then press downward again and repeat the process. The result is a figure-eight motion of your hands (figure 12.1f). A steady pressure is thus maintained throughout the sculling. Sculling for support without moving through the water is called a *neutral scull* or *sculling in place*.

## Figure 12.1    Sculling

### TILT PALMS INWARD

1. Hold arms just underwater, wrists straight
2. Hold palms 3 feet apart
3. Tilt hands inward to 45-degree angles

*a*

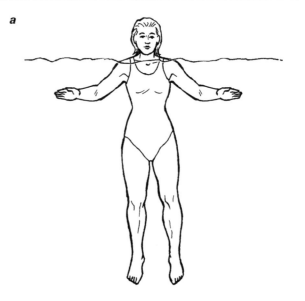

## BRING HANDS INWARD

1. Keep wrists and hands rigid
2. Press inward and downward
3. Move slightly uphill

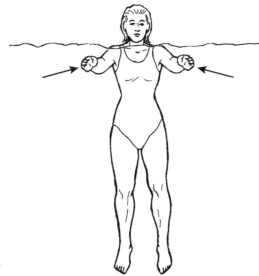

b

## ROTATE HANDS

1. Bring thumbs close together
2. Press down
3. Rotate arms
4. Turn palms to slant outward

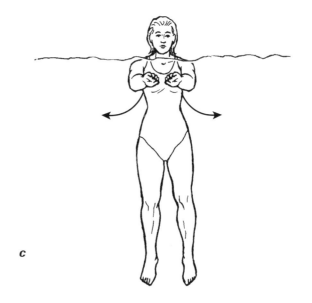

c

## PRESS OUT

1. Press outward and downward
2. Move slightly uphill

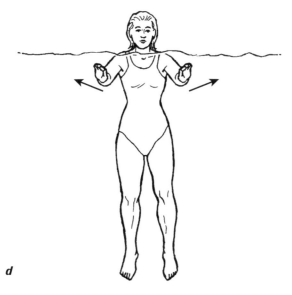

d

## BRING HANDS OUTWARD

1. Pull hands apart
2. Press down and rotate arms
3. Tilt palms inward

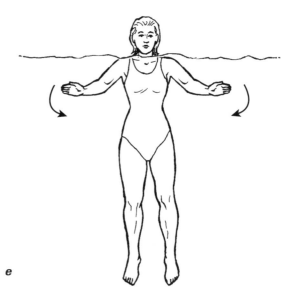

e

*(continued)*

## Figure 12.1 *(continued)*

**CONTINUE**

1. Continue figure-eight motion

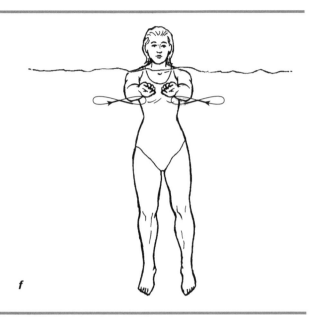

*f*

---

**Misstep**

You produce inadequate downward force and fail to support yourself.

**Correction**

Check the angle of your hands. Scull faster.

## Universal Sculling Drill 1. *Neutral Scull*

Stand in chin-deep water. Extend your hands in front 30 to 36 inches (76.2 to 91.44 centimeters) apart and 6 to 8 inches (15.24 to 20.32 centimeters) underwater, with elbows bent, wrists straight, and hands tilted 45 degrees facing inward. Press down and in to bring your hands together in a nearly horizontal plane, allowing them to rise slightly. Press directly down as you rotate your forearms to turn your palms out at 45-degree angles. Press down and out in a nearly horizontal plane, allowing your hands to rise slightly, until they are about 30 to 36 inches apart. Once again press directly down as you rotate your forearms again to turn your hands inward at 45-degree angles.

Continue this figure-eight motion, pressing on the water hard enough to maintain your position as you lift your feet from the bottom (figure 12.2a).

Continue the sculling motion as you extend your elbows and scull farther in front of you. As your elbows straighten, the rotating motion to maintain the 45-degree slant will become a rotating motion from your shoulders. Your entire arm will rotate to turn your hands. Keep your wrists rigid and perfectly straight.

Allow your feet to rise, straighten your hips, and lie back. As your feet come to the surface, you will be sculling at your hips on either side of your body (figure 12.2b). Continue to scull until your hips and feet are at the surface of the water. Drop your fingertips slightly by bending your wrists, not your knuckles, to negate any headfirst motion of your body. Bring your body from vertical to horizontal and maintain your hips and feet at the surface for 3 minutes.

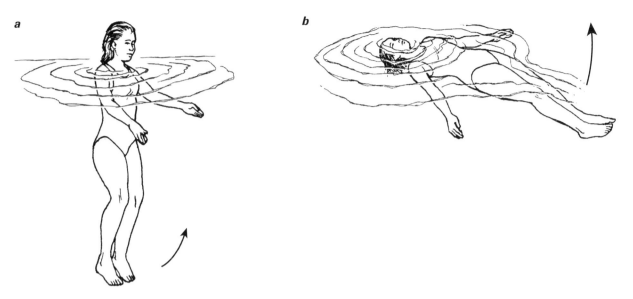

**Figure 12.2** Neutral scull: *(a)* lift feet from the bottom of the pool; *(b)* bring legs and feet to the surface of the water.

**To Increase Difficulty**

- Scull your body as high out of the water as you can.

**To Decrease Difficulty**

- Bring your hips and feet up slowly, and only high enough to be at the surface.

## *Success Check*

- Start sculling and lie back in the water.
- Scull only hard enough to maintain your position. It will be easy.

### *Score Your Success*

Maintain a horizontal position for 3 minutes = 2 points

Accomplish this feat on the first try = 1 additional point

Your score ___

## Universal Sculling Drill 2.    *Neutral Scull on Your Back*

Start in a back-float position with your toes just 6 inches from the edge of the pool. Scull at your hips to maintain your hips and your feet at the surface and to keep your toes within 6 inches of the wall. If your feet move out from the wall, it's because your wrists are bending slightly back and your fingertips are rising slightly. Flex your wrists forward to lower your fingertips as you scull. If you dig your fingertips in too deeply, you will move toward your feet. Practice until you can hold your neutral position without moving toward either your head or your feet. Maintain your horizontal position within 6 inches of the wall for 5 minutes.

**To Increase Difficulty**

- Hold position within 6 inches of the wall for 10 minutes.

**To Decrease Difficulty**

- Hold position with feet and legs at the surface, but just under the water.

## *Success Check*

- Raise your fingertips from your wrist to move headfirst. Scull.
- Drop your fingertips from your wrist to move feetfirst. Scull.

**171**

## Score Your Success

Complete 5 minutes of neutral scull = 2 points

Complete 10 minutes of neutral scull = 4 points

Your score ___

## Universal Sculling Drill 3.

# Headfirst Sculling on Your Back

Start in a back-float position, sculling at your hips to maintain position. Gradually bend your wrists back until your fingertips point up at about 45 degrees. Continue to scull, rotating your arms from your shoulders so that the heels of your hands move alternately inward (figure 12.3a) and outward (figure 12.3b), leading your fingertips. Maintain downward pressure also so that your hips and feet remain at the surface. You will move headfirst. Scull headfirst for 45 feet (13.716 meters) with your hips and feet at the surface.

### To Increase Difficulty

- Scull up from standing position to back position before moving.

### To Decrease Difficulty

- Scull only as fast as you must to maintain position and slow headfirst motion.

### Success Check

- Maintain your position with your face out of the water but with your body just barely under.
- Maintain downward pressure by keeping your palms turned partly downward.

## Score Your Success

Scull for 45 feet = 1 point

Scull for 45 feet with your feet at the surface = 3 points

Your score ___

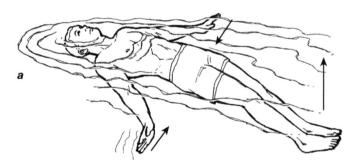

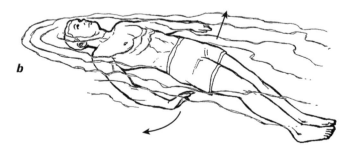

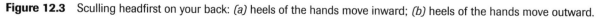

**Figure 12.3** Sculling headfirst on your back: *(a)* heels of the hands move inward; *(b)* heels of the hands move outward.

172

## Universal Sculling Drill 4. *Feetfirst Sculling on Your Back*

Start in a back-float position with your head toward the edge of the pool. Scull in position (neutral scull) until your hips and feet are at the surface. Gradually flex your wrists forward so that your fingertips point deeper toward the bottom of the pool. Keep your elbows locked straight and continue to scull, rotating your entire arms from the shoulders so that your fingertips lead alternately inward and outward from your hips. Maintain downward pressure to keep your hips and feet up, but pull yourself forward with your fingertips as you scull. Scull 45 feet with hips and feet at the surface.

**To Increase Difficulty**

- See how fast you can go.

**To Decrease Difficulty**

- Do not arch your back or let your feet drop.

### Success Check

- Take hold of the water with your fingertips and pull in and out with flexed wrists.

#### Score Your Success

Scull feetfirst for 45 feet = 2 points

Keep toes at the surface for 45 feet = 1 additional point

Your score ___

## Universal Sculling Drill 5. *Sculling Pivot*

Start in a back-float position, doing a neutral scull (sculling in place). Flex one wrist forward, pointing fingertips down; bend the other wrist back, pointing fingertips up. Continue sculling. Keep your body rigidly straight. The hand pointing down will pull on that side; the hand pointing up will push on that side. The result should be that your body pivots as though it were turning on a post at your hips. You should not move in a circle but should pivot in place. Reverse your hand positions to pivot in the other direction. Pivot 360 degrees in place in each direction.

**To Increase Difficulty**

- Scull headfirst for 10 feet (3.048 meters), then pivot 180 degrees and return. Pivot again.

**To Decrease Difficulty**

- Use hand paddles or web-fingered gloves until you master the concept.

### Success Check

- Keep your body and legs rigidly straight.
- Scull equally as hard on each side.

#### Score Your Success

Pivot 360 degrees = 2 points

Pivot 360 degrees in the opposite direction = 2 points

Your score ___

## Universal Sculling Drill 6.    *Circular Sculling on Your Back*

Start from a neutral scull on your back, sculling at your hips. Keep one wrist absolutely straight, the hand twisting by shoulder rotation. Bend your other wrist back to elevate the fingertips. Continue to scull. The elevated fingertips should propel that side of the body headfirst, causing you to move in a large circle. Reverse the hand positions to reverse the direction of the circle. Do not let your body bend at the hips. Scull in a complete figure eight on your back with hips and feet at the surface. You can use the backstroke turn flags as a centerline to guide your course. Make three complete figure eights.

**To Increase Difficulty**

- Wear a 5-pound weight belt.

**To Decrease Difficulty**

- Try hand paddles or web-fingered gloves for a few minutes.

### Success Check

- Do not bend your body sideways.
- Make large circles.

### Score Your Success

Score 2 points for each figure eight, up to 6 points.

Your score ___

## Universal Sculling Drill 7.    *Canoe Scull*

*Canoe* is simply a name for sculling in this position. To do this drill, start in a prone-float position. Keep your elbows in close to your sides, and bend your elbows so that your hands are pointing to the bottom of the pool. Bend your wrists back so that your palms are turned partly toward your feet and partly toward the bottom of the pool. Your wrists will have to be bent back about as far as you can bend them (figure 12.4). Start sculling, leading with the heels of your hands and moving your hands alternately in and out from your body. Scull near your hips, under your body. Rotate your forearms to change the direction of your palms. Your elbows will move out from your body to lead the hands away, then they'll lead your hands in again. You should be able to apply enough downward force on the water so that you can lift your head forward and hold it up, chin on the water, for breathing. By strongly arching your back, you will keep your heels at the surface. You also will apply force back on the water, which should move you forward as well. Hold a good canoe position and scull forward 25 feet (7.62 meters). Make five attempts at 25 feet.

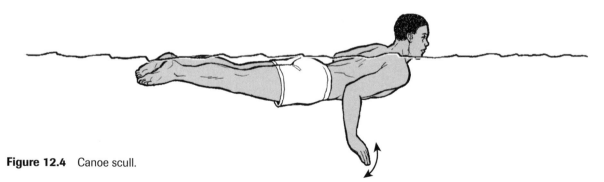

**Figure 12.4**  Canoe scull.

**To Increase Difficulty**

- See how fast you can move forward without losing form.

**To Decrease Difficulty**

- Move forward 15 feet (4.572 meters).
- Wear a mask and snorkel and keep your face down.

## Success Check

- Use an extreme back arch with head up.
- Bend wrists back to maximum.

### Score Your Success

Complete 25 feet = 1 point

Complete 25 feet with your head completely out of the water = 3 points

Your score ___

## Universal Sculling Drill 8.

# Headfirst Overhead Scull in Prone Position

Start in a prone-float position with both arms stretched overhead. Flex your wrists forward to point your fingertips at the bottom of the pool (figure 12.5). Keep your elbows rigidly straight and rotate your arms from the shoulders to point your fingers alternately inward and outward. Leading with your fingertips, pull outward about 12 to 18 inches (30.48 to 45.72 centimeters). Rotate the fingertips inward and let them lead as you pull inward again. This sculling motion will feel as though you are pulling your body along by your fingertips (you are!). Scull forward, lifting your chin for a breath, then dropping your face into the water again. You will get no upward support from this scull, but your forward motion and buoyancy will help bring your feet to the surface. Instead of pressing down on the water, you use this sculling motion at the beginning of the crawl stroke and butterfly arm pull. Scull 15 feet (4.572 meters) forward in prone position. Complete three trials.

**To Increase Difficulty**

- Think of it as beginning a butterfly stroke. Make it pull with great force.

**To Decrease Difficulty**

- Wear a mask and snorkel to practice.

## Success Check

- Keep body rigid.
- Do not bend at the hips.
- Use maximum wrist bend.
- Fingertips lead in and lead out.

### Score Your Success

Scull for 15 feet (4.572 meters) with no aids or for 30 feet (9.144 meters) while wearing a mask and snorkel = 2 points

Work the scull into a butterfly stroke = 2 additional points

Your score ___

**Figure 12.5**   Headfirst overhead scull in prone position.

# Universal Sculling Drill 9.   *Torpedo Scull*

Do the following short land drill first. Stand erect with both arms over your head. Imagine that the ceiling is just within reach of your hands. Bend your wrists back to place your palms flat against the ceiling. Now move your arms and hands alternately apart and together sideways, leading with the heels of your hands, as if you were polishing the ceiling. Allow your elbows to bend to reach behind you somewhat. Continue—heels lead out, twist from the shoulders, heels lead in, twist again, and so on.

Now put on a nose clip, take a back-float position in the water, and "polish the ceiling" beyond your head (figure 12.6). Take and hold as much air as you can hold to produce maximum buoyancy. You should move feetfirst rather rapidly. To keep your feet from sinking, tighten your abdominal muscles to eliminate the arch in your back, bend very slightly at the hips to raise your legs a little, and point your toes until the soles of your feet are slanted up 45 degrees. The faster you go, the better your feet and legs will stay at the surface.

If you don't bend your wrists back far enough, they will be turned partly up toward the surface of the water, causing an upward push that will sink your head. Bend your wrists farther back—you can even bend your elbows more, if necessary—to make your palms face directly overhead. Scull feetfirst for 30 feet, like a torpedo in the water. Repeat two more times.

**To Increase Difficulty**

- Race your buddies across the pool in torpedo scull.

**To Decrease Difficulty**

- Practice while wearing a float belt for buoyancy, then do it without the belt.

## Success Check

- Reach back behind your head to help keep your head from sinking.
- Use maximum wrist bend and bent elbows to "polish the ceiling."

### Score Your Success

Scull for 30 feet without letting your head drop underwater = 2 points

Complete three successful 30-foot (9.144 meter) runs = 2 additional points

Your score ___

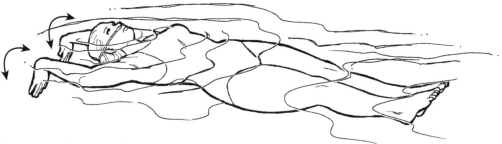

**Figure 12.6**   Torpedo scull.

# Universal Sculling Drill 10.
## *Sculling Sideways*

When you're doing a neutral scull, your hands slant alternately out and in. The slant positions create both inward and outward pushes against the water. Because the outward push of the right hand exactly counteracts the outward push of the left hand, no sideways motion is possible—or is it? Suppose one hand were slanted more than the other. Then the forces would be unequal, and sideways motion would result.

Stand in the shallow end of the pool and place both hands and forearms flat on the pool deck, palms down. (If your pool doesn't lend itself to this exercise, get out of the water and use a table.) Move your hands apart about 2 feet. Now carefully slant your left hand, thumb up, about 10 degrees from the horizontal (still nearly flat). Slant your right hand, thumb up, about 80 degrees from the horizontal (nearly perpendicular). Now move them slowly together (figure 12.7a). You can see that the right hand would have more pull on the water than the left; this would tend to move you to the right. When your hands are close, reverse the slant. This

time slant the left hand about 80 degrees, palm out, and the right hand about 10 degrees, little finger high (figure 12.7b). Now push them apart. The left hand will push harder than the right, causing you once again to move to the right. Continue to scull, carefully varying the hand tilt as before. Remember, the flat hand cannot be perfectly flat and the steep hand cannot be perfectly upright. If they were, all the downward pressure would be lost and no supporting force would remain.

Now take a back-float position in the water, hands at your hips, and do a neutral scull. Slowly begin to change the tilt of your hands until you are pushing and pulling more to one side than to the other. Voilà! The "impossible" sideways movement occurs. Take a position with your toes 6 inches from and perpendicular to the pool edge. Keep your toes 6 inches from the edge as you scull sideways 10 feet (3.048 meters) in one direction, then reverse and scull sideways back to the starting position. Control the hand slant and wrist action very carefully.

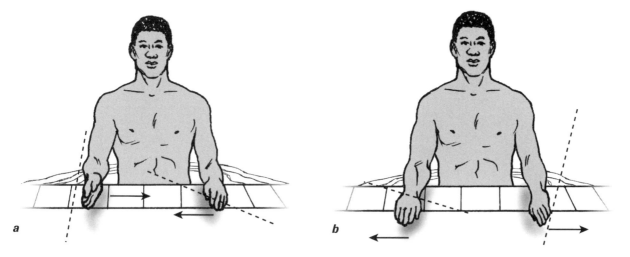

**Figure 12.7** Sculling sideways: *(a)* left hand 10 degrees from horizontal, right hand 80 degrees from horizontal, hands move inward; *(b)* right hand 10 degrees from horizontal, left hand 80 degrees from horizontal, hands move outward.

**177**

**To Increase Difficulty**

- Scull headfirst, then stop and scull sideways.

**To Decrease Difficulty**

- Start very slowly without trying to move, then increase speed with movement.
- Wearing hand paddles or web-fingered gloves may help.

- Keep wrists rigid to avoid headfirst or feetfirst motion.
- Pull or push harder on the hand that is nearly vertical.

### *Score Your Success*

Understand the concept = 2 points

Scull sideways for 10 feet in each direction = 4 additional points

Your score ___

## Universal Sculling Drill 11. *Ultimate Sculling Test*

You can now scull headfirst, feetfirst, and sideways. You can turn, pivot, and do a canoe scull on your belly. Can you put them together?

Take a back-float position in one corner of the pool. Your objective is to move diagonally across the pool from your corner to the far corner. You are to keep your body perfectly rigid, your feet together, and your toes pointed the whole time.

Start moving forward and sideways and begin to pivot as you go, always moving along the diagonal line (figure 12.8). Add a roll from your back to a canoe scull on your belly. Roll again to return to your back, all the while sculling forward and sideways, or feetfirst and sideways, along the diagonal line. Make your continuous pivot in a counterclockwise direction.

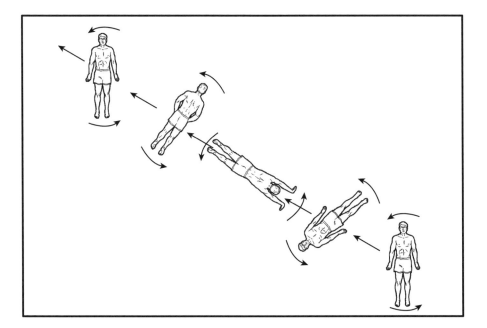

**Figure 12.8** The ultimate sculling test.

## To Decrease Difficulty

- Wearing hand paddles might help.

## Success Check

- Keep your body rigid and straight, toes pointed.
- Take your time. Think about what you need to do next.

## Score Your Success

Attempt the drill = 2 points

Complete the drill = 5 additional points

Your score ___

# SUCCESS SUMMARY OF UNIVERSAL SCULLING

As you have seen, sculling is truly universal in character and use. Sculling plays some part in every aquatic activity, but it's most prominent in the sport of synchronized swimming. Are there other uses we haven't mentioned? How about sculling in an inverted vertical position to lift the lower half of your body higher out of the water? This move is used a lot in synchronized swimming; it's called an *inverted lift*. Have fun thinking of other uses for sculling.

If you scored at least 20 points, you have shown great ability to adapt to new challenges. If you scored 21 to 30 points, you are showing mastery of aquatic skills. If you scored 31 to 40 points or more, try synchronized swimming—you'll like it.

*Universal Sculling Drills*

| | | |
|---|---|---|
| 1. Neutral Scull | | ___ out of 3 |
| 2. Neutral Scull on Your Back | | ___ out of 4 |
| 3. Headfirst Sculling on Your Back | | ___ out of 3 |
| 4. Feetfirst Sculling on Your Back | | ___ out of 3 |
| 5. Sculling Pivot | | ___ out of 4 |
| 6. Circular Sculling on Your Back | | ___ out of 6 |
| 7. Canoe Scull | | ___ out of 3 |
| 8. Headfirst Overhead Scull in Prone Position | | ___ out of 4 |
| 9. Torpedo Scull | | ___ out of 4 |
| 10. Sculling Sideways | | ___ out of 6 |
| 11. Ultimate Sculling Test | | ___ out of 7 |
| *Total* | | ___ *out of 47* |

# Additional Strokes, Stunts, and Games

We are weightless in water. We can therefore perform feats of physical prowess unattainable on land. We can, with some diligent application, combine parts of various swimming strokes to create new, interesting, and challenging strokes. This step challenges you to do just that—create new strokes, stunts, and games.

You should have fun in the water, and the following new strokes are fun to try. You should also experiment with new combinations of skills; research of this kind leads to the development of practical aquatic skills. Challenges are also useful to competitive swimmers because some of these strokes are now finding their way into competition at the national championship level. Why don't you become famous by inventing a new and even faster stroke? It could be named after you!

## DOLPHIN CRAWL STROKE

This stroke has actually been used in competition. A competitive swimmer has won a big swim meet by introducing the stroke into a freestyle event. He used the stroke to produce a burst of speed during the last lap of a middle-distance race. It worked!

In prone-float position, start a slow, rhythmic dolphin kick in sets of two. (Review figure 8.1, page 104, if necessary.) After the second set of two kicks, add a one-arm butterfly arm pull to the next set of two kicks. Then pull with the opposite arm on the next set of two kicks. Turn your head to the side and inhale during the pull of one arm. Turn your face down and exhale during the pull of the other arm. Continue pulling with alternate arm strokes to the butterfly stroke rhythm. Smooth out the timing so that your legs are kicking a constant four-beat rhythm: down, up, down, up. Now begin to feel that it is not a butterfly stroke you are swimming, but a crawl stroke instead with two dolphin kicks accompanying each arm stroke.

**Misstep**

You try to work in a butterfly arm stretch count ("a-a-n-d") with this stroke.

**Correction**

Kick an even four-beat dolphin kick with no variation.

# DOLPHIN BACK CRAWL STROKE

After you learn the dolphin crawl stroke, the next logical step would be to learn the dolphin back crawl stroke. Over time competitive swimmers learned that using a dolphin kick while on their backs after a turn was faster than actually swimming a back crawl. Some could even swim an entire pool length using nothing but the dolphin kick. This prompted a rule change at the national level. The rule now states that backstroke swimmers can stay underwater on their backs after a turn for only 15 meters before their heads must break the surface. These swimmers did not use their arms while underwater, only their legs, but in the future we may discover that using the dolphin kick with the back crawl armstroke is faster still. It is perfectly legal to do so under the current rules.

Start with a back glide, arms stretched overhead. Do an inverted dolphin kick, undulating from your hips and emphasizing the upward lift of your feet and lower legs. Kick in pairs of upward beats, counting as for the prone dolphin kick: "one, and, two, a-a-n-d." Do the two upward beats as a pair, then slow the downward recovery of your legs on the slow "a-a-n-d" count. Pull through a back crawl arm stroke on the next pair of upward kicks, getting your arm all the way through the pull on counts 1 and "and." Return your arm to the water overhead on count 2. Rest both arms overhead for the longer "a-a-n-d" count. This is the same coordination as for the butterfly stroke, except it involves only one arm at a time. On the next set of two kicks, pull through with the opposite arm, returning it to the water overhead on the count of 2 also. Rest both arms again for the long "a-a-n-d" count. Repeat, alternating arm pulls with each set of two kicks, but don't forget to pause for a slow count as your feet drop deeper in preparation for the next two upward thrust beats. Inhale during an arm pull and exhale during the pull of the opposite arm. Try to pull exactly as in the back crawl stroke, bending your elbow during the pull and recovering your arm straight and vertical. Slow down the kick rhythm so that you don't have to pull so fast. Again, slow down until you master the rhythm!

**Misstep**

You fail to match dolphin rhythm with back crawl stroke. This is the most common misstep in this stroke.

**Correction**

Think butterfly stroke with one arm at a time.

# BUTTERFLY BACKSTROKE

Rules for swimming backstroke in competition say only that you must stay on your back for the entire race (except for turns). You may move your arms and legs in any pattern you wish. It's even legal to swim the stroke using a double overarm recovery if you wish!

The butterfly backstroke is not an important stroke in current competitive swimming, but one day it may be as important as the butterfly stroke is now. That is the point of this step—to use the research on new strokes to discover ways to incorporate elements into existing strokes.

Start in a back glide position with arms stretched overhead. Begin an inverted dolphin kick in paired kicks as for the butterfly stroke. Just before kicking up to begin the second pair of kicks, pull both arms in a wide, sweeping pull just beneath the surface and toward your feet. Bend your elbows slightly to bring them closer to you. Kick up with the dolphin kick as your arms reach midpull. Count 1 comes as you kick. Finish the arm pull all the way to your thighs and immediately lift both straight arms over the water as you drop your feet on the "and" part of the kick. Kick up again (count 2) as your arms enter the water stretched overhead. Rest your arms in glide position for the longer "a-a-n-d" count while you drop your feet in preparation for the next. You have completed one stroke.

Keep the coordination for this stroke exactly as for the butterfly stroke. Pull on count 1, then hit the water with your arms on count 2 for a glide. Be sure your arms glide for a long count between strokes. Keep your arms straight for the recovery over the water and bend them slightly on the pull. Do not try to pull deep; your arms should pull horizontally about 6 inches underwater. Inhale during the pull and exhale during the glide.

**Misstep**

You fail to maintain the long interval before each new kick begins.

**Correction**

Slow way down until you master the coordination.

# BUTTERFLY BREASTSTROKE

The term *butterfly* refers to an arm motion. A butterfly breaststroke, then, is a breaststroke with a butterfly arm motion. The butterfly breaststroke was discovered in the 1940s. It was developed during a search for greater breaststroke speed by eliminating the underwater resistance of the arm recovery. The competitive rules at that time did not anticipate such a move and so did not prohibit an over-the-water recovery. The kick and the timing remained the same as the breaststroke, but the new overarm recovery broke all existing records, and its peculiar appearance was the origin of the term *butterfly* in swimming. Shortly thereafter the rule makers outlawed the overarm recovery, but they coupled it with the dolphin kick to create the butterfly stroke and added a fourth stroke to the then-three-stroke individual medley event.

Begin in a prone glide position, arms stretched overhead. Recover your legs for a breaststroke kick, then kick as you pull through a butterfly arm pull. At the very end of the arm pull, recover your legs quickly and kick a second time as your arms recover over the water. Use a standard breaststroke kick. Glide while your legs recover, then repeat the action. Inhale during the pull of your arms and exhale during the glide. Double-kick on the arm pull and recovery, and glide as your legs ready themselves for the next double kick.

# STUNTS AND CHALLENGES

The word *swimming,* as in the declaration, "I am going swimming," denotes more than just swimming speed or utility strokes. It usually means having fun in the water. Water stunts and games are a large part of the meaning of *swimming.*

There are many, many fun things to do in the aquatic habitat. Here are a few more examples to get you started; then you can invent as many as your heart desires. Having fun is always important to your life and health. Let your imagination run wild! Try things that are impossible on land but are great fun in the aquatic world.

## Marlin Turn

The marlin turn is a basic movement in synchronized swimming. It's easy and fun to do. It does not move you through the water, but it changes your position by exactly 90 degrees in relation to the pool edges. The marlin turn opens a new area of water mastery, which we touched on only briefly in step 12 of this book.

The marlin turn starts with a horizontal back-float position parallel to the edge of the pool. Arms are stretched to the sides at shoulder level. From this position, do a complete roll. During the roll, your feet slide sideways so that your body turns in place, finishing not parallel but perpendicular to the edge of the pool. Thus you do a complete roll and a quarter turn. Precision in the roll and the turn is a measure of success.

From the start position—floating on your back parallel to the edge of the pool, arms stretched to the sides at shoulder level (figure 13.1a)—sweep your right arm up overhead and your left arm down to your side, rolling onto your right side (figure 13.1b). Continue to sweep your arms back to the outstretched position as you roll onto your belly (figure 13.1c). Sweep your left arm overhead and your right arm down to your side as you roll onto your left side (figure 13.1d). Continue to roll onto your back and sweep your arms back to the starting position (figure 13.1e). This entire stunt should be done in one continuous, flowing motion with your arms, legs, and body rigidly straight.

If you keep your body rigid and make your arms push against the water as they move, you will also make a quarter turn in place, finishing perpendicular to the edge of the pool. As you roll onto your belly, you may wish to raise your head until your chin is on the water. Keep your torso, legs, arms, and wrists straight throughout the turn; move only from your shoulders. Continue to turn three more times to complete a full circle, finishing in the same place and position from which you started.

You may, of course, roll in the opposite direction. Simply reverse the movements and make quarter turns in the opposite direction.

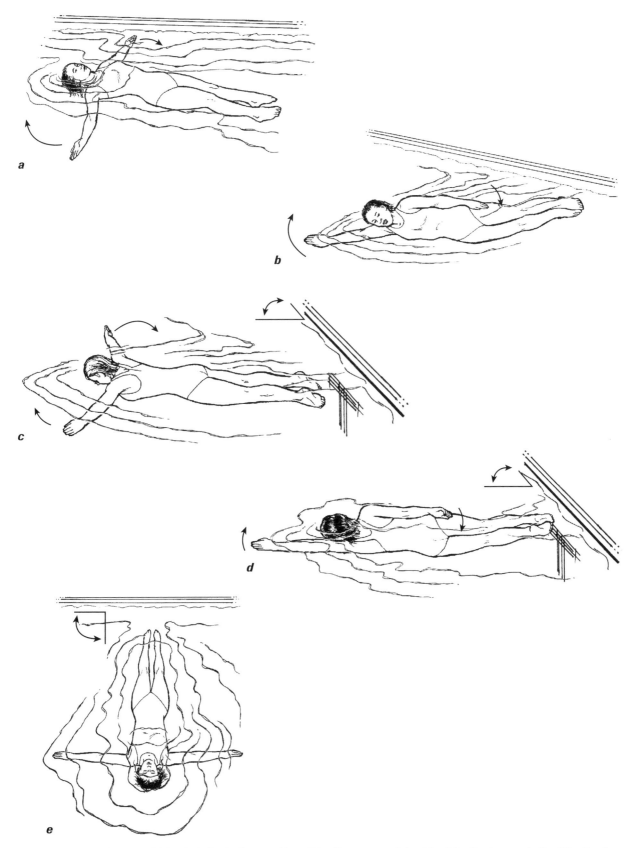

**Figure 13.1** Marlin turn: *(a)* begin in back-float position; *(b)* roll onto your right side; *(c)* roll onto your belly; *(d)* roll onto your left side; *(e)* roll onto your back.

## Back Scull Underwater

The back scull underwater is a new method of propulsion that you probably have not tried. It may surprise you, though. Because of the small expenditure of energy relative to the speed you obtain, you may find that you can swim underwater farther this way than by any other method. How will you know until you try it?

For safety, wear defogged goggles and a nose clip or a mask and snorkel. Start by pushing off from the end of the pool, underwater, on your back, arms extended overhead, as from a backstroke turn. As you glide, drop your head back until you can see where you're going. Bring both arms toward your feet until your bent elbows are at your sides, fingertips pointing directly up toward the surface (figure 13.2). Begin sculling as if you were polishing a tabletop at waist height. The resultant force from this sculling motion will propel you headfirst.

**Figure 13.2**  Back scull underwater.

If you begin to rise toward the surface because of buoyancy, bend your wrists a little so that your palms are slightly turned up toward the surface. The resultant force will push you headfirst and slightly deeper. Occasionally drop your chin to look up at the surface to see how deep you are, but for safety look back over your head most of the time. Relax your legs and feet as much as possible, but keep them streamlined—do not try to kick. If you scull efficiently, you will move rapidly with little fatigue. When you need a breath, drop your chin to your chest and scull to the surface.

## Centipede

Have you ever seen a centipede swim? This is a multiperson stunt strictly for fun. After a swimming lesson, drill, or workout, lighten up the atmosphere by using a stunt like centipede as a cool-down activity.

Get two, three, or more people to participate (try to see how many you can get into one centipede). Line up single file, facing the other end of the pool. The first swimmer lies prone and presses his feet on the waist of the second swimmer, who puts his feet on the next swimmer, and so on. When every swimmer (except the last) has his feet on the swimmer behind, they all start swimming crawl stroke in rhythm with the lead swimmer (figure 13.3). The last swimmer provides the kick for the centipede. Start with two swimmers and build to as many as possible. Next try a centipede on the back, using a back crawl stroke.

**Figure 13.3**  Two-person centipede.

## Underwaterball

You can create a strange and wonderful creature from a water polo ball. Insert an inflator needle into a water polo ball or a rubber volleyball and squeeze out *all* the air; flatten the ball completely. Now attach a piece of tight-fitting rubber tubing to the needle and put the other end of the tubing into the nozzle of a water hose. Turn on the water carefully to fill the ball completely with water. Try to work all of the air out before withdrawing the inflator needle.

Take the ball into the water and try dribbling it like a basketball on the bottom of the pool. Then dribble it off the surface of the water from underneath the water. See whether you can pass it underwater. It simply will not go straight for more than 2 feet before curving away in some wonderful, unpredictable direction.

You can do the same thing with an ordinary balloon filled with water, but it won't last long, and you must get all the torn scraps of rubber out of the pool when it breaks.

## Champion Underwater Diver

No aches, no pains, no falling flat.

Wear a nose clip and goggles. Wear a weight belt with enough weight to make you neutrally buoyant when holding a full breath. (With neutral buoyancy, you neither sink nor rise when motionless under the water.)

Take a deep breath and do a feetfirst surface dive in 8 feet (2.4384 meters) of water. When your feet touch bottom, immediately push off as though from a diving board and float in slow motion through a perfect one-and-one-half somersault with a full twist.

Invent any dive you wish. In the weightless environment, you can be the perfect diver without the pain of failure.

## Underwater Target Practice

Target practice is more fun from the under side.

Find a hula hoop that floats. Make a small ring of plastic tubing about 8 to 10 inches (20.32 to 25.4 centimeters) in diameter. Tie it to the hula hoop in three places so that it becomes a bulls-eye in the center of the hula hoop (figure 13.4). Collect a few worn-out badminton shuttlecocks. Use two colors of waterproof felt-tip pens to mark eight shuttlecocks, four in each color.

Float the hoop target on the surface and swim under it. As you pass under the target, release one or more shuttlecocks to float up toward the target. Keep score if you wish.

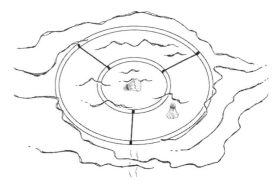

**Figure 13.4** Target ring using a hula hoop.

# SUCCESS SUMMARY

Ask a synchronized swimmer how to do a water-wheel. Try it, then see if you can do it vertically instead of horizontally. Can you maintain a steady lifting motion in an inverted position to hold your legs out of water up to your knees? How about a frog crawl (a crawl stroke with a frog kick)? Can you do a plank? Try a chain dolphin. How about a tub? Synchronized swimming books are loaded with good stunts.

Have you tried water polo or underwater hockey? Both are nationally recognized sports. Why not take a course in lifeguarding from the American Red Cross or the YMCA? Become a certified water safety instructor and teach others the joy you have found in aquatics. Join a swim club and become a competitive speed swimmer. If you love the aquatic medium, you will soon find yourself immersed in it.

You have attained many goals in this swimming course. You've probably improved your skills, but just as important, you've probably developed an enthusiastic attitude toward water and toward aquatics in general. Are you pleased with your progress?

# ◪ About the Author

**David G. Thomas** has been a swimming teacher and coach since 1948, when he became a water-safety field representative for the American Red Cross. In 1955 he became swimming coach and aquatics director at Berea High School in Berea, Ohio. Eight years later he moved to the State University of New York at Binghamton, where he was director of aquatics and swimming coach until retiring as professor emeritus in 1985.

Thomas gained nationwide prominence in 1972 by producing a textbook, teaching guide, exams, and visual aids for training swimming pool operators. The *Swimming Pool Operators Handbook* and the other materials were published by the National Swimming Pool Institute as the basis for its Certified Pool Operators program.

Since retirement, Thomas has focused much of his attention on writing. He has published numerous articles on aquatic subjects and is a contributing author to several books on swimming pool design and operation, including *Professional Aquatic Management*. He is the author of *Teaching Swimming: Steps to Success, Advanced Swimming: Steps to Success, Competitive Swimming Management*, and the video *Water Is Friendly: The First Step in Learning to Swim*.

A consultant in aquatics and pool design and operation, Thomas lives with his wife, Virginia, in Anderson, South Carolina. He swims each day for fitness.

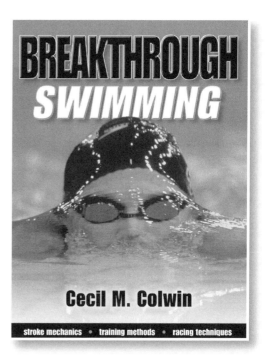